HAMP

AN AUTOBIOGRAPHY BY

LIONEL HAMPTON
WITH JAMES HASKINS

Discography by Vincent H. Pelote

Amistad

New York, New York

1271 Avenue of the Americas
New York, NY 10020

Distributed by:
Penguin USA
375 Hudson Street
New York, NY 10014

First published in November 1989 by Warner Books as an Amistad book. First
issued as an Amistad Press, Inc., trade paperback with new introduction in
February 1993.

1   2   3   4   5   6   7   8   9   10

Library of Congress Cataloging-in-Publication Data

Hampton, Lionel.
    Hamp : an autobiography / by Lionel Hampton with James Haskins.
        p.   cm.
    Originally published: New York : Warner Books. c1989. With new
introd.
    Discography: p.
    Includes index.
    ISBN 1-56743-019-8 (pbk.) : $12.95
    1. Hampton, Lionel.   2. Jazz musicians—United States—Biography.
I. Haskins, James, 1941–   .   II. Title.
[ML419.H26A3 1993]   93-102
786.8'43'092—dc20   CIP
                                                        MN

To Gladys Hampton
God gave me the talent. Gladys gave me the inspiration.

ACKNOWLEDGMENTS

The author and his collaborator are grateful to the following people for their help: the late Irving Ashby, Kathy Benson, Charles Bowen, Halimah Brooks, Patricia Allen-Browne, Orleen Caballero, Betty Carter, Will and Kay Clanton, Gene Grissom, Milt Hinton, Chuck Jones, Charlie Mack, Patricia Marsh, Dan Morgenstern, Albert Murray, Vincent Pelote, Jerome Richardson, Marshall Royal, Phil Schaap, Audrey Smaltz, Bill Titone, and George Wein.

CONTENTS

1

EARLY YEARS IN BIRMINGHAM

I *was* born on April 20, 1908, in Louisville, Kentucky, to Charles Edward and Gertrude Morgan Hampton. My father and mother met the year before I was born in Birmingham, Alabama, her hometown. They were both in school there, and they got married. He went to work for the railroad, and they moved to Louisville.

After I was born my father was away a lot. My mother didn't want to be alone with a baby, so she moved back to Birmingham. I don't remember anything about Louisville, I was still a babe in arms. I also don't remember anything about my father. When America entered World War I, my father went into the Army and was shipped to France. Within a few weeks he was declared missing in action.

The news eventually reached my mother in Birmingham, and she wrote all kinds of letters trying to find out what happened. She wrote to the War Department, to his regiment, to everybody she could think of. But she never found out what happened to him. An investigation was started, but it was complicated by the fact that my father had been attached to a French unit. Colored soldiers weren't allowed to fight with white American soldiers.

I was about six years old when it dawned on me that I didn't have a father like the other children I played with. I was happy living with my mother and grandparents and aunts and uncles, and that seemed like family enough to me. But the other kids had fathers. So I asked about mine. I was told that he'd died in the war.

I felt sad that I never would know my father, but I was also proud. I was the son of a war hero, and my playmates envied me. I wasn't much interested beyond that. I knew my mother had written letters and that she hadn't found out anything. I wasn't curious. To me, Charles Edward Hampton was a stranger who had vanished in a strange country.

Years and years later—it must have been about 1939, because I was still with Benny Goodman's orchestra—we were giving some concerts in Dayton, Ohio. A boy named Johnny Lyttle used to hang around the bandstand wherever we played. He was about ten, and he told me he wanted to become a vibraharpist. He's a good vibraharpist now.

One day, Johnny said, "Why don't you ever visit your father when you are in Dayton?" I said, "I don't have a father. My father died in the war."

Then Johnny told me about the old gentleman in the VA hospital who said he was the father of Lionel Hampton, the vibraharpist. His name was Charles Edward Hampton, and he'd been exposed to mustard gas in France. He'd come home blind and spent many years in the Veterans Administration hospital in Dayton. The story sounded so unbelievable that it didn't register in my brain. I said, "Okay, if you say so," and went on about my business.

A lady who was a relative of Johnny's was taking care of the gentleman, going to the hospital to visit him and taking him things. I think one of the reasons she took an interest in him was because she knew Johnny wanted to be a vibraharpist. Anyway, this lady and some teenage guy and members of her family took me out to see him at the VA hospital.

We walked into the room, and they took me over to this distinguished-looking man who looked to be in his seventies. I had never seen a picture of my father before, but when I looked at that man I knew he was my father. There was no shadow of a doubt. He looked just like me, and I looked just like him. We looked just alike.

I spent a whole day with him. He asked about my mother, who was still living then, and I said she was fine and I was going to tell her that I'd seen him. He talked about the years of darkness and loneliness. He said he started hearing about me being a big musician and was proud to tell people, "That is my son." I felt very bad about never knowing him until then, but I was happy that I saw him.

I was going to send for him and bring him to New York. My wife and I had decided to do that. But he died before I got through with that tour. A few months later, I was in my dressing room at the Grand Terrace in Chicago when I was called to the phone. It was 2:00 A.M., and I had just come off the stage. "This is Mrs. Lyttle," a voice said. "Your father just died in his sleep."

Today, I am as old as he was when he died. When I look in the mirror, I see my father. It's not that I resemble him. I look identical. I wish I'd had more time with him, but I'm glad I did find him after all those years.

The only "father" I knew in my early life was my grandfather, Richard Morgan. He was born near Selma or Tuscaloosa, Alabama—some little town—a few months before the start of the Civil War. He married my grandmother, Louvenia, and they moved to Birmingham.

My grandmother was an evangelist. She worked for the Church of God in Christ. My grandfather had a job working as a fireman on the railroad. That was the biggest job you could actually have in the South. For blacks it was like being a bank vice president.

He was a full-fledged fireman, shoveling that coal. He was on the Special—either the L & N, Louisville and Nashville, or the Southern, the one that ran from Birmingham to Atlanta, Georgia. I think it was the Southern.

In the South at that time, the trains were a major form of entertainment for people, especially black people. We had no circus, no ball game. And since we didn't go anywhere, the trains let us dream about faraway places. People sat along the railroad tracks on summer afternoons and watched the trains go by. The greatest show was the Special, which left Birmingham every evening about six o'clock. Hundreds of people came every day to stand just outside the station and cheer the spectacle.

The train was in slow motion as it pulled away from the platform, so you could see every detail. The dining car with its white tablecloths, the coaches filled with passengers, the berths being made up for the night. But the big locomotive was the star. The engineer, who was always white, blew the whistle. The fireman, who was always black, rang the bell. The different duties of white and black were clearly defined in those days.

How proud I was when the fireman was my grandfather, mas-

tering the biggest engine in the world. When he spotted my grandmother and me in the cheering crowd, he'd salute like a soldier. I'd
wave back, and then sometimes I'd look around to make sure everyone knew who he was saluting at. The other boys envied me.

One day a boy on our block didn't want me to play with his
ball. "All right," I said, "then I don't allow you to watch the train."
Right away he handed me the ball. Being the grandson of a railroad
fireman had clout.

Railroad jobs were the best jobs. Porters were important, too.
And they used those jobs to help the people. When that train came
through the black part of Birmingham, at six o'clock, we all lined
up beside the track. And that's when my grandfather went into his
act. He started shoveling that coal, and the old white engineer—
you'd see him with his foot hanging out of that cabin, and they were
ringing that bell and blowing that whistle—*ring, ring, ring, wow-
wa*. And the black people would be applauding the train.

And the porters would throw out food to them, and my grandfather would shovel out some coal on the side of the road so those
people would keep warm. My grandfather kept a lot of black folks
warm in his time. I knew he did that. That's where we got all our
coal from! He was kind of a hero.

My grandfather had very dark skin and high cheekbones. We
decided he must have Indian blood. When he dressed up, he cut a
fine figure. He always dressed up after a hot bath had cleaned all the
smoke and grime off. Everybody in our part of town dressed up after
he returned home from work. On Sundays, Grandfather would put
on a three-piece suit with a golden watch chain. He carried a black
cane with a silver knob. My best memory of him is sitting in his
rocking chair, on the front porch, all dressed up.

The house was at 1513 Seventh Avenue, at the corner of Fifteenth
Street. It was a big white wooden house, bigger than the other houses
in the neighborhood. But it contained a large family.

My grandparents had five children. Archie was the oldest son.
He drove a truck for the candy company down there, had all kinds
of sweets in it, and he would deliver to people. He was kind of
middle-class, a good-living cat.

Richard was the other son. He was quite an operator. History
remembers him only as the driver of the car in which Bessie Smith
got killed. He was never the same after that, but up to that time he
led a charmed life. He was a born winner. He always had several
jobs at a time. Wherever there was a buck to be made, Richard could
smell it and be there before anybody else. Like most of the men in

Birmingham then, he worked at a foundry. But he also ran a shoeshine business. He owned the chairs and the brushes and provided the polish, and then he leased out the equipment to youngsters in the neighborhood.

He had a letter-writing business on the side. People who couldn't read and write would pay him to write their letters. His love letters were in real demand. He copied passages from books and charged twenty cents a letter. If he decorated them with a drawing, he added a nickel to the charge.

For his eighteenth birthday, my Uncle Richard bought himself white shoes, a straw hat, and a silk tie. My grandmother was proud of him and happy about the money he brought home. She also agreed that he deserved to buy whatever clothes he wanted and that he looked stylish in them. But she couldn't quite make up her mind whether God wanted man to be that flamboyant.

Aunt Pherebia was the oldest Morgan daughter. She married the owner of the grocery store, Mr. Ford. He was probably about thirty-five at the time, but to me he looked elderly. Aunt Pherebia looked a lot like Grandma and acted like her, too—very dedicated to her faith.

My mother, Gertrude, was the second daughter. She remarried a couple of years after we moved to Birmingham. My stepfather, Samuel Davis, also worked for the railroad as a porter. He was a tall man who dressed with great style. He lived across the street, and after they got married, my mother moved in with him. She left me with Grandma and Grandpa. I never called my mother "Mama." That was what I called my grandmother, but that's what all southerners did in those days. When the grandmother raised you, she was your mama. I called my mother "Gertrude."

My mother and Samuel Davis had a son, who of course was called Sammy Davis, Jr. He was my half brother, but I'm ashamed to admit I never claimed him. He was a very gentle man and in his field very successful.

When he died in March 1981, he left me quite a bit of money. It seems that none of the Morgan clan has any talent for staying poor. But I hadn't paid much attention to him or what he had done with his life. In going through the papers I found in Sammy's house in Los Angeles, I found out more about him.

He'd studied law while living on a farm and working in an automobile factory. At that time I was already wealthy and could have helped him, but he never asked me for help. He always sent his blessings, and I never inquired about his situation.

Sammy taught law in Texas. Later on, he received a Ph.D. in education and became a specialist in working with retarded children. He even wrote a well-known textbook on the subject.

In his papers I also found a letter that had belonged to our mother. It read: "This is to certify that Mrs. Gertrude Davis has been in our employ as a waitress in the lunchery for the past four years, and have always found her to be honest, obedient and a hard working person and can highly recommend her to any one wanting a girl in this kind of business. Wm. Schwarzenbach, Manager, The Busy Corner, Birmingham."

The third daughter was Anna Mae. She was several years older than I was, but we grew up together like brother and sister, fighting every inch of the way. Anna Mae got slapped by everybody in the house, because in those days that was the way you brought up children. Then she'd turn around and slap me. When Sammy got old enough, I turned around and slapped him.

When Anna Mae graduated from Birmingham High School, the whole family attended. It was the first ceremony I'd ever been to outside church, and I was impressed. It was the first high school for colored girls in the South, and Professor Parker, the founder, gave a thundering speech about the rights of colored people. I didn't understand much of it, not knowing what the rights of white people were. An orchestra played, and all sorts of black dignitaries, mainly ministers, were present. All the graduates wore black skirts and white blouses. On the way home, my grandmother said, "Now you know how beautiful it is to finish high school."

Anna Mae was skinny as a rail when she was a young woman. Everybody said it was because she didn't have a man. She would blush when she heard that kind of talk. She'd lock herself in the bathroom. She was the spinster of the family. Even after I was a grown-up man, she'd follow me around like a chaperone, convinced I'd fall into sin without her guidance. Later on, she made up for it by getting engaged half a dozen times and marrying twice. She became a wealthy real estate agent in California and started the Foundation for Cats and Dogs, a kind of animals' union. She died only recently.

The success of the Morgan clan owes a lot to both my grandparents. But whatever success I've had in life is due to my Mama Louvenia. Grandpa was important to me, but he died when I was still a boy. And even before he died, Mama was the undisputed head of the family. Even Grandpa called her "Mrs. Louvenia," and the family used to say that he never disagreed with her. In fact, he would agree with her before she even said anything.

Mama Louvenia was born a few months after the start of the

Civil War. She had very light skin and straight black hair and was very tall. My preference for tall women probably goes back to my grandmother. By the time I came along, Mama Louvenia was wearing round eyeglasses. Combined with her height and her erect posture, they made her look like a schoolmistress, not the daughter of southern farm slaves.

Mama Louvenia was born and raised on a farm near Selma. There was no school for the children of slaves, and she was taught to read and write in church. The second most important thing to her was education. She made sure that all five of her children graduated from high school. She also nagged them to take college courses. She sent my mother to Erskine University to major in liberal arts. She sent Uncle Richard to night school. When he couldn't attend evening classes anymore because of his various businesses, she made him take early-morning classes. Whenever there was a correspondence course of any kind offered—shorthand, medical massage, or in the proper use of baking powder—Mama Louvenia would register everyone in the family who was eligible.

The most important thing to Mama was her faith. I used to pray with her all the time. She taught me how to pray. My early childhood memories are of going to church and coming home from church. Sunday was all-day church. We'd go to six o'clock prayer service, nine o'clock prayer service, service at eleven o'clock. There was young people's meeting at two or three o'clock, and then prayer service at night. I'd always have to get dressed up—starched shirt, tie, neatly pressed pants, and shiny black shoes. The only part of that outfit that was store-bought was the shoes. Everything else was homemade by Mama and the other women of the house. That wasn't true just for my clothes, but for everybody's in the household. They sewed and turned and knitted and embroidered and darned and mended day and night. The family budget didn't allow for ready-made clothes. We were quite a sight when we all set out for church. We looked like we'd just stepped out of a band box. All that was ever said about Jewish mamas applies to Mama Louvenia. She believed in God and in clean fingernails. She told me that God wanted little boys to be clean, courteous, never to interrupt the conversations of adults, and to go to bed without complaining. She read to me from the Bible, and I could spell by the time I was five years old.

I was her favorite. I went everywhere with her. And she was everything to me. If it was hailing outside and she said, "There's fire," I'd say, "Yeah, there's fire out there."

My grandmother lived and breathed religion, and hers was that old-time religion, too. She left the Baptist Church when she decided it was getting too worldly. There was a Congregationalist Church right next to our house, but she joined the Holiness Church on Twenty-fourth Street, about ten blocks away. I was happy she made that choice, because the Holiness Church was more fun.

That red-brick building rocked on a Sunday! There was a big band with all kinds of instruments, but especially rhythm instruments. It was important to keep a steady beat going. My favorite instrument was the big bass drum. The sister who played it was pretty big, too. She'd beat that drum for hours, and then, all of a sudden, the spirit would grab her. She'd start dancing and her eyes would roll up into the back of her head. In my imagination, when her eyeballs disappeared, her soul left her body and was on its way up to God. Seemed to me that drumming was the best way to get close to God.

One Sunday I picked up the mallet she had dropped, and started hitting the bass drum with it. My grandmother let me continue. She saw that I was trying to get close to God, too. So from then on, I was a drummer. I drummed on pots and pans, chair seats, the front porch railing, the front porch steps. The rest of the family complained, but Mama Louvenia thought I showed real talent. She looked forward to me playing in the church band one day. Maybe even being famous.

Mama Louvenia had a way of always being number one. She quickly became the holiest sister in the Holiness Church. She had a reputation as a healer, and she deserved it. Nobody in my family ever went to a doctor while my grandmother was alive. She would go to the houses of sick people in the congregation to pray them well. She even held prayer meetings in nearby towns. More impressive, even white people needed her help. I will never forget the time a shining limousine driven by a white chauffeur pulled up to our door. Mama Louvenia and her friend, Sister Draper, climbed into the backseat, and the car drove away. I don't think I ever asked the name of the person they were going to heal. The fact that it was a white person was enough for me.

We didn't have much contact with white people. Everybody in our neighborhood was black, everybody in our church was black. We didn't do much shopping in white stores. I can't remember ever going to downtown Birmingham when I was a child. But I knew that there were people called white people, who were different, and that if they respected you, that was a source of pride.

Sister Draper almost always traveled with Mama on church or healing business. Sister Draper lived on the small pension she collected as the widow of a soldier who'd died in one of the wars. She also worked as a seamstress in white homes. She had a gold tooth, which always fascinated me. She and Mama would be dressed in long black skirts and woolen stockings and black hats. They always wore white gloves. Sometimes they took a train to other towns to conduct healing sessions or prayer meetings. The Southern Railroad gave them free tickets, because my grandfather worked for the company.

Mama Louvenia and Sister Draper were out of town the day I came down with pneumonia. I was about five or six at the time. My mother happened to be taking care of me, and she didn't put much store in prayer as a healing device, at least not her praying. She rushed to the pharmacy and came back with the pharmacist. (We didn't have any doctors in our community, which was one reason why my grandmother was so important.) He took my pulse and temperature and said I had pneumonia. He also prescribed a medication. But I wouldn't take it. Mama Louvenia had taught me that we didn't need medicine because we had faith. Hanging over my bed was a drawing of Jesus bending over a bed with a little blond girl in it. Under the drawing were the words, "The great physician who forgiveth sins and healeth our diseases."

My mother tried to force my mouth open, but I fought her. By the time my grandmother returned home that night, my mother was distraught, and I had a raging fever. Louvenia Morgan and Sister Draper went right to work, not even stopping to take off their hats.

"Do you really believe in Jesus?" Mama wanted to know.

"Yes," I cried.

She poured a few drops of castor oil on my forehead and made the sign of the cross with it. Then the whole family started praying. It took about four hours, but at last the fever broke. In two more days I was feeling fine.

Just a few months earlier, I'd had another serious illness, appendicitis. Once again, my body was racked with fever, and the pain in my side was so bad that I remember it to this day. The family gathered around my bed and began praying. In a matter of hours the appendix got tired of being inflamed. I don't remember if that was my idea of how I got well or whether my grandmother told me that. At any rate, the pain went away and I felt well again. After that, I believed wholeheartedly in the healing power of prayer, and especially in my Mama Louvenia's abilities. No wonder I refused to take the pneumonia medicine from my mother a few months later.

The problem for a small boy was that there wasn't any place for death. When I heard talk of everlasting life, I thought they meant that true believers didn't die. But Grandpa died. It was confusing, and nobody wanted to talk about it. To this day, I am not comfortable thinking or talking about death.

My grandfather had retired from the railroad, but he didn't just sit around and collect his pension. When he came off the railroad, he got another job. The family probably needed the money. He went to work in the boiler room of Birmingham's biggest department store, Loveman, Joseph and Loeb. He shoveled coal in the hot, dark, unventilated basement. The only good thing about that job was its title—"engineer." He would come home at night just covered in soot. My grandmother or one of my aunts would heat water on top of the stove and pour it into a big galvanized tub, and he would scrub and scrub until all the soot came off. And then he'd get dressed in clean clothes and we'd have supper.

I still have memories of when my grandfather died. He died on the job, shoveling coal. His corpse was delivered to our house the next morning. It was hard for me to understand that he was lying in a coffin in our living room. The rocking chair on the front porch stayed vacant from that day on. Then a few months later, the rocking chair disappeared. I suspected that my uncle Richard took it away. But since nobody commented on its disappearance, I didn't ask.

A big change came for the family around 1919. World War I was over by that time, and the end of the war had a big impact on Birmingham's economy. Thousands of workers were laid off from the foundries, including my uncle Richard, and his income from his other businesses was not enough to support the family. Mama Louvenia decided it was time to leave Steel City and move north. Besides, she knew I wasn't going to get the kind of education she wanted for me in the South.

She picked Chicago, probably because it was one of the most progressive places for the black population. It was like the center of the United States. There were only two railroads that went east to west, the Twentieth Century direct from New York to Chicago, and then you had the Santa Fe from Chicago to California. It would take almost a week to go all the way across the country, so a lot of companies had their headquarters in Chicago and that's where people from both coasts got together for meetings. And it was the easiest northern city to get to from places like Alabama and Mississippi in those days. You could take the L & N direct, or if you couldn't afford a ticket, you could follow the river.

My grandmother was probably influenced by the *Chicago Defender*, the black weekly newspaper that was building its circulation with a campaign to get southern blacks to move north, promising jobs and opportunity and a chance at dignity. The biggest stockyards in the country were in Chicago—Armour, Cuddahy & Smith was there—and they needed unskilled labor, which there was plenty of in the South. The *Chicago Defender* was always talking about how you could get a good job and a decent place to live. Then there were the stories brought back by the blacks from Birmingham who'd gone to Chicago. They came back in new suits, some driving cars. Chicago was the Promised Land. Hundreds of thousands of southern blacks were moving there. And the Morgan clan was going, too.

My grandmother got the pension from the railroad after my grandfather died, and she decided she was going to use that as a stake to move the family up north. She sent my uncle Richard up first. When he left, he carried with him half of Mama's life savings in an envelope, which probably amounted to no more than a few hundred dollars. As the son of Richard Morgan, my uncle Richard applied for free passage north on the Southern Railroad. But his application was denied. So my stepfather, Samuel Davis, the porter, hid him under the lower berth of a sleeping car on a train from Birmingham to Kansas City. Then, in Kansas City, he had his porter friends smuggle Richard aboard a sleeping car on a train to Chicago.

It was a long time before we heard anything from my uncle. He was gone so long my grandmother started to get worried. But he finally came back. He said, "I got a place for the family to stay." And that's when the rest of the family started moving up.

Anna Mae went first. Then my mother went, with my stepfather and half brother, Samuel Davis, Sr., and Jr. Finally it was time for Mama Louvenia and me to go. Uncle Richard sent a check and a note that said, "That is for the purchase of leather suitcases."

In those days, southern blacks traveled with cardboard suitcases, if they could afford suitcases at all. *Leather* suitcases were unheard of. They were for rich people. We decided that Uncle Richard must be rich. In fact, Uncle Richard was doing very well. But he knew that there was a lot of resentment of the "southern niggers" who were arriving in Chicago by the trainload, dressed in their "country" clothes and carrying raggedy cardboard suitcases. Uncle Richard didn't want his mother and nephew being sneered at, or causing him embarrassment.

I'll never forget the day Mama and I left Birmingham. Seemed as if half the city had turned out to see us off. The entire congregation of the Holiness Church was there, and Sister Draper was swooning like she was at a funeral. I looked out the train window at my neighborhood friends, and I had a feeling I would never see them again. I didn't even care. All I could think about was riding on the train and getting to Chicago.

Mama Louvenia and I traveled on free passes, which she got

because my grandfather had worked for the railroad. It was my first train ride, and I studied every inch of wooden paneling and leather seats. The train actually had a colored sleeping car, which my grandmother said was a big step forward. She and the porter exclaimed about the importance of this bit of progress. But there was no colored dining car, and we couldn't share the white dining car, so we ate what Sister Draper had packed for us.

I was too excited to eat. After all those years of watching trains go by, I was finally on one. I wouldn't have cared if we'd had to sleep on the roof of the car. And I was also excited about Chicago. I didn't know much about it, but it sounded like a pretty exciting place to me.

2

CHICAGO

When the train pulled into Chicago the next day, I wasn't impressed with my first views of the city. From a train, you saw the backsides of cities even then. But all the ugliness was forgotten when I saw my mother on the platform. I hardly recognized her. She had cut her hair short and was wearing a short dress that I know Mama Louvenia didn't approve of, though she didn't say anything. But I thought my mother looked beautiful, and I was kind of proud that she was my mother. She didn't look like a country woman just up from the South.

I guess her attitudes changed, too, after being in Chicago for a while. She later divorced Sam Davis and married a Mr. Whitfield.

Most southern blacks who went to Chicago at that time got jobs in the stockyards. Chicago was called the meat butcher to the world. Those were the days when the white meat packers thought chitterlings were garbage and threw them away, and for black employees one of the perks of the job was carrying home chitterlings by the pailful. Down the line somewhere, someone got wise to the secret, and now the packers and caterers get rich selling chitterlings as delicacies at fancy prices.

Uncle Richard didn't go in for a manual labor job when he got to the North. A much better opportunity presented itself in the form of Prohibition. The Volstead Act was passed in 1919, and Richard Morgan saw right away how he could make the much older laws of supply and demand work for him.

The bootleg liquor business was really disorganized. Every petty thief was making bathtub gin or passing wood alcohol off as home brew. Richard had the idea of bringing up some real southern moonshiners to Chicago, guys who knew what they were doing and took pride in their work. He could make good money by selling good stuff.

My uncle also had sense enough to look around and see who ran the Chicago underworld businesses. He didn't just start freelancing. It didn't take him long to figure out that he needed a mob connection, and that was none other than Al Capone. Capone was young then, and not the major mob kingpin that he later became. He liked my uncle, who was probably a couple of years older than he was, and he liked the idea of importing some real bootleggers from the South. I don't know what their deal was, but it turned out to be very profitable for both of them.

By the time Mama Louvenia and I arrived in Chicago, Uncle Richard had his own car, an open-door Nash. We rode from the train station in that limousine, which just happened to be my first ride ever in any kind of automobile. He also had a brownstone house at 2837 Wabash Avenue. By this time, my grandmother was just about overcome with amazement at what Richard had managed to do. "Son," she said, "what have you got here?"

He had four floors. The kitchen was in the basement, and a food elevator connected it to the dining room on the floor above. The bedrooms were on the floors above the parlor and dining room floor. There were *two* bathrooms, which to me seemed like the real height of luxury.

There was not much furniture in the main, public rooms of the house. There wasn't room for it. Most of the space was taken up by barrels bubbling away with bootleg liquor, which had to be stirred constantly. In fact, Richard had a couple of apartment buildings on the city's South Side, and most of the apartments in those buildings were factories for the manufacture of his product. Capone's organization must have provided those apartment buildings, because Richard didn't have the money to buy whole buildings.

Of course the police were always on the lookout for the bootleg operations. They'd get suspicious if a building didn't seem to be "lived in." So Richard called on family and friends to help give his buildings a nice, "lived in" appearance. This meant turning lights on and off at normal times of the day, running the record machine sometimes, pulling the curtains closed when it got dark outside, and of course, stirring the booze in the dozens of bubbling barrels in the empty apartments.

Richard kept moving his operations into more apartment buildings. I remember that Anna Mae moved into a building at the corner of Thirty-second Street and Rhodes Avenue. Mother and Mr. Davis and Sammy moved to 5945 South Michigan Avenue. Mama Louvenia and I stayed at the Wabash Avenue brownstone. Uncle Richard's official residence was at 5848 South Michigan Avenue, but he slept in different places. Other buildings were assigned to my uncle's many girlfriends.

I remember in our house, in the basement, was a tub and a couple of stills. Richard had a setup for making both gin and whiskey. I learned how to make them. We put potato peels in to make gin. They used corn to make the whiskey. They had some kind of mash—hops—and they put yeast in on top of it and let it ferment. And it would start popping—*pop, pop, pop*. To give color to the whiskey, we used brown sugar—burned brown sugar. Bubbling brown sugar—that's where the title comes from.

Richard used to carry the gin and whiskey over to the headquarters, or wherever the distributors were, in the back of his car. He used to drive it over himself. He'd have it in those five-gallon cans, and the whole back of the car would be filled with those cans. He had a cover to put on top of them. There may have been a false bottom, I don't really remember.

My family had never been poor, we were always middle-class. But in Chicago, we were really well-to-do. Uncle Richard dressed in Hart, Schaffner & Marx suits, silk shirts, Borsalino hats, and handkerchiefs and ties that matched. He bought me the same kind of wardrobe, only a few sizes smaller. I was twelve years old and looked like a miniature Bugsy Malone. Mama Louvenia stayed with her same basic, conservative wardrobe, but I remember she acquired quite a collection of black straw hats, and each was decorated with a different flower arrangement. She also bought a dead fox to wear around her shoulders—a whole, stuffed fox, with beady eyes and a sharp nose and claws.

After years of scrimping and scraping, Mama Louvenia was enjoying all this luxury. But she stayed pretty levelheaded. "Vice doesn't pay," she was always telling my uncle. "But whiskey does" would be his retort. She continued to control the family purse strings, only now Richard brought her stacks of hundred-dollar bills instead of a few bucks here and there. She saved a lot of money that he would have just spent on girls and clothes.

One time two cats caught on to what my uncle was doing. They sent him a letter, or called him up, and said they wanted to see him. They said they were from the FBI, and they wanted ten thousand dollars from him. Ten thousand dollars was a lot of money in those days. So he went and told the Capone boys about it, and they said to set up an appointment—tell them to meet him at Wabash Avenue and State Street, under the el. He set that up, and the cats were fool enough to come down and meet him, and the Capone boys had the place staked out. They beat those SOBs, almost killed them, and told them to get out of town. They said, "We're gonna know if you're ever in town again, and if we catch you, we're gonna kill you." Those cats never showed up again. They weren't FBI guys; they were just trying to hold my uncle up.

My uncle Richard and Al Capone had a good business relationship, and Capone and his men were always polite to Mama. More than once, she prayed away illnesses for him, and one time she prayed a bullet out of one of his lieutenants. Capone called my uncle every day. When he called our house, my grandmother always answered the telephone, and I'd hear, "Good morning, Mr. Capone." Mama Louvenia loved that telephone. No one answered it more "elegantly" than she did. "Elegant" was her favorite word once we got to Chicago.

When my aunt, Anna Mae, Mama's youngest, got a job as the maid in the employees' ladies' room at Saks Fifth Avenue, Mama thought that job was elegant. And for that time, it was. It didn't pay much, but it was a cut above being a servant. Anyway, Anna Mae got a 10 percent employee's discount, and that was a nice bonus for the family.

Once we were in Chicago, my grandmother didn't waste any time getting back into the church and healing business. Soon after we arrived in the city, she started looking for the local Holiness Church. What she found wasn't much: an abandoned grocery store at 2916 South Dearborn Street. It only had about twelve members, but Mama didn't worry about that. She moved in and took over, and in about two years there were one thousand members. They had to attend in shifts, because there wasn't enough room for everyone. They hired a minister, M. E. Dunn, and started raising funds for a new church. My grandmother wanted it to look like her old church in Birmingham, and when it was dedicated in 1927 at the corner of Langley Avenue and Sixty-second Street, it did look a lot like the one where I first got inspired to play the drums.

Meanwhile, Mama was in more demand as a healer than ever, and now she appeared before even bigger audiences. She also had an "advance team," three women gospel singers who fired up the congregations before she came on. Their names were Agnes Coleman, Sarah Pitts, and Willetta Moffett.

I think my grandmother also prayed that the rest of her family would join her in Chicago, because after a while Aunt Pherebia and her husband, Mr. Ford, came up. He sold his grocery store in Birmingham and came to work for Uncle Richard. The only one of her children that she couldn't summon up through prayer was Archie, the oldest. He stayed in Birmingham.

Mama told herself that she could continue to lead a Christian life even though most of her family was living on money from bootleg whiskey. But she wasn't so sure about me. I was having a hard time adjusting. Those were some mean streets, and I didn't fit in at all with my silk shirts and my slow southern drawl. The public schools in the neighborhood were rough places where it was more important to carry a knife than a book. I wasn't good at self-defense. Mama worried that I wasn't getting an education.

The first school I attended in Chicago was the Doolittle School. The kids were beating up each other in the school. They had gangs and cliques. They fought and carried on there so, my grandmother was afraid I'd get killed.

She also worried about me growing up around bootleggers and mobsters. She'd watch me stirring the sour mash and then drumming on the wooden barrels. She worried that my basic "exuberance," as she called it, was going to get out of hand. So she decided to send me away to school.

I don't know how she found out about Holy Rosary Academy in Collins, Wisconsin. But when she announced that I was going to a Catholic school, the rest of the family were shocked. Years later, my aunt Anna Mae was still saying, "Making you a Catholic was really reckless of Mama." I wasn't too keen on being educated by a bunch of nuns, either, but once Mama made up her mind, there wasn't much anybody could ever do about it.

I remember that it was a Sunday in the springtime when Uncle Richard drove Mama and me to Collins, which was about ninety miles north of Chicago. The car was a touring car, open, so my uncle and I had on goggles and leather caps like the Red Baron. My grandmother had a silk scarf wrapped around her black straw hat and tied under her chin. She was also wearing her dead fox around her shoulders.

We caused people to do double-takes as we tooled along the country roads. Needless to say, most of them had never seen black people like us before. We stopped for a picnic lunch along the way, and a guy came up to us and asked, "Do you speak English?" He probably thought we were foreign dignitaries.

No matter how elegant we looked, we still had to eat a lunch brought from home. And that night, we threw blankets over the car, wrapped ourselves up in other blankets, and slept on the seats. Blacks couldn't get rooms for the night in the towns we were driving through.

Holy Rosary Academy was pretty new. It was a branch of a school in Milwaukee called St. Benedict's. Father Stephen Eckhardt was the head of the school. He belonged to the Franciscan fathers, and he had dedicated himself to helping blacks and Indians. The school was for blacks and Indians—exceptional children who couldn't get a good education anywhere else—and most of the students were black. The few whites were tokens.

All the teachers were nuns—Dominican sisters. They wore white habits. The one who made the biggest impression on me was Sister Petra, and she would be my guiding force while I was at Holy Rosary. She was a hard-hitting, no-nonsense type of person who also happened to be a virtuoso on the drums, and she taught me some musical lessons that I will never forget.

The school was forming a drum and fife corps. Looking back, I realize that it must have been in financial trouble even then and hoped to get more support by getting some of the students out in public to show what they could do. So they got instruments donated from Catholic organizations and started their group. Sister Petra was in charge. I applied for drums. I didn't know what I was getting into. Her philosophy was to impose the rudiments, you know. She taught me the twenty-six rudiments on drums—drums have a scale just like the horn. She taught me the flammercue and "Mama-Daddy" and all that stuff on the drums. She was great. You're supposed to play drums holding the sticks evenly, but most people favor one side or the other. I'm right-handed, so I favored the right-hand side, and I held the right stick the way I should have been holding the left stick. Boy, whenever she saw me doing that, she'd make me stand up. And then she'd take and kick me in the behind, and she wore pointy-toed shoes, too. I'd change to the other side quick. So that's where I got my rudiments on drums, and I played drums in the drum and fife corps.

We practiced four hours a day. We'd get up in the morning and pray and take some classes. Then after lunch we'd practice for four hours. We did that every day. And when we weren't serious, we'd get hit on the knuckles or kicked in the behind. It's a wonder any of us lived to get to Kenosha, Wisconsin, about two months later for our first Catholic band competition. We won second prize! Out of all those bands, we won second prize, and after being together only two months. That was due to Sister Petra, who made us practice and made sure we were correct.

We went to a lot of other contests after that. Parades, too. Sometimes it wasn't easy parading through a town full of whites, who also happened to be Lutherans. We were an integrated group, but in those days that was almost as bad as being all black. Since I played the drum and marched in the first row, I got the brunt of the crowd reaction sometimes. I remember one time—I think it was a Veterans Day parade in Milwaukee—when a man in the crowd shouted out, "Look at that colored kid. What big eyes he's got . . . and a big mouth, too." That was not my best day. But if I had shown any emotion, Sister Petra would have kicked me good.

I played other instruments—xylophone, orchestra bells, snare drums, and timpani. I loved everything about music, and I'd pick up any instrument I found. I was getting good at reading music, too, thanks to old Sister Petra. But I didn't stay long at Holy Rosary. The school had to close for lack of funds. After about fourteen months, I was back in Chicago. I enrolled at St. Monica's School, at Thirty-seventh and Wabash. My grandmother wouldn't let me go to public school.

St. Monica's was run by the Sisters of the Blessed Sacrament, and they had a dedication to helping blacks and Indians, too. Mother Drexel was their founder. They started Xavier University in New Orleans—I'm on the board of trustees at Xavier. I was happy to continue my education under the Catholics; I liked Catholic training. The Catholic church has done a lot in black education, and the sisters who taught me had a special desire to help blacks. Besides, St. Monica's was very convenient for me, just half a block from where I lived.

I became an altar boy when I was at St. Monica's. Archbishop Mundelein—he wasn't a cardinal then—was coming to the parish for confirmation, and they were short of altar boys. Up at Holy Rosary Academy I had been baptized and confirmed—Archbishop Messmer of Milwaukee was the one who confirmed me. So since I was already baptized and confirmed, they trained me to be an altar boy. Sister Esther, who taught at the school, was Archbishop Mundelein's cousin, and she was the one who taught me the prayers for the regular services and the special prayers for the occasion.

I enjoyed being an altar boy, but they overworked us. We served at regular services, weddings, and other special occasions. I liked to serve with a boy named Joseph Porter, and we were good together. We'd ring the bell, and instead of the usual *bling, blong, blong,* we'd go *bling, bling-bling-bling*—we'd put a little soul into it. We were serving a wedding one time, and Joseph Porter went into the sanctuary and drank the wine. Father smelled the wine on Joseph Porter, and he slapped him, right up there on the altar. That's when I quit serving.

They didn't have a real music program at St. Monica's, but they let me play the snare drum for the other kids. At noontime, I'd be speaking the drums, you know. But I didn't get a chance to develop my music much until I joined the *Chicago Defender* band.

Mr. Robert Abbott, the owner of the *Chicago Defender* newspaper, was one of the few blacks in Chicago who had big money. A couple of the others were Madam C. J. Walker, who made millions with her beauty products and her Poro Beauty Schools, and Mrs. Annie Malone, who owned a bunch of Poro schools. They took over the big mansions on Grand Boulevard after the whites moved. My friend Milt Hinton, the great bassist, likes to talk about how it was called Grand Boulevard until the black neighborhoods started getting too close. Then, after the whites moved out, the name was changed to South Parkway. Now it's Martin Luther King, Jr. Drive.

Anyway, Mr. Abbott was always interested in helping black youth, and he decided to start a band with the black newsboys who delivered his paper. He got Mrs. Schumann-Heink, the most famous singer with the Chicago Opera, to donate her house at Thirty-seventh and Michigan for a kind of conservatory where the boys could study and practice.

Now that Mr. Abbott had his rehearsal place, he wanted a teacher. He got the black musical director from Wendell Phillips High School, Major N. Clark Smith, to be the director of the Chicago Defender Youth Band. He was the next biggest musical influence on my life.

Major Nathaniel Clark Smith was from Kansas, and his father was in the army, so the major grew up with an army education. He joined the army, too, and got to be a major. He had the reputation of being the bandmaster for Theodore Roosevelt's Rough Riders. He always carried himself like a military man and sometimes dressed in military clothes, with a hat and a cape, and wearing medals. One was for his musicianship, and one, I think, was for marksmanship. He was kind of portly and had a handlebar mustache. He was always well dressed, and when he wasn't wearing military clothes, he always wore a vest, morning suit, striped pants. He had both flop tails and the short-tail coat for dress.

Major N. Clark Smith was a graduate of Heidelberg College in Germany, and he was a master in French Solsege harmony, a chording system. He played violin and other instruments. Trumpet was his horn. He taught in Kansas City before he came to Chicago. Walter Page and all those great musicians from Kansas City studied under him, including a couple of guys who later joined Jimmie Lunceford's band. Then he moved to Chicago and Wendell Phillips High School, and Eddie South, Ray Nance, Hayes Alvis, Happy Caldwell, Milt Hinton, Jimmy Fletcher, and Nat and Eddie Cole studied under him there. Later on, he moved to St. Louis and taught Clark Terry and other great musicians from St. Louis.

Major N. Clark Smith taught all those great jazz musicians, but he never taught jazz. The only time we'd play jazz was when Major N. Clark Smith wasn't in the room. He'd throw a stick at you in a minute. He taught harmony and reading, playing what you see. He taught you to play all kinds of instruments. He was a demon, about the greatest musician I guess I have ever known.

I became a *Chicago Defender* newsboy just so I could be in that band. Every Saturday afternoon I delivered those newspapers, and I swear I had the route with the most climbing. All my subscribers seemed to live on the top floors of ten-story walk-ups. But it was worth going through to be in the Chicago Defender Youth Band.

We got out of school at three o'clock, and at three-thirty we'd start the band rehearsals. We practiced from three-thirty to six-thirty every Monday through Thursday. We had private lessons with him for an hour, and then there was an hour for band and an hour for concert, and that would take us up to six-thirty at night. We had Friday, Saturday, and Sunday off. Not everybody was in the concert band, because you had to be special to be in the concert band. We copied the Chicago Symphony. A lot of great musicians came out of the Chicago Defender Youth Band, and they all got a strong grounding in harmony and reading there.

I got ear training from Major N. Clark Smith. I'm still thanking him for that training. In April 1988 I was playing a recording session, and I used that training. I played a whole piece and didn't know what key I was in. With ear training you know every tone on the keyboard; you know what note follows the other. We had a good piano player at that recording session—Bobby Scott. Bobby plays some of the most funky piano you want to hear, and I was listening to him and said to myself, "Well, I'm going to play some, and where he is with this funky stuff. I'm black, he's white. I'm gonna see where he is. I'll just follow him." I didn't know what key he was in, I was going by his sounds, and I was playing all those runs, majors and flatted fifths, nineteenth and twentieth chords. Afterward, the guy said, "I don't know what key you're in, but the way you were playing was a bitch."

On weekends, the *Chicago Defender* band and the concert band would give performances all over Chicago. For some of us, there was also more practicing. After I got good, Major N. Clark Smith had me to practice on weekends the music that he had composed himself. He was real close with Lyon and Healy, the owners of a big music store in Chicago. He often sent boys down there to get instruments. Lyon and Healy had sponsored him on a trip to the Caribbean to write music about black people, and he'd written all these pieces. One was called "Pineapple and Mint." On weekends he had us practicing his compositions, and he had a dream of taking a black youth band down to the Caribbean.

My favorite instrument was still the drums, and all the guys liked to play with me because I was two-time good on drums. But Major N. Clark Smith had a strict seniority system. You had to pay your dues. I had to wait almost a year before I was allowed to appear with the marching band in a parade. And even then I didn't play. My job was to pull the cart that carried the big bass drum.

I'll never forget that day. It was Columbus Day, 1924, and we were the first band. We also had the nicest uniforms, courtesy of Mr. Abbott's money and Major N. Clark Smith's taste. Mama Louvenia was so proud, she had everyone we knew to come out and see me pulling that rope and dragging that cart with the drum on it. Uncle Richard and his musical friends were there, including Jelly Roll Morton. Al Capone and a bunch of guys from his gang made a real commotion when I marched by. And Mama Louvenia looked like she was about to burst.

A little while after that, something happened to the bass drum player, and I started beating the bass drum. And then I moved up to the snare drum. And finally I was the senior drummer, and younger boys had to carry my equipment. They even put the drum sticks into my hands. I had to move up, I'd paid my dues.

Milt Hinton was in the Chicago Defender Youth Band with me. He tells me that I didn't want him to be in the band because he was still in short pants. Graduating to long pants was paying some dues, too. I remember that Mama Louvenia didn't want me to grow out of short pants. She wanted me to still be a boy. But by this time I had graduated from St. Monica's and was at St. Elizabeth's High School, and in high school you wore long pants.

People ask me if I wanted to go to Wendell Phillips High School so I could study under Major N. Clark Smith. But I was happy in Catholic school. Anyway, I was already studying under Major N. Clark Smith because I was part of the Chicago Defender Youth Band. Later, Sam Davis, Jr., got to go to Wendell Phillips, but not me. Milt Hinton remembers being at Wendell Phillips High School with Sam and that Sam was a dancer, which was a dangerous thing for a young boy to be back then. Milt says he ought to know, because he caught hell for playing the violin.

I got a lot of instruction from Major N. Clark Smith after school and on weekends. I first started to play the cymbals. Then it was the bass drum and then the snare drum. After about a year studying under Major N. Clark Smith, he had me to play timpani and then xylophone. He said everybody should know harmony. He got mad with some of the cats in there who didn't want to study xylophone, and he taught me the flute parts of the xylophone. I was playing The William Tell Overture and all those big heavy overtures. Uncle Richard took me to the Dixie Music Shop and bought me the longest xylophone in the place. And after I did that for about a year—I was listening to jazz records by Louis Armstrong and Coleman Hawkins—I got so that I could take their solos off those records and play them note for note on my xylophone. So I was getting into jazz then, heavy.

There was no way not to get heavy into jazz in Chicago in those days. All the big white bands were in Chicago because it was the crossroads of America, and all the great white hotels were there— the Edgewater Beach, the Palmer House, the Congress, the Blackstone. Paul Whiteman, Ted Lewis, Ben Bernie and all the big white bands were playing at those hotels. And as soon as black people started moving to Chicago, they wanted their type of music, and that's when King Oliver and Louis Armstrong and Charlie Christian and the New Orleans bands started coming up in the Mississippi riverboats. They had the whole South Side to play in, and Chicago was a magnet for black musicians from Kansas City, St. Louis, everywhere. You had Jimmy Noone, Freddie Keppert, Jelly Roll Morton.

The black bands and the white bands didn't play together, but they played off each other, and so they were inspiring each other, and it was quite a scene. And there was no way a kid with music on his mind in Chicago wasn't going to be into jazz and dreaming of playing in a big band.

Plus, I had jazz on my doorstep. My uncle Richard was a great jazz fan, and he used his connections to help southern jazz artists get to Chicago. He'd send them train tickets, promise them jobs. My grandmother would find a place for them to stay with one of the members of her congregation. It didn't take them long to find a place of their own once they got familiar with the city. There were so many speakeasies that almost every musician with any talent could get a job.

History has proved that Al Capone was the savior of the black musician in those days. His nightclubs alone employed hundreds. Louis Armstrong, Earl Hines, Jimmy Noone—all those guys got jobs because Capone made the managers get black musicians and black singers. Alberta Hunter was one of Capone's favorite singers. I'm proud of that connection, because even though he was a booze peddler, he set the standard that a lot of big clubs run on today.

I met just about all the greatest jazz artists at Uncle Richard's parties, which he seemed to give all the time. I remember Jelly Roll Morton, with that diamond in his front tooth, and Jimmy Noone, the great clarinet player. Joe "King" Oliver and His Creole Jazz Band played at Uncle Richard's parties, and I remember when he brought a young, unknown trumpet player named Louis Armstrong around.

One thing that struck me about Louis was how he looked. He had great big eyes and an even bigger mouth. I guess those things made an impression on me because of what had happened to me when I was marching in the front row of the Holy Rosary Academy drum and fife corps in the parade in Milwaukee. But I forgot all about how he looked when I heard him play. He had the sweetest trumpet in the world. Eddie South, the great violin player, was also at that party, and they jammed together like they were made to play together. I'll never forget that night.

From time to time, white musicians came to Uncle Richard's parties and jammed with the black musicians. I remember Mugsy Spanier and Frank Teschemacher and Bix Beiderbecke. They would jam until my grandmother put breakfast on the table. Bix Beiderbecke once did a solo at our house that gave me goose bumps. Of course, they couldn't play in public together.

It's kind of sad to think about all those black and white musicians going around admiring each other, playing off each other, jamming privately together, and yet knowing they couldn't be seen together in public. But they just accepted that that was the way things were, and got together privately as often as they could. Some of the younger cats were doing the same thing. Milt Hinton talks about how he and Benny Goodman took music lessons at Jane Adams' Hull House for twenty-five cents a lesson, and about how they could play together there, whereas they couldn't play together anywhere else—they went to segregated schools.

Other whites besides musicians came to my uncle's parties. Mostly they were members of the mob, paying "courtesy" calls. But some were real jazz lovers, like John Hammond, who was an industrialist at that time. They got to hear some of the greatest jazz and blues in Chicago.

Uncle Richard also had all the greatest singers. Alberta Hunter came to my uncle's parties. So did Ma Rainey—she would be accompanied only by Jelly Roll Morton. And then there was Bessie Smith, when she was just up from Birmingham. Uncle Richard knew her from back home. He'd met her when she was working in a laundry across the street from the luncheonette where my mother worked. He may have helped her get to Chicago or helped her get a job once she was in Chicago. They were just friends, then, but I know from personal experience that my uncle thought Bessie Smith's music was the greatest that God had ever put on earth.

Every time Bessie sang, Richard went around shushing people. Nobody was allowed to interrupt her. One night she was singing "Empty Bed Blues," and I got so into the tune that I started to cry. I cried loud, and Uncle Richard told me to leave. In fact, he told me not to ever come back to one of his parties.

A few nights later I was sitting in the kitchen, trying to hear as much music as I could from exile, when Bessie came in, looking for food. She wanted to know what I was doing in the kitchen. I told her. She told me that I'd paid her a big compliment by crying over one of her songs. "You come back with me," she said, and that was the end of my punishment.

Later on, Uncle Richard and Bessie Smith got real close. In fact, he became "Mr. Smith," or so the gossips put it. But he helped her a lot in the early days in Chicago, when she was just up from the South and had no money and he was a big-time bootlegger with Al Capone.

With all that jazz going on in my own house, I was bound to be into jazz. I couldn't get enough of it. I listened to jazz records all the time. I went to every party of my uncle Richard's that I could. I went to jazz matinees at local clubs.

Mama Louvenia didn't disapprove. She said I had a "gift from God." In fact, in the few free hours when I wasn't doing my homework, practicing for Major N. Clark Smith, attending my uncle's parties, or delivering papers for the *Chicago Defender*, she had me give drum or xylophone concerts for her.

I used to hang out at the Vendome Theater, because Erskine Tate had a big orchestra there with Louis Armstrong, Barney Bigard, Stump Evans, and some other cats. I'll never forget the first time Louis Armstrong played with the Erskine Tate band. My uncle Richard bought tickets to the Vendome for the entire family. We were in the front row of the first balcony, and we could see the entire audience go crazy after his first, fifteen-minute solo.

Jimmy Bertrand was the drummer, and he taught me a lot about drums. I learned from him how to please an audience. He was the favorite musician there, the star of the grand finale. He'd do a great solo, then he'd throw his sticks in the air, and then the house lights would go off and all you'd see was a spectacular light show, from his drums. Uncle Richard gave me a set of drums for Christmas—a set just like Jimmy Bertrand's, with flashing lights and all. He was my idol, one of the few people I ever asked for an autograph. I remember one day I waited for him at the stage entrance, before the matinee performance. When he showed up, I was too excited to ask him for his autograph. He gave it to me anyway. Maybe he understood.

When I was in the second year of high school, I was with Les Hite's band. Les Hite was an alto sax player who lived across the street from me. He was about three years older than me, and he had an all-teenage band. I was the youngest in the band, but nobody minded because I could keep good time with the drums. Les Hite's band was doing a lot of gigging, and I got some good experience working with a jazz band. I was sorry when he went out to California and the band broke up. He promised me and the other guys that he would send for us once he got himself established out there. After he left, I worked with Detroit Shannon's band for a while, other local bands. We played Chicago and ranged into other parts of the midwest, including Hastings, Nebraska, where I can remember getting stranded once.

After a while, Les Hite wrote back and told me, "If you come out here I'll get you a job in a big band." I was the only one from the old band that he sent for. He wanted me because I had a different style on drums. I was already playing with a heavy afterbeat, getting that rock-and-roll beat that wouldn't even get popular until the 1950s. I wanted people to dance, have a good time, clap their hands, and they would do it to my drumming. So I was ready to leave the next day, but there were a few details to take care of first. I had to get my grandmother's permission. She didn't give me a hard time. She knew I had to follow my talent.

But she wanted to make sure I would finish high school. At that time, the University of Southern California had an extension course that you could go to right from middle school, graduate from high school, and then go right into college. I promised that I would finish up high school at the university. I didn't promise to go to college. Gertrude, my mother, had to sign some papers, because I was a minor.

Mama Louvenia also wanted to make sure I didn't forget my religion, and I promised to pray every day and go to church on Sundays and write to her at least once a week. But just in case, she started writing to everybody she could think of in the Holiness Church out there, asking them to take care of me and look out for me.

My instruments were crated up and sent on ahead by train. And my aunt Anna Mae arranged for me to travel with the baggage belonging to a rich lady she knew who was going out to California. All I had to do was count about fifty trunks, suitcases, and hat boxes when they were put on board the train, and count them again when they were taken off the train. I never even saw the lady. I got a free ride for this, though my family could have afforded to buy me a ticket. My family was never in distress, and especially not after my uncle started working for Al Capone.

The day I left, Uncle Richard went around slipping bottles to the porters and waiters, so they'd take good care of me. Mama Louvenia made me promise for the hundredth time that I would pray every day and write to her every week. When the express started out of Pacific Union Station, she was crying, Uncle Richard was crying, and I was crying. But I wasn't sad for long. Those railroad workers couldn't do enough for me, and I was the best-cared-for passenger on that whole train—probably even better than the rich lady. It didn't take long for the guys to get into those bottles, and that was one happy ride.

As for me, I was feeling grown, and I couldn't wait to play in a big band.

3

HOLLYWOOD

I arrived in Hollywood with several hundred dollars in my pocket, thanks to Uncle Richard, and the addresses of some Holiness Church families who would let me stay with them, thanks to my grandmother. I went to one of the homes and paid my three dollars a week for room and board for a couple weeks in advance. Then I got in touch with Les Hite.

He wasn't doing as well as he had let on in his letter. When he wrote, he was with Reb Spikes' band, which was called Reb Spikes' Sharps and Flats at the time, but then he left to start his own group. He was getting only a few gigs. He thought that adding me to the group might make a difference. But we still didn't get much work. I was going through Uncle Richard's money fast, treating the guys, buying stuff, traveling around the city.

Hollywood was a pretty town, but I didn't think much of the attitude toward blacks there. It was my first real experience with discrimination. Back in Chicago, the black population was so big that you could live and go to school and work and never even have to talk to a white person. And even if you went downtown, you didn't have to sit in the back of the bus or anything. But out in

Hollywood, it was like the South in some ways. You had to sit in the back of the bus, go into the white nightclubs by the back door. Taxis wouldn't stop for you. Also, black musicians didn't get paid as much as white musicians—in fact, blacks got about 20 percent of what whites made. So even when Les Hite did get a gig, none of us made much money from it.

I figured I'd better get some kind of a paying job, make some kind of money some way. So I went to work as a counter man at a drugstore over in Culver City. It was right near the Metro-Goldwyn-Mayer studios, and a lot of the stagehands and cameramen and extras hung out there, and I liked that. I also liked having all the ice cream sodas and banana splits I could eat. I didn't get a salary, worked for tips, but I usually managed to make about two dollars a day, which was plenty, considering that I was getting room and board for three dollars a week.

The worst thing about that job was the long hours. Quitting time was whenever the manager felt like sending me home. That may have been one reason why I broke so many dishes. But the main reason was that I was just fast. I'd snatch and grab, and a plate would fly this way and a cup that way. After about two months, the manager let me go, warning me never again to work with things that were breakable.

I didn't mind losing that job. The long hours kept me from my music. And luck was with me, because about three days later I got a job as drummer with Reb Spikes' band. By this time the band was called Reb's Legion Club Forty-Fives. Reb had a music store at the corner of Twelfth and Central on the east side of Los Angeles, and he needed a drummer, and a friend of his, a trumpet player named George Orendorff had met me and recommended me to Reb. Soon after I joined, Les Hite came back to Reb, so I was playing with Les after all.

As I remember, I made my first recording with Reb's Legion Club Forty-Fives. It was around November 1924, and the group consisted of Reb on bass sax, me on drums, Andrew Blakeney and Andrew Massingale on trumpet, Leon White on trombone, Les Hite on clarinet, alto sax, and vocals, Gene Wright on piano, and William Calhoun on clarinet, tenor sax, and vocals. We did "My Mammy's Blues." I also played on a cut with Les Hite and William Calhoun called "Sheffield Blues." These were 78-rpm records, and I don't even remember what company we recorded them for—and the discographies aren't any help. All I knew was that I had actually made a record.

Reb didn't do much recording. His main work was a steady gig at a dance hall, the kind where the girls sit around and a guy pays a nickel to dance with one. The girls split fifty-fifty with the house.

Timing was very important in that job. When the place got crowded, the manager always wanted us to speed up so the numbers would be shorter and the guys would have to pay more nickels. Since I was the drummer, I controlled the tempo, and the owner always gave the signal to me. I liked experimenting with the tempo of songs anyway, and I liked things fast, anyway.

When I wasn't playing with Reb, I sat in sometimes with Curtis Moseby's Blue Blowers. We didn't record. Then Paul Howard, who played alto sax, offered me a job with his Quality Serenaders, and I said good-bye to Reb Spikes and Curtis Moseby. There were eight of us in the Quality Serenaders: Howard on alto sax, Charlie Lawrence on alto and clarinet, George Orendorff, the guy who had recommended me to Reb Spikes, on trumpet, Lawrence Brown on trombone, Thomas Valentine on banjo and guitar, James Jackson on tuba, Harvey Brooks on piano, and me on drums. The band was the most popular band among the quality black folks. Paul Howard was secretary and treasurer of the Black Musicians Union in Los Angeles, Local 767, for years. His band played every dance and ball and cotillion there was. We did a good ten gigs a week and made the huge sum of fifteen dollars a week, plus tips. The music was not too exciting. It was mostly slow, romantic tunes, and I didn't beat the drums so much as I brushed them. All this was fine and mellow. We jammed together when we were off duty.

I got more chances to record when I was with the Quality Serenaders. We recorded for Victor, which at the time didn't have studios in Hollywood. The old discographies say we recorded in Hollywood, but we didn't. Instead, Victor rented talking-film studio space from the producer Hal Roach in Culver City.

I remember it was in April 1929, and it was like a steambath in that studio—to keep out the noise, they kept out the air. Every once in a while, when the musicians were about to drop, we could have a break and go out to the street for five minutes. There was a huge microphone in the middle, and the musicians moved up close or far away from it, depending on what kind of sound they wanted. That was the 1929 version of "mixing." The engineer sat over in a corner trying to get the sound on wax, and you usually didn't get a good cut the first time, so you had to do it over and over until he got it. But for me this was a little piece of heaven—recording for a label that at least somebody had heard of.

As I recall, we started out just doing instrumentals, but the studio manager told Paul Howard that he should have a singer on some cuts. Howard turns around and wants to know who can sing. I volunteer. I imitate Louis Armstrong, the greatest jazz voice I'd ever heard. Back in Chicago, I used to go out on a winter night with no coat on, hoping to get laryngitis so I could sound like Louis.

We only did two cuts that first date—"Overnight Blues" and "Quality Shout" (which was supposed to be a play on the name of the band). "Quality Shout" was rejected. But we did better the next time out, which was about a week or two later. I played drums on "The Ramble" and "Charlie's Idea," and I sang on "Moonlight Blues." The next day we tried "Quality Shout" again, and this time we did it right. We also did "Overnight Blues" twice, because the first one didn't come out well, plus "Stuff."

Six months later, in October 1929, we did "Harlem" and "Cuttin' Up," but they were both rejected. This was ten days after the stock market crash, but our problem was not that we'd lost money in the market. In fact, the problems with the recordings weren't our problems at all. The techniques were so primitive in those days that you made more mistakes than you got things right. There were always mechanical troubles. And then if you didn't all start at exactly the same time, you had to scrap the whole ball of wax, or disc in this case—melt it down and try again with a new one. Maybe we were having problems because Paul had added on two new guys—Lloyd Reese on clarinet and alto sax and Earl Thompson on trumpet—and we still weren't all used to working together. It also didn't help that the studio we were in was for talking films, not records.

By the late winter of 1930 Victor finally had its own recording studio in Hollywood, and we didn't have any rejections after that, although there were some sides that weren't issued for one reason or another.

I remember that first session in the new Victor studios because it was the first time I played piano on a record. You worked on a schedule, just like you do now, and when it was time for us to record, the piano player, Harvey Brooks, hadn't shown up. Paul Howard asked who could play the piano, and this rookie volunteered. Jelly Roll Morton had given me a few piano lessons, and I'd listened to every record Earl Hines ever made. I sat down and played in my best Hines style on "New Kinda Blues." By "Hines style," I'm talking about how he stressed the right hand in his playing, with strong chords and great runs. After that, Harvey showed up, so that was the end of my debut as a pianist.

I sang on both "California Swing" and "Cuttin' Up" for that session, in my best Louis Armstrong imitation. I also played drums on "Harlem" and "New Kinda Blues." For me this was a tour de force—singing, playing piano, and playing drums in the same session—and I wrote home about what a big recording star I was. Uncle Richard bought the records and gave them to all his friends as Christmas presents. I must have had copies, too, but I didn't have sense enough to hold onto them. I was traveling light in those days, and I wasn't thinking about history. I was thinking about having a good time and playing my music.

I wasn't content with the kind of music I was playing with the Quality Serenaders, but I was working steady, and there was a certain advantage to playing with the group that gigged at all the parties for the black middle class. We played for afternoon dances for the teen-agers. There was a dance hall down at Fifty-fifth and Central, and all the kids went upstairs there for afternoon dances. They didn't let kids go to parties at night in those days. In the evenings we played the big parties for the grown-ups. That's how I met Gladys. If I'd just been playing small dives, I never would have met her.

The Quality Serenaders played at the annual ball of the Antique Art Club, one of the biggest black clubs in Los Angeles. A lot of the members were maids and butlers to the rich white Hollywood folks, or porters and attendants in the "comfort rooms" of the big stores on Rodeo Drive, and in those days if you worked for the high and mighty, you were pretty high and mighty yourself. The chauffeurs were the hottest things out there, with those slick outfits on—the chicks went for that. You also had a lot of "opportunities." I still feel like I should say this in a whisper: they stole. The women would steal those white women's dresses and wear them out at night. Steal their champagne—here's a bottle for you and two for me. My lord, they had a big society thing going out there, all those maids and butlers and chauffeurs. And this Antique Art Club was the crème de la crème.

During an intermission, Paul Howard and the rest of us in the band were invited over to the president's table to share a toast with the members of the board. A group of young women were sitting at the table. They all wore orchids, and we called them the orchid girls. After the toast, we were standing around talking. They were asking us where we lived, and I mentioned that I was living with a funda-mentalist family but that I was looking to move. I was getting tired of them watching over me and wanting me to play at their church and always writing home to my grandmother about me.

One of the orchid girls said that her mother operated a board-inghouse for railroad men, and before we left to go back to the bandstand, I had the address, and somehow it had been decided that

I would move the next morning to 1109 Central Avenue. I didn't even know the girl's name, and already she'd made a major decision for me. That was Gladys. It was 1929, and from that day until she died, she made all my major decisions.

She was a beautiful girl—tall, light complected, carried herself well. She was part Indian and had been born on a reservation in Lehigh, Oklahoma, but she had grown up in Dennison, Texas. She'd attended Fisk University in Nashville, Tennessee. She was older than I was by about three years, and she had also been married before, to a guy named Neal. She never talked about him much. All she would say was that he was very mean and that he beat her, and that's why she divorced him. Her maiden name was Riddle, but she was using the name Gladys Neal when I met her. She was a lot more sure of herself. She was a career woman—worked for the movie studios as a seamstress. Later, I realized that Gladys was a lot like my grandmother, but I didn't make the connection at the time.

Anyway, I admired Gladys right from the start, but I didn't have any ideas about going out with her. The fact that she was older and so sure of herself kept a shy young guy like me from even thinking about asking her out. Plus, I was concentrating on my music and becoming a jazz star. But Gladys showed an interest in me, wanted to know about my plans for the future and all, and pretty soon I was telling her about my family and my dreams.

It was Gladys who made me keep my promise to my grandmother and enroll in that extension course at USC. And she told me that I should save my money, though I admit I didn't pay much attention to that bit of advice. And she'd do little things for me. She'd bring home the silk drawers that she made for some guy. Either it was Douglas Fairbanks, Jr., who was married to Joan Crawford; or else it was Lord Mountbatten, who was friends with Hearst and who found out about Gladys from Marion Davies after she and Hearst got together. Whichever one it was liked handmade silk underwear with his initials embroidered on them, and he would wear a pair only three, four times. Well, Gladys was never one to waste anything, and so when he got rid of those drawers, she'd take them back and bring them home to me.

I enjoyed the attention and took some of the advice, and the living arrangement was just fine with me. I shared a big first-floor room with a cousin of Gladys—cousin Rudolph, who was a bank teller—and ate her mother's great cooking and all for nine dollars a week.

Meanwhile, Les Hite was finally doing better. He'd gotten together with a couple other guys and formed a band, Elkins and Hite. Leon Elkins really started it. He was an old trumpet player who used to play the circus. He got out to the West Coast and got a job, and he brought Les in and gave him half the band, and Les brought me in. I left the Quality Serenaders without thinking twice. It didn't matter to me that the country was going into a depression and that I might be better off with an established group. I don't think I was far enough along in my relationship with Gladys at that point to have asked her advice. The Quality Serenaders weren't playing my kind of music. I wanted to swing, and with my old buddy from Chicago, Les Hite.

It wasn't long before Les Hite had the whole band. Elkins had asthma or something and gave it up, and Les put in some new, younger guys. We played together for a few months and were very popular, too, in and around L.A. We could swing, but we could also play romantic music, and we got a lot of gigs playing those Antique Art Club dances and the balls for the Holy Girls (we called them the Holy Girls, but they were church clubs). We played for these kinds of affairs about four, five times a week.

One night we played one of these balls, and the porter in the men's room at Frank Sebastian's Cotton Club was there, and he heard us and liked what he heard. Frank Sebastian was looking around for a new band because the band at the club had been there for about eight years. So this porter tells Frank Sebastian, "I heard a band the other night that was real great. If you want to hear them, I'll set up an audition for you."

So he called Les Hite, and we did the audition for Frank Sebastian, and he *loved* our band. We were a bunch of young cats and we could swing, man. And I made a big difference because I kept time like a big band swinger. And the thing about it was that we could play popular songs, and we all could read music good, because we all had a high school education and some had college or junior college, and we could play the shows and back up the headline acts. When Frank Sebastian hired us for his Cotton Club, man, we all felt we'd made the big time. We went in under the name Leon Hereford's New Cotton Club Orchestra, because Sebastian wanted Hereford to front us, but very soon we were Les Hite and His New Sebastian Cotton Club Orchestra.

Frank Sebastian must have had some kind of connection with the mob back east, because he named his club after the Cotton Club in New York, and that was run by the mob. The club was across the street from the MGM lot, and Frank used to hire the big headliners from back east to come out there and stay for a month or six weeks, and all the Hollywood stars would go there to see them. Frank Sebastian put on a good show. He had a big show with beautiful black girls who danced in big production numbers, and comedians, and then a big headliner. The Mills Brothers were playing there when we auditioned and got the job in the spring of 1930. We played behind them for about two weeks.

Then, between acts, the house band—us—would play. We weren't Les Hite's band any longer. Now we were Frank Sebastian's Cotton Club Orchestra. He had fancy uniforms made for us, and he decided that the leader and the drummer, Les and I, should wear gray top hats. I thought that was cool.

We played good dance music for the people to dance to. We didn't have our own arrangments. In those days you didn't have professional arrangers, and you couldn't buy scores for jazz bands. We copied other bands—that was our "book." They had a band out at the Coconut Grove called Les Arnheim and His Orchestra, and we'd listen to him, get his arrangements. We played to the same clientele, and we could play all those pretty numbers like "Roses Remind Me, Remind Me of You" and "I Surrender, Dear." We would listen to recordings of Duke Ellington's band, and every number he'd play we'd take it off the record. Les was a great fan of Ellington, and every time Sonny Greer hit those cymbals in a number, I did, too. One time Duke and his band came out to Hollywood to do a movie, and Frank Sebastian gave us the night off and presented Duke instead. Afterward, Sebastian told Duke he wasn't that great—his own house band played all the same arrangements. But Duke got his revenge—he hired Lawrence Brown away from Les, and that's where Lawrence Brown made his big, big reputation as a trombone player, with Duke.

But I'm getting ahead of the story. Back to what kinds of numbers we played: Les Hite would mix them up. We played the pretty numbers, but we had all kinds of jazz numbers to throw in there. Old Les really knew how to put those numbers together. I learned a lot from him, and that's how I can play today—I can play in front of any type of audience because I know how to judge them.

Louis Armstrong came into Frank Sebastian's Cotton Club that summer. His manager, Irving Mills, was out there ahead of him to take care of the negotiations, and he heard us, and he said to Frank, "Keep Hamp in there, and I'll bring Louis Armstrong out with his music and leave his band in New York and let your band back up Louis." So that's what happened. Frank Sebastian got the idea of handing out contracts to individual members of the band, and the only ones he gave contracts to were Lawrence Brown and me. We stayed regardless of who came. I think I was making ninety dollars a week under that contract. I had started at Frank Sebastian's Cotton Club at fifty-six dollars a week, and even then I was making a little more than the rest of them because I was the drummer, and I was a good drummer, and if a tap dancer came on the floor, he didn't need any taps on his shoes because I could make all the taps for him on the drum.

In fact, I actually did that for a tap dancer named Bo Diddley. He would finish his performance standing on his head, while I made the tap noise on the drums. We had a good time together working up new variations on this theme. Frank Sebastian liked this kind of novelty number, and once he found out that I had a good time doing them, he had the idea of having a second set of drums brought to the dance floor while I was doing a solo on stage. Then the band would start playing "Tiger Rag," and I would suddenly run to the other set and start running around the drums and throwing my sticks in the air. The band would point their instruments like guns, and the crowd would yell out, "Where is the tiger?" while I screamed as if the tiger was biting me. Then, at the end, I would jump on top of the drums to safety.

I loved doing those antics. To me it was showmanship, and I have always been Mr. Showmanship. I used to study other drummers who clowned around, because there was a long, honorable tradition of clowning in black performing that I wanted to carry on. My biggest influence back then was a guy named Rastus Crump who was with Norman Thomas's quintet. He was a small little man and probably the biggest showman there ever was on drums in those days. I picked up a lot from Rastus Crump—walking around the club beating on people's glasses and that sort of thing.

Les Hite was still fronting the band when Louis came in. Les brought in a lot of young cats—got modernized, you understand. We had George Orendorff and Harold Scott on trumpet, Luther "Sonny" Craven on trombone, Marvin Johnson on alto sax, Charlie Jones on clarinet and tenor sax, Henry Prince on piano, Bill Perkins on banjo and guitar, and Joe Bailey on bass and tuba. Later on, Marshall Royal came in on clarinet and alto sax. He was a young cat, only about eighteen and the baby of the band. His father, Marshall Royal, Sr., was president of Local 767 of the Black Musicians Union. His mother had helped to raise Gladys back in Dennison, Texas, and his mother and Gladys's mother had been friends since the time Gladys's mother married her husband, who was a miner in one of those little towns in Texas. After Louis came in, we were Louis Armstrong and His Sebastian New Cotton Club Orchestra.

Louis fell in love with us. At first, he was kind of disgruntled about not having his own band with him, especially his drummer, Frank Barbarin. But it didn't take him long to realize we could back him just as well as his own band. He really liked me. He didn't remember me from Chicago even after I told him about Uncle Richard's parties and how I used to walk the streets in the winter nights trying to catch a cold so I could sound like him. He liked the way I could play drums, and the way I could play the bells when he wanted that kind of sound, and the way I knew all his solos. He said to me, "You swings so good, I'ma call you Gates," and from that day since I have been proud to carry that nickname. Some of my friends still call me by that name.

Right away Louis took us on a recording session with him. We did "I'm a Ding Dong Daddy," "I'm in the Market for You," "Confessin' (That I Love You)," and "If I Could Be with You for One Hour Tonight" for Okeh and Columbia in July, and then we did one cut, "Body and Soul," in early October. But the recording session I remember best was on October 16, 1930. We were recording for Okeh, and the recording studio was also the NBC studio and sitting in the corner was a set of vibes. Louis said, "What's that instrument over there?" And I said, "Oh, that's a new instrument that they're bringing into percussion, into the drum department. They call it a vibraharp, some call it a vibraphone." At that time they were only playing a few notes on it—*bing, bong, bang*—like the tones you hear for N-B-C. All that big beautiful instrument and nobody could do anything with it.

To give you a little history of the vibraharp: It was invented about ten years before that. It looks like a xylophone, but the vibrato is produced by the rotation of electrically operated fans at the upper ends of the resonator tubes. It hadn't been used for anything except incidental chime notes—the intermission signals on radio programs —but it was important in those early days of radio. With all the programs live, and since it took quite a bit of time to switch from one studio to another, the intermission signal filled the gap. I'd never played it, but I'd heard about it, seen it, and just hadn't gotten around to trying it out.

It is still probably the most misunderstood instrument in music. People don't know whether to call it a vibraharp or a vibraphone or a xylophone. Both vibraharp and vibraphone were originally trade names. Vibraharp was the oldest, and that's what I've always called it. To avoid the problem, just call it the vibes.

We started to record, and then the equipment broke down or something—equipment was always breaking down in those early recording studios. We're standing around waiting for the technicians to repair the equipment, and Louis noticed the vibraharp again. So he said, "Can you play it?" I was a young kid, full of confidence, and I said, "Sure." So I looked at it, and it had the same keyboard as the xylophone had. He said, "Pull it out in the middle of the floor and play something on it." So I pulled it out, and Louis plugged it in. Everybody's standing around waiting to record, and I played one of his solos, note for note, that I had taken off one of his records. That ear training came in handy. And boy, he fell out. He said, "Come on, we going to put this on a record. You can play on this record."

Eubie Blake had sent Louis a copy of his song, "Memories of You," and I played the introduction on it. I'm playing vibes all through that. That's the first time jazz had ever been played on vibes. Not long ago I met a guy who said he had the original record that I played on, and he's supposed to get it for me.

I played with Louis for eight or nine months out at Sebastian's Cotton Club, and it was great, man. We had a ball. I proudly sent a picture of the band home to my mother, and wrote on it:

1. Mama, that is Les Hite who has the band.
2. That is Louis Armstrong. We play a lot of numbers together.
3. That is you know who. Pray that I become the world's greatest drummer.
4. That is George Orendorff. He and Les and I started playing together.

At Sebastian's Cotton Club with Louis Armstrong, I wasn't the world's greatest drummer, but I was getting pretty good billing. The announcer would say, "Louis Armstrong, the world's greatest trumpet player, and the world's fastest drummer, Lionel Hampton." They would broadcast over radio live from the club, and it went all up and down the coast. We recorded again, too, in December 1930 and in March 1931, and the records sold really well because of the publicity we were getting. On those last two sessions with Louis, I was on drums and vibes. That first experience with the vibraharp didn't excite me enough to switch instruments. Besides, that one cut, "Memories of You," wasn't enough to get the whole music world behind the vibraharp as a standard instrument.

When Louis left to return to New York, later that spring, he told me he would send for me. But I didn't sit around waiting. Frank Sebastian still wanted me at the Cotton Club, and I was happy there.

It was after Louis left that Buck Clayton came into the Cotton Club band. The legend has gotten around that Buck Clayton worked for me, and he doesn't like that. It isn't true. He and I played together for Frank Sebastian. We kind of ran the band together. Then Buck left to go to China, and a boy by the name of Ike Bell came in.

It was also after Louis Armstrong left that Gladys stepped in and started acting as a kind of unofficial manager for me. She was taking a real interest in my career, and she didn't think I should be running around the stage pretending to be bitten by a tiger, at least not for what I was getting paid. She thought I should be paid better, and she thought I should get individual billing. She knew just how to handle Frank Sebastian, who had an ego that was of major dimensions even by Hollywood standards. At least once a week we had to have a photo session. Every formal photograph of the orchestra had him in it—even when we didn't notice it at the time. Gladys understood that. She'd always start a business discussion with him with "You, who knows how to appreciate music" or "You, who has such good taste." She negotiated such a good salary for me that the other guys asked her to act for them, too. I still remember the *Hollywood Reporter* headline, "Frank Sebastian pays highest wages in show biz!" This was big news, especially for black musicians.

Then, Gladys went to work on the issue of billing, which was even harder, because the only name Frank Sebastian liked to see in lights was his own. But Gladys did it. He finally changed the marquee so it read "Frank Sebastian's Cotton Club"; then below that, "Appearing / Les Hite and Frank Sebastian's Cotton Club Orchestra"; and finally, below that, "New! Frank Sebastian features the World's Fastest Drummer, Lionel Hampton!" "This is a giant step forward," said Gladys.

Then she started urging me to form my own band. She had good reasons. I was famous on the West Coast because of the radio broadcasts from the club, and I was packing people in every night because my name was out there, and the booking agents just kept on worrying me to play here and play there.

Gladys went around asking the guys at her mother's boarding house if anybody had heard of me outside of L.A. Most of them were railroad men, and so they traveled around a lot. They told her that nobody knew who I was east of the Rockies, but on the West Coast, as far up as Vancouver, people in every little town knew about Lionel Hampton, the world's fastest drummer. Gladys decided there was a market for me out there. She didn't go so far as to suggest that I ought to try to compete with the established bands in L.A. Les Hite and Paul Howard's Quality Serenaders and a couple other bands had a corner on the market—there were only so many Antique Art Club balls to play at. But outside L.A. was a different story. Anyway, she talked me into it, and finally I took the plunge.

4

FIRST BANDS

I got together a ten-piece band—four brass and a rhythm section. Meanwhile, Gladys was looking around for a manager. She was getting pretty good at the business angle of music, but even she knew she wouldn't get far in those little towns outside L.A. All of them put together didn't have a big enough black community to support a ten-piece band. No Antique Art Clubs in those little places. So we were going to have to go after white audiences. That meant dealing with white club and theater managers. Then, too, we were going to have to travel and somebody was going to have to see about hotels and all. Gladys was self-assured and businesslike, but that didn't take away from the fact that she was "colored," as we put it in those days. She couldn't even go in the front door of some of those white theaters, much less sign contracts. Being a woman wasn't the problem so much as being black. So we had to find a white "front man," and that wasn't easy either. Even in those Depression days, white guys willing to manage a black band were few and far between.

We finally found an Englishman named Jack Hamilton who was willing to take us on. He had red hair and freckles. He was a nice guy. We couldn't ask for much beyond that, because at least he said he'd take the job. He started lining up some booking for us, and it seemed like he was doing what he was going to get paid for. We hired him on a percentage—he'd get 25 percent of our take from every gig, before expenses. When we started to travel, he didn't travel with us. He went on ahead. He said he had to make preliminary arrangements. He said he would leave us an envelope with our 75 percent share.

We set off on our first road trip in two cars. One was Gladys's 1929 Dodge, which she drove. The other was a 1927 Ford, which I think she borrowed. She needed a driver for the Ford, so that's how Johnny Miller got hired as bassist. He was a good bassist, but the main reason he was hired was because he was willing to drive, too. I didn't know how to drive, and I have never learned. We squeezed everyone plus instruments into or onto those two cars. The bass, the drum, and the vibes were all strapped on the roofs. It was uncomfortable enough riding, but sometimes we also had to sleep in those cars.

Jack Hamilton would take a gig for the money, without taking into account the fact that it took some time to get from one place to another. So sometimes we didn't have time to stay overnight anywhere. Most of the time, though, that wasn't the problem. The problem was accommodations. In the larger towns, especially towns with railroad stations, there were boarding houses for blacks where we could stay for five dollars a night plus all the fleas that could bite us. In some of the smaller towns, we could stay with local black families in their homes. We had clean sheets, good food, and paid a lot less than we had to pay at the flop houses. But there were some towns that didn't have any blacks at all, or where the blacks didn't have any room. Then, we slept in the car.

The same conditions went for eating. We couldn't go into most restaurants except through the back door to order takeout. Many's the time that we bought bologna and cheese and bread at a grocery store and ate sandwiches in the car. We were always glad to find a Chinese restaurant. They didn't segregate us, and we could eat a good big meal cheap. We had to eat cheap. Sometimes all we could afford was rice. We'd put ketchup on it. This was embarrassing to some of the guys, so Gladys would go in, order ten cartons of takeout rice, pour ketchup into the cartons, and bring it out to us.

Gladys was a strong woman. She could have been back in L.A., living in comfort and making good money at her job with MGM. But Gladys believed in me. She had quit her job, or taken a leave of absence (I can't remember which), and there she was sleeping in a cramped car and eating rice and ketchup when she could have been attending Antique Art Club balls. She believed in me, and she was convinced that we could make big money.

We had some serious problems with money, thanks to Jack Hamilton. Time after time, all we found in the envelope he left us —which was supposed to contain our 75 percent—was a note explaining why he couldn't leave us any money this time. He always had an excuse. Gladys kept getting madder and madder, but there wasn't much she could do. If she fired him, who could she get to replace him?

That first road tour ended in Seattle when most of the musicians decided to sign on with a ship that was taking a pleasure cruise somewhere. I couldn't blame them. At least on the ship they got to travel in style and have three square meals a day. Gladys and I could not offer them that. We were a sorry group returning to Los Angeles—the remains of a band in two practically empty cars, with no money to show for our grand tour.

Of course, Gladys announced to Frank Sebastian that we'd had a "triumphant tour," and that's how he introduced me every night after I returned to the Cotton Club to play with the Charlie Echols Cotton Club Orchestra (Les Hite had gone off to work someplace else by then). I didn't put him right about that. Still, I was pretty discouraged. But Gladys wasn't. She reminded me that people had stood in line to get tickets to see the band and that they had danced and cheered and applauded everywhere we went. That was true. In those same towns where we couldn't get a hotel room or a meal in a decent restaurant—even if we could pay for it—the people treated us like kings once we got up on the stage. I'll never forget Portland, Oregon. It was the only time in my life I couldn't get served at a hotdog stand. But at the McEnroy Ballroom it was standing room only to hear Lionel Hampton and His Orchestra. Gladys said it was important to keep trying. "The money will come," she said. So I let her talk me into getting a new band together and trying another road trip.

I know it's hard to believe, but we let Jack Hamilton book us again. He swore he'd do better, and Gladys negotiated a different money arrangement so he didn't get it all. We couldn't find anybody else. If we wanted to go on the road, we had to let Jack Hamilton act as the front man.

This time we traveled in three cars. The third was owned by Buster Wilson, the piano player. We also had a small trailer for the instruments. Now, when we had to sleep in the cars, at least there was some room to curl up. This time, Jack had gotten us some better bookings, and we were really looking forward to eating better and maybe having some profits. But pretty soon old Jack started scamming us again.

He booked us into a nightclub in San Diego promising that our girl singer would sing all of Duke Ellington's tunes. We did not have a girl singer. When we arrived in San Diego, Jack was on his way to Bakersfield (with the advance money), and the manager of the club wanted to know where our girl singer was. He informed us that if we didn't get a girl singer who could sing Duke Ellington's songs by show time, he'd haul us into court for breach of contract.

We couldn't hire a temporary girl singer because Jack had our money. So Gladys became our girl singer. We rehearsed "Sophisticated Lady," and she didn't sound too bad. Meanwhile, she'd called her mother to come down from Los Angeles by bus with an evening gown. Mrs. Riddle arrived in the nick of time, and Gladys went on in a beautiful red dress covered with sequins. When the time came for her to sing, she launched into "Sophisticated Lady," and for the first few bars everything was fine. Then she started changing keys. I am telling you, we went up and down the scale with Gladys, and the audience loved it. The audience wanted an encore, and since that was the one Ellington song she knew, she just kept singing it. And the other musicians and I got the biggest workout of our lives trying to follow her up and down that scale. Talk about improvisation!

That whole trip was one case of improvising right after another. Jack Hamilton did it to us again when he booked us into the Trianon Ballroom in L.A. It was my first appearance in L.A. as a bandleader, and I wanted to make a good impression. But Jack had told the manager that we dressed in white tuxedos, and we didn't have any tuxedos. Gladys got on the phone to her friend, Dr. Chops.

His real name was Nelson Creswell, and he'd been raised up with Gladys in Texas and was like one of her family. Later, he was like one of our family, too. He just died out in L.A. a couple of years ago, and I miss him a lot. Dr. Chops was Gladys's Mr. Fix-It. He was a hustler, a utility man. He was in merchandising. He'd get stuff wholesale and he'd say, "Man, I got a great suit here for you," and you'd give him ten dollars on the deal and it was all right. Sporting life type.

Anyway, when Gladys told him we needed tuxedos, he said he'd see what he could do. His job was to round up ten white tuxedos and ten pairs of white shoes. He got our sizes and said he'd be back in touch. We waited all afternoon, but no call. We were scheduled to go on at nine that evening, and we had no alternative plan. Finally about eight o'clock, he called. "Be ready to put on the tuxedos as soon as I get there," he said. So we got dressed in our white shirts and ties and stood around in our shorts wondering if he was going to get there. He arrived just before nine, and we rushed into the tuxedos and shoes. The only trouble was, my shoes were about two sizes too tight. Dr. Chops told me to jump around a lot and I wouldn't notice. So that's what I did.

Gladys made a mental note to get in contact with a tuxedo rental place and have all our sizes on file there, so we wouldn't have to go through that again. Of course, the ideal was to have a whole wardrobe of tuxedos, white and black. But we weren't making that kind of money.

We were getting maybe sixty-five dollars a night. But after expenses the musicians made only about ten or fifteen dollars a week. Gladys and I made a little more, but we're not talking big bucks here. There were a lot of expenses, especially for the cars—new tires, gas, other repairs. We needed those cars, because we traveled up and down the coast from Tijuana to Vancouver. At one point, money was so tight that Gladys mortgaged her mother's house to tide us over. Her mother never found out.

There were always problems. In Oakland, Buster Wilson got sick and so did his car, and we needed both another car and another pianist. By this time Paul Howard had lost his band and was with me. He knew that Lawrence Brown, the trombone player who had gone with Duke, had a brother in Oakland. The brother was a mailman, and mailmen knew everybody in those days. The mailman got us Ernie Lewis, who was not only a piano player but a piano player with a car. He later became president of the American Federation of Musicians. Back in those days, most black musicians weren't even in that union, much less officers.

I remember that it was also that time in Oakland that I found myself without an alto player. I asked around, and somebody told me about this young kid named Jerome Richardson. By young, I mean he was only thirteen or fourteen, and he didn't even play jazz, but he could read well. So I sent somebody to ask his father if he could join me for a gig at a theater there in Oakland, and the father said okay, as long as he could drive the kid to the club and then pick him up afterward, and that was all right with me. So this young Jerome Richardson comes to rehearsal, and he is really just a kid, but I remembered that I could play real good when I was a kid. And this kid could read, and he played so well that I wanted him to stay with us. But his father said no, he had to go to school. But about fifteen years later Jerome Richardson played with my band.

Oh, we had some times on the road in those early days. I remember our first trip to Las Vegas. Jack booked us into one of the casinos as a fifteen-piece show orchestra at a time when we only had eight or nine musicians. He told us he'd arranged to have Al Durham, a trumpeter out of Kansas City, join us with six musicians to make up the difference.

Well, Durham didn't arrive on time, and we had to play the first night with just the usual number of musicians, and the club manager was fit to be tied. And then finally Durham shows up in his old car with six people, but only four musicians. Two of them were hitch-hikers he'd picked up on the way. They were a dancing couple that called themselves Bodmer and Bodmer, and since I needed them to make up the right number I included them in the show. They were a big hit. He was tall and skinny, and she was as fat as the fat lady in a sideshow. The audience howled when they did "Swan Lake."

Las Vegas wasn't much of a town then—mainly just one strip of casinos. Real segregated. Across the tracks were some wooden buildings; they called the section Dustville. The Chinese had places there where you could play poker and dance, and that's where the black entertainers went. We stayed over there, and that's where we were allowed to gamble. We couldn't even go in the front door of the casino where we played.

Things were about the same in Reno, but during that same trip we got to stay in the same casino where we were playing. That gig was memorable for two reasons. One was that Jack Hamilton was actually waiting for us. Some of the guys in the band didn't believe until that day that Jack Hamilton was real. They thought he was somebody Gladys and I had made up to explain why we couldn't pay the musicians half the time. Old Jack was there to tell us he didn't have a place for us to stay. "I booked you into the hotel," he said.

We said, "What?" We knew we couldn't stay in that hotel. But Jack said we should try to wing it. So we walked in the front door and Jack told the woman at the desk that we had reservations, and the woman didn't even blink an eye. Jack stayed in Reno at that hotel the whole time we were there, just in case we had any trouble. But we didn't. We paid more for those hotel rooms than we made playing that gig, but it was nice to stay in style for a change. Later, the manager told us he knew it was all pretty unusual, but he thought that maybe the usual rules didn't apply to us because we were famous.

I had to give Jack Hamilton credit for staying with us that time. And not long afterward he made up for all the rest of the trouble he'd caused and the money he stole. We were in San Jose when Gladys got real sick. In fact, she collapsed on her bed one day, and she was bleeding and I was afraid she was going to die. Jack was in San Diego, but I got on the phone with him and told him what was happening, and he got on the phone to the local hospital, and then the hospital called us to say to take her there. And there a German doctor named Schufeld, who was a famous surgeon, operated on her and took out her appendix.

Jack sent his wife, Marley, to stay with Gladys while she recuperated. I stayed close by with the band, but I wasn't very good around sick people or hospitals. Growing up with Mama Louvenia around, we never even took aspirin, and part of me felt real uncomfortable around doctors and hospitals. So I was glad that Marley Hamilton was around. Jack never managed any situation as well as he did that time Gladys had appendicitis. And when Gladys got out of the hospital and I asked for the bill, Dr. Schufeld told me I could pay him by playing at a party he was having at his house. It's one of my nicest memories about the days when I had my first band.

I wanted to stay in San Jose until Gladys was well enough to rejoin the band, so I got us a gig at a little club that was owned by a guy named Sam Ervine. We were working for very little money, and we brought in so much business that Sam wanted us to stay. I told him we couldn't. Los Angeles was our home base, and even if we played on the road most of the time, we didn't want to relocate. Well, it turned out that Sam had a club in L.A., too, and when I convinced him I wasn't staying in San Jose, he offered us a long-term deal at a beer hall he had there. He said he'd turn it into a jazz club if we'd be the house band.

I later found out that Sam Ervine owned a lot of clubs, almost all of them in his sister's name. Sam himself was a detective with the Los Angeles Police Department, and that helped both when liquor was illegal and later, after it was legal again and clubs had to get liquor licenses.

I should mention that Prohibition was over by this time, 1933. Back in Chicago, the ride was over for my uncle Richard. He'd seen it coming anyway. The Depression had hurt the bootlegging business, and there was talk of repeal for years before the states finally voted on it. Around 1930 he and Bessie Smith really got together.

Before then, they were just friends. She had become famous and started traveling on the TOBA entertainment circuit. (The initials stood for Theater Owners Booking Association, but black entertainers said they stood for Tough on Black Asses.) Bessie wasn't around Chicago that often. She got married to Jack Gee, a nightwatchman from Philadelphia, and Richard was living with a woman named Lucy. Then Bessie and her husband separated, and she went to see him one time when she was in Chicago, and they were both free and they got together. From then on, he became her manager and started traveling with her and her troupe. Thanks to Mama Louvenia, Richard had invested his money and had plenty of it to help Bessie out. More than once he had to bail her out of jail after she got drunk and was arrested for violating the Volstead Act. He worried about her drinking, but he never gave her a hard time about it. He respected her too much, as a singer and as a person.

The two of them moved to Philadelphia, and Richard helped Bessie get her son, Jack, Jr., back with her. Around the same time —this was about 1932—Lucy decided she wanted Uncle Richard back. But Richard wanted to stay with Bessie. Lucy died not long after that, and to this day I still think she grieved herself to death. I wasn't around for any of this, because I stayed pretty much on the West Coast, but after I went with Benny Goodman, I met up with Richard in Philadelphia and he filled me in.

Anyway, after Gladys got sick, her mother told her to stay home and not go on the road anymore. I was tired of being on the road so much, and I wanted to have a steady gig in L.A. That's where all the jazz, such as it was, was happening on the West Coast. The big-time jazz center had shifted from Chicago to New York by then, and the hottest band was Duke Ellington's. He came out regularly to be in movies, but he didn't stay around long. Louis Armstrong came out for movies, too, but his home base was New York. I didn't have any ideas about changing coasts. I liked California, and anyway, that's where Gladys was.

So Sam Ervine's offer sounded good to me, and it fit in with Gladys being permanent in L.A. There, she could look after my business and have her own business, too. She set up a partnership with a woman named Beazie DeVaughan, and they sewed for all the big stars.

We went into the Red Car Club, which was located at the corner of Sixth and Main Street in downtown L.A., right at the spot where the red car trolley line that connected the piers with the central city ended. Motormen and conductors hung out there, and so did all the sailors who came in on the ships and then took the trolley into the city. The club was a big beer garden—it seated about four hundred—with sawdust on the floor. The chicks who worked there wore blue-jean overalls—didn't care how they looked. The only liquor sold was beer—a pitcher cost a quarter. Needless to say, we didn't need white tuxedos to perform there.

But I liked it. It was a steady gig, and I could have kind of a normal life. I played with Nat Shilkret's Studio Orchestra from time to time. I took courses in harmony and music theory at the University of Southern California. I did my practicing at the Red Car Club. That was another nice thing about that gig. The guys who went there were interested in beer and girls, not music, and because nobody was all that interested in the music, we could try out a lot of new stuff. A lot of guys came to me looking for work because I had that kind of freedom. Plus, it was a steady gig. I got Teddy Buckner as my lead trumpet because he would play for any wage as long as he didn't have to leave his new wife. Later on, he was out at Disneyland playing Dixieland jazz for years. And I got a lot of young guys with so much talent that even I can't believe it.

Paul Howard left and went back to ballroom music, and that's when I got Don Byas on alto. Tyree Glenn came along, and he could play any instrument I put in front of him. He could play the vibes, too, and I liked experimenting on the vibes with him. It was still not a popular instrument, and so there weren't a lot of guys around to talk about it with. What I liked about having Tyree around was that he gave me more room. When I wanted to play vibes, he could take over on the drums, and when I wanted to drum, I didn't have to lose the sound of the vibes, because he could take over for me. After a while, I was on the vibes more than I was on the drums.

Ever since I'd first tried out a couple notes on the vibraharp, I'd been interested in seeing what it could do. Plus, Gladys was convinced that I would make my fame with that instrument. She laid on that. She gave me a set of vibes for my birthday way back when I was playing with Les Hite at the Cotton Club, but Les didn't like the sound. "Just play the drums, man," he'd say. But Gladys was persistent. Every time I'd go to play in a telephone booth, she'd say, "Take those vibes with you."

I really studied that instrument. The way I did it was I would go out after work to the after-hours clubs, and I'd sit down at the piano and get a piano player to play the upper part of the piano—what we call comping, or complementary parts—and I'd play two-finger piano down at the other end. That's how I got my ideas and style for playing the vibraharp. I would do that for hours. I'd get off work at three o'clock in the morning, and I'd play two-finger piano until daybreak. I'd wear out two or three piano players before I got done. I was very studious as far as the vibraharp was concerned, and I was *the* innovator in making the vibraharp a jazz instrument.

With all that talent and all the creativity we were allowed, it wasn't long before we were the hottest band in town. Sam took the sawdust up off the floor, put cloths on the tables, put the waitresses in short skirts. He changed the name of the club and upgraded it, instituting a one-dollar admission charge. Now, we were the house band for the Paradise Nightclub. Gladys negotiated a nice contract for us, and we were on top of the world.

Of course, once we got so good, other band leaders started raiding my group for talent. Those who wanted to go to New York or with another band someplace did. I didn't mind. Almost all musicians moved around a lot, and I knew I could always get somebody else who was good. There was so much talent out there. The Depression and talking movies had taken their toll on jobs for musicians, and guys who could play sounds made in heaven were begging for work.

The Depression closed a lot of the small clubs, because people didn't have the money to spend in them. The bigger problem was talking movies. When that first Al Jolson movie came out in 1929, that was the beginning of the end for all those musicians who made their living playing in theater orchestras. When there was no sound in the movies, those orchestras, or sometimes just piano players, made the sounds. They also made the emotion. But as soon as sound movies came in, the movies came along with their own music, so the theaters didn't need musicians anymore. That put a lot of guys out of a job. That's what happened to Milt Hinton back in Chicago. His instrument was the violin, but after 1929 he couldn't get work. The theater orchestras had always included violins, but the jazz bands weren't using them. Milt had to switch over to bass.

So, as I said, there was a lot of talent, and a lot of moving back and forth. Once in a while, I got a guy from one of the big bands back east. That's how I got Al Morgan. He was out of New Orleans, and a great bass player. He was with Cab Calloway in New York, and Cab came out to Hollywood to do a movie with Al Jolson. Well, Cab does his usual stuff, dancing and shaking his head, but the camera's always on Al Morgan. And the movie people tell Al Morgan that anytime he's in California, if they have a picture that uses jazz musicians, he's got the job. So Al quits Cab right then and there and decides to stay in L.A. He joined me soon afterward. As a matter of fact, that's when Milt Hinton signed on with Cab. Cab picked him up out of the Three Deuces in Chicago where Milt was playing with Zutty Singleton and Art Tatum.

Meanwhile, Gladys was doing great at her business. She made all the outfits for the big stars like Joan Crawford and Marion Davies. Joan Crawford wouldn't wear a dress unless Gladys had sewn it, and they were friends all their lives. Even years after Gladys could afford all the designer dresses she wanted, she was sewing for Joan Crawford out of friendship, because Joan Crawford liked only Gladys's designs and work. That should tell you something about Gladys right there— if she could keep up a friendship with Joan Crawford, she had to be sure of herself. In fact, she was designing so many dresses for so many stars that she didn't need the added headache of looking after me. But she believed in me. When she couldn't be around, she had Dr. Chops take her place. She made sure that Dr. Chops took me to the Paradise Nightclub and picked me up every night, or almost every night.

I'll have to say that Gladys wasn't just being generous. She had her reasons for having Dr. Chops spend so much time taking me places and picking me up. That was the only way she could keep track of me. Gladys did not understand that a musician needs to unwind after playing his heart out all night.

Nobody who isn't a performing artist understands that. You got to unwind. You put so much of yourself into your music, you can't just put a breaker on the energy. That's why so many musicians drink or use drugs or eat too much. I never was into any of those things. Louis Armstrong smoked reefer. He offered me a reefer once, and man, I was flying. Dinah Washington boozed and binged. Me, I just wanted to go out and have a good time.

A lot of the club owners knew this, and they'd have "breakfast clubs," which were after-hours clubs where the musicians could go and drink and where wealthy white patrons could go and meet black girls. There were always a lot of girls. I don't know what bothered Gladys most—the boozing or the girls—but she didn't want me in those places. That's why she always had Dr. Chops waiting to pick me up. To outsmart her, I had to climb down fire escapes, make my getaway over roofs. Oh, what we didn't try to get away from Gladys and Dr. Chops.

It got to be a game. We'd make our getaway, and then wait for Dr. Chops, or Dr. Chops and Gladys, to find me. One time we were at an after-hours place. I didn't have any money, as usual, because Gladys always collected the checks. I was playing the piano for some change, and the guys tied me to the stool. In walks Dr. Chops. Without saying a word, he picks me up, stool and all, and deposits me in front of Gladys in the limousine outside. "You don't have to make a fool of yourself because you already are one," she said.

Between them, Gladys and Dr. Chops had antennae that spread over the whole L.A. area. There was no place to hide. The guys and I heard about a secret place out on the highway twenty miles from L.A. When we got there, who was sitting at the bar but Dr. Chops. "I figured you would try this place next," he said.

Gladys never had a more loyal friend than Dr. Chops. When she got to be Miss Big—she used to wear half a million dollars' worth of diamonds—he made a point of telling all the fellows, "I'll kill any of y'all if any of her rings are missing." And during the time when we were still struggling, he was her right-hand man when it came to watching over me.

I was a bad boy. Anyone will tell you. Ask Milt Hinton. He says I was crazy, absolutely crazy. As I remember it, I was just having a good time.

Milt came out to Los Angeles in 1933. Now, this was my old buddy from the Chicago days. He and I played in the Chicago Defender Youth Band when Milt was still in short pants. He had gotten a job with Eddie South, the big violinist who was in Erskine Tate's band with my idol on the drums, Jimmy Bertrand. Eddie South had a gig at the Club Alabam on Sunset Boulevard. It was a quartet— South on violin, Everett Barksdale on guitar, Antonio Spalding on piano, and I was going to be on bass. Gladys knew Eddie South, and that's how she found out that Milt was coming to L.A. She told me, and we all decided we were going to give Milt a big welcome.

We all met him at Union Station. The whole band was there, and Eddie South and Gladys, and when Milt got off the train, we hugged and kissed. Gladys said, "Now, Lionel, you and Eddie and Milt and everybody come out to the house." She turns to Milt and says, "I can't let Lionel out because I can't find him half the time, so you all get checked into the Dunbar Hotel, come over to the house, and I'll have a big spread for you." Well, Gladys went back to the house, and Milt and Eddie and the other guys and I got Milt checked into the hotel, and then we went across the street to the barbershop, and one thing led to another, and Gladys couldn't find me for two, three days. Even Dr. Chops couldn't find me that time.

It was great having a steady gig at the Paradise Nightclub, and by the time Milt Hinton arrived, my band was big in L.A. The Paradise Nightclub was getting big, too, thanks to us. A couple of years after I started playing there, Sam Ervine had to put ropes up, there were so many people trying to get in. There was a doorman. There was a $1.50 cover charge. I got a singer named June Richmond. Later, she was with Jimmy Dorsey. Marie Bryant, who taught the Hollywood stars how to dance, got me four little chorus girls, and we put on a show. It was turning into a real class place. People came from miles around to hear us.

They included a lot of musicians. Nat Cole and his guitarist, Oscar Moore, came in one night. Nat hadn't been on the coast from Chicago long. He didn't even have a steady gig. He'd come out to California with a show and got stranded and didn't have anywhere to go. He and I used to jam every day, and I was going around town trying to hip people to him. I liked his style of piano playing, but even more I liked his singing. I was the one who kept telling him, "Man, you sing. You sing." I knew he could sell the public on his singing. Finally, the manager of the Swanee Inn on North LaBrea had told him that if he could get a quartet together, he had a job. So Nat got Oscar, and then they started looking for a bassist. Nat took my bassist, Wesley Prince, away from me. But I couldn't complain. Nat was a home boy out of Chicago. Nat never got a quartet together, but the King Cole Trio became famous, especially with Nat singing.

Wesley wasn't the only musician I lost to Nat over the years. Later, around 1948, he hired Joe Comfort away from me, and around 1950 he hired Charlie Harris, who had played bass for me, to replace Joe Comfort. I never begrudged a guy leaving my band—if they could make more money or get more solo time with somebody else, they should go for it.

Louis Armstrong also caught my band at the Paradise when he came to Hollywood to make a movie that summer of 1936. He asked me to record with him on the Decca label, and that's how I got to be part of Louis Armstrong and the Polynesians for one day. There were three real Polynesians in the group—Sam Koki on steel guitar, Joe Nawahi on bass, and Andy Iona on ukulele and vocals. The rest were Louis, me on drums and vibes, and George Archer and Harry Baty on guitar and vocals. We recorded "To You, Sweetheart, Aloha" and "On a Cocoanut Island."

I also played with Louis in the movie he'd come out to do—"Pennies from Heaven," with Bing Crosby. I was the masked drummer in Louis's band in that movie.

John Hammond also started hanging out at the Paradise when he was in town. I remembered him from the Chicago days when he used to come to Uncle Richard's parties and listen to Louis Armstrong and Bessie Smith. He'd been a businessman then. By the middle 1930s he was in the music business. Benny Goodman would later marry his sister. He came to the club and heard us and started talking us up. When Benny Goodman arrived in L.A. for a two-week engagement at the Palomar Ballroom, Hammond told Goodman that he ought to hear me. Before Benny got around to coming by, two of his guys, Hymie Schertzer and Pee Wee Erwin, dropped in, and I guess they told Benny he ought to come and hear me, too.

Benny had just come off a gig in Denver, Colorado, where his band didn't take. In fact, I heard that after that Benny was thinking about breaking up his band because he wasn't having any success. It was John Hammond who thought he should get a more exciting sound—and who decided my sound might be what Benny needed.

Now, John Hammond knew that I was black, and by recommending me to Benny, he was leading Benny into uncharted

territory—an integrated band. Benny did have Teddy Wilson traveling with him, but Teddy didn't play with the band. Teddy only
played intermission piano. By recommending me, John Hammond
was pushing Benny into a completely different arrangement.

Benny was busy, so he sent his brother Harry out to the Paradise.
Harry must have brought back a good report, because the next night
Benny came himself. He sat at one of the front tables, and I remember
thinking he looked familiar. But I didn't try to place him in jazz circles. With his granny glasses and his business suit, I thought maybe
he was a politician or somebody whose picture I'd seen in the papers.
Then, during a break, Sam Ervine whispered to me that Benny Goodman was in the audience, and then I knew why the guy looked so
familiar.

After the break, he got up on the bandstand with me, pulled his
clarinet out of his case, and we started to jam. We jammed all night
and into the morning—it must have been about six o'clock when he
finally said, "Pleased to meet ya," and left. For me, it was a night to
remember. I had all his records and had copied his solos and his riffs.
But he was white and we moved in different circles. I was honored
to jam with Benny Goodman.

The next night was even more exciting. I'm up onstage playing
as usual, and I hear this clarinet player next to me, and I turn and
there is Benny Goodman, playing right next to me. He had brought
Gene Krupa and Teddy Wilson along, and the four of us got on the
bandstand together, and man, we started wailing out. We played for
two hours straight, and Benny liked the sound we made so well that
he said, "Come on and join me at a recording session tomorrow at
RCA Victor, out in Hollywood."

Well, I was so excited that I couldn't sleep. I didn't get to sleep
until about seven or eight o'clock the next morning. Around eleven,
Gladys's mother shook me awake and told me that a Mr. Goodman
had called and he was waiting for me at the RCA Victor studio. I
was wide awake in an instant. I jumped out of bed and into some
clothes and hailed a taxi for the Paradise to pick up my vibes. On
the way, I decided I should tell Gladys, so I had the taxi driver stop
at her shop. She decided that she should come with me.

When we walked into the RCA Victor studio, Benny gave me a
look, but he didn't say anything. Teddy Wilson and Gene Krupa were
there. We didn't do much rehearsing before we started to record. We
did two numbers—"Moonglow" and "Dinah." I had a great time.
I felt as if I'd been playing with those guys all my life. That was
August 19, 1936, and I'll never forget it.

I recorded two more times with members of the Benny Goodman

Orchestra before they left Los Angeles. About a week later, I played vibes with Teddy Wilson and His Orchestra. Benny was on clarinet, but for that session he was part of Teddy's group. I liked that— Benny was very unselfish when it came to recording, and he had no problem with his guys recording on their own, and even playing in "their orchestras." Teddy had his own deal with Brunswick Records, and we did "You Came to My Rescue" and "Here's Love in Your Eyes." And after that, without Benny, we did "You Turned the Tables on Me" and "Sing, Baby, Sing."

Benny and his band finished their gig at the Palomar and went back to New York, and I went back to the Paradise. A few weeks later, the records I had made with Benny and Gene and Teddy were released. They really took off. Every one of them was a sensational success. When the impact of that success hit Benny, he decided he wanted me as part of his orchestra. One night, a couple of months later, Tyree Glenn tells me that Benny Goodman's on the phone. Now, Tyree was in the habit of playing practical jokes on me, and I thought this was just another one of those. Part of me wanted to believe it, but nobody had ever called me to come east before. I didn't think that was going to happen to me. So I just ignored Tyree. Over the next week or so, Tyree kept shouting, "Benny's on the phone from New York," but I thought he was just joking.

Then one night Gladys answered the phone, and she and Benny got to talking serious. After she hung up, she said that Benny had offered me a one-year contract at $550 a week. He also said that she could come along and travel with the band. I couldn't believe it. That was big money. But that was also a big change. Going with Benny meant moving to New York, and I wasn't sure I wanted to relocate. But Benny Goodman had the biggest big band in the country; he had Gene Krupa and Teddy Wilson. Playing with them was like being in heaven. I couldn't make up my mind. I did know one thing: I wasn't going to New York without Gladys.

Gladys never really asked me how I felt about it. She talked it over with everybody but me. She even had her brother, Dr. Riddle, come from Texas to discuss the matter. For Gladys it meant leaving her business, so she talked it over with Beazie DeVaughan, her partner. Beazie agreed, and Gladys and Beazie remained close friends for the rest of their lives. She talked it over with Dr. Chops. She used to like to tell how everybody said to her, "Go, Gladys. This man is going to be a star." She gambled on me. She finally told me, "We're going to New York," and next thing I knew I was on my way to join Benny Goodman in New York City at the Hotel Pennsylvania, the Madhattan Room.

5

WITH BENNY GOODMAN

e drove from Los Angeles to New York. Benny Goodman offered to pay for train tickets, but Gladys wasn't taking any chances. She said, "No, I'm going to take my car so if anything happens we can get in the car and come back home." So we set out in the early hours of the morning on November 9, 1936. We had a white Chevrolet, and my drums and vibes were in the back. Allen Durham, a trombone player with me, helped us drive. We were going to stop only when we had to, and make that cross-country drive in record time.

One stop we had to make was in Arizona. You see, we had to get married. Gladys's mother wouldn't let us go unless we promised to get married. Said she wouldn't have us living together in New York City. We had to get married, and we had to send her back the marriage certificate. Gladys's mother said, "You don't do it, you come on back home."

Now, Gladys and I had been together a long time by then. We were shacking up. We acted like we were married. In fact, a lot of people thought we were. Milt Hinton thought we were married when he came out to Los Angeles in 1933. But we'd never gotten around to that formality. But now Gladys's mother said we had to. I said, "It's all right with me," and Gladys said the same thing. So we drove until we got to Arizona, where you could get married right away and didn't have to wait, and we got married in Yuma in about five minutes. It was Armistice Day, 1936, and the next stop was the post office so we could send the marriage certificate to my new mother-in-law.

I don't remember much about that trip. We were so excited we weren't worrying about hotels or anything. We just slept in the car and kept on coming. Route 66, Route 80. When we had to stop we went to the black part of town. But we were rushing so fast that we didn't stop much. We had to stay on the road because we were due in New York to play with Benny on November 21, 1936. Gladys drove night and day, and we made it in record time. We even had some time to settle into the Big Apple before my debut with the Benny Goodman Orchestra.

Gladys had a friend from California in New York, who she'd gone to school with. Her name was Hazel, and Gladys had asked her to find a place for us. When we got there, Hazel had a place all picked out. She said, "I'm gonna take you on Sugar Hill. You're with Benny Goodman, you gotta be on Sugar Hill." It was a really nice neighborhood of tall apartment buildings that overlooked the Polo Grounds and the rest of Harlem. The 500 block of Edgecombe Avenue and the buildings right around that block were Sugar Hill, and we lived at 409 Edgecombe. The big shots lived in that building, including W. E. B. DuBois. Paul Robeson lived in the neighborhood. Duke Ellington lived right down the street, and every Sunday when we were off we used to have dinner together with Duke and his son, Mercer, and his sister, Ruth. She lived about a block down, around 375 or 390 Edgecombe, and she and Gladys were very good friends. Every Sunday after dinner, Duke and I and whoever else was around would have jam sessions in Ruth's apartment. She was good to us, a wonderful person.

A couple of years later, we decided we were in New York to stay, so we got our own apartment at the Doris E. Brooks Houses on 137th Street. We stayed there for more than thirty years. In fact I didn't move out of there until after Gladys died.

When I got in touch with Benny to let him know we were in town, the first thing he wanted me to do was go to a doctor so he could get insurance on me. Benny didn't leave anything to chance— he wanted his musicians insured. The doctor checked me out, and afterward he said, "The doctor who operated on your appendix did a tremendous job. Who was it?" "Dr. Jesus," I answered.

The next item on the agenda was a photo session. Benny and Gene Krupa and Teddy Wilson and I all went to a studio and the photographer made pictures of the four of us, in all different poses. By this time the record we cut back in Los Angeles was selling like hotcakes and everybody wanted a picture of the "Benny Goodman Quartet." Well, they couldn't supply those pictures until the fourth member of that quartet arrived.

Then, Benny asked me if I needed an advance, and he handed me two weeks' pay in cash. Since Gladys was the banker in the family, I wasn't used to having this much cash. But I was glad to have it, because I wanted to buy her a wedding present. I asked the guys where I could get some nice jewelry and furs, and they sent me to Seventh Avenue, and I rushed up and down Seventh Avenue, and I ended up buying Gladys a half-carat diamond ring and a secondhand mink coat. When I got back home, I proudly presented Gladys with her wedding gifts. She accepted them, and I could tell she was pleased. But she wanted to know, "How much money do you have in your pocket?" I had about thirteen dollars. Gladys got on the phone with Benny right away and told him never again to give me that much money. Benny promised not to do it again, and from then on, Gladys and Benny wouldn't even talk about money to me.

I made my debut with Benny Goodman at the Madhattan Room of the Pennsylvania Hotel across the street from Penn Station. It was November 21, 1936, and it wasn't exactly the kind of debut I had planned. I found out at rehearsal that I wasn't going to be in the Benny Goodman Orchestra, I was going to be part of the Benny Goodman Quartet that only played for part of every show.

I wasn't the only one who was surprised. So was Gene Krupa. He didn't like that arrangement any more than I did. Gene had been with Benny for a long time, and Benny hadn't even told him. That was Benny—he made these major decisions and forgot to tell anybody else. Gene calmed down when Benny told him that he would be getting a double salary.

Gene had more reason to be upset than me. There were good reasons why Benny couldn't put Teddy and me in the orchestra. I don't know why it hadn't occurred to me before that he was going to have a lot of trouble booking his band into those big white places with two black musicians. Teddy Wilson wasn't part of the Benny Goodman Orchestra, either. He couldn't sit on the stage with the white musicians. He came on for specialty numbers and also played intermission piano. I was going to play under the same arrangement. That's how it was in those days—you didn't have mixed bands.

Sometimes a black musician would be featured with a white

band, or the other way around. Louis Armstrong recorded with Jimmy Dorsey the same year I joined Benny Goodman. Later on, after Gene Krupa got his own band in the early 1940s, he featured Roy Eldridge. But they didn't live and travel together.

Benny had Teddy and me traveling with the band, and both of us were on the regular payroll.

I wanted to play with the Benny Goodman Quartet, and Benny was paying me good money. And my name was getting out there. At the Pennsylvania Hotel they had live broadcasts of Benny's music, and so through radio I was getting famous on the East Coast just as I had on the West Coast.

We were still playing at the Pennsylvania Hotel when we went into the Paramount Theater for a gig. Benny planned on doubling at both places, because he didn't hold out much hope for big success at the Paramount. He hadn't usually done very well in theaters. But when we arrived at the Paramount for an early-morning rehearsal, we were astounded to see a couple of hundred kids already lined up at the box office. By ten o'clock that morning there were over four thousand kids. An integrated band was such an unheard-of thing, even in New York in those days, that some people actually worried that there would be a race riot. I remember that *Down Beat* carried the headline, "Predicted Race Riot Fades As Crowd Applauds Goodman Quartet." In fact, we were so popular at the Paramount that we had kids screaming and dancing in the aisles, and parents clucking just like they later did about rock and roll. Something like twenty-one thousand people heard us that first day, and every day after that. It was some kind of record. We ended up leaving the Madhattan Room and just playing at the Paramount for several weeks.

It was with the Benny Goodman Quartet that I became famous as a jazz vibraharpist. There was another guy, named Adrian Rollini, who was a vibes player and had made a name for himself before me. But he played cocktail-lounge music, not jazz. By the time I joined Benny, I had developed my style, and it really hasn't changed much since. With my background as a drummer, it made sense for me to drum on the vibraharp. (By the same token, my famous two-fingered piano style comes from playing the vibraharp—I use my fingers like mallets.) The effect was like a percussion instrument. The Goodman quartet played things very fast, and that suited me, the fastest drummer in the world, just fine. But something I did that was unique was to make use of the silences—I used long rests between phrases, and that made for some high drama.

Benny also took good care of Teddy and me. After a show, he'd have a limousine drive us up to Harlem so we wouldn't have to worry about getting a taxi. Back in those days, too, taxi drivers would pass by a black man, and would refuse to go to Harlem at night.

But I had an edge when I arrived in New York. Not only did I have a job with the hottest white big band of the day, I also had my own following. *Down Beat* magazine named me the most exciting artist of the year 1936, and that was no small bit of recognition in those days. I was with Benny, but I was my own man.

It was exciting being in the Big Apple. Jazz was everywhere, and the big bands were revolutionizing the tempo and becoming the major sound. We learned about augmenting the fifth and ninth chords. We could hype, and we made what were considered freaky sounds then. We came up with half-diminished chords. We used to use just G-flat, A-, C-, and E-flat. Now we had F-G–flat and B-C– and D-E–flat. Every chance we got, we'd go over to Fifty-second Street—West Fifty-second Street, the street that never slept. All up and down both sides of the street were these little clubs—they'd been speakeasies during Prohibition—and you'd go in one after the other, and every place you'd go, you'd hear the greatest jazz.

I got back in touch with Milt Hinton, my old buddy from Chicago, once I got to New York. He was with Cab Calloway, and they'd opened up the new Cotton Club, the downtown club after it closed in Harlem. They had the same show schedule at the Cotton Club, Broadway and Forty-eighth Street, as we did at the Pennsylvania Hotel—eight-thirty to ten, then off from ten to eleven, and then back on at eleven. We used that hour off, man. We'd rush up to the Cotton Club and pick up Milt and some of the other guys, and then we'd all go to Fifty-second Street to hear who was playing. We had an hour and we were going to make as many joints as we could to hear what was going on. We could hear Art Tatum, Billie Holiday, the King Cole Trio, Joe Bushkin, Stuff Smith. And everywhere we'd go we'd meet other musicians doing the same thing we were—just soaking it all up.

A lot of record producers hung out on Fifty-second Street, too, and pretty soon they started asking me to make records. I didn't have any contract with Benny that said I couldn't make recordings on my own.

Eli Oberstein, head of repertory at RCA Victor then, liked my playing. He said, "When the bands are in town, how would you like to get some musicians and have a recording session—*your* recording session?"

I said, "Great."

Victor was trying to compete with Brunswick Records, I later realized. Brunswick was doing a series of records featuring Billie

Holiday and Teddy Wilson. Victor had also had good luck with Benny Goodman's trio and quartet recordings, so they figured why not try me and the guys I could round up.

I started making records with a bunch of guys, and we called ourselves Lionel Hampton and His Orchestra, even though I only had an orchestra on records, not onstage.

That was a great time. You could get a bunch of guys together and try out different combinations. You didn't have to worry about who was black or white. The first time I recorded as Lionel Hampton and His Orchestra, I had Ziggy Elman on trumpet, Hymie Schertzer and George Koenig on alto sax, Arthur Rollini and Vido Musso on tenor sax, Jess Stacy on piano, Allan Reuss on guitar, Harry Goodman on bass, and Gene Krupa on drums. Now, you know that wasn't a combination you'd be likely ever to see on a bandstand!

The next time, I had a rhythm section made up of guys from Duke Ellington's orchestra—Cootie Williams on trumpet, Lawrence Brown on trombone, Mezz Mezzrow on clarinet, and Johnny Hodges on alto sax—and guys from Benny Goodman's, Fletcher Henderson's, the Mills Brothers', and Stuff Smith's bands as well—Alan Reuss on guitar, John Kirby on bass, and Cozy Cole on drums, respectively. The next time I had Buster Bailey on clarinet and John Kirby on bass. In 1938 I did a whole session with a group drawn entirely from the Earl Hines band.

These recording sessions also gave me a chance to play whatever instruments I wanted, so on one recording session in April 1937 I played vibes, piano, and drums. On another, I played vibes and sang. Sometimes we just jammed, but most of the sessions were arranged—a lot of them by Benny Carter—and built around my playing and singing. But I always let the other guys get a chance to solo, with the result that the sides were very long, longer than most cuts were in those days.

I recorded off and on for Victor with pickup orchestras for about four years altogether, and today these sides are considered classics. In 1939 Harry James, Benny Carter, Herschel Evans, Billy Kyle, John Kirby, Jonah Jones, and I and some other guys recorded "I'm in the Mood for Swing" and "Shoe Shiner's Drag," which was a Jelly Roll Morton composition arranged by Benny Carter. That same year I had Chu Berry and Russell Procope doing solos on "High Society" and "Shufflin' at the Hollywood" and "Sweethearts on Parade." What a time that was. I did better solo work with those guys than I did with the Goodman quartet and sextet, though the sides I recorded with these Goodman groups are classics, too.

My job with the Goodman combos was to create a balance. There was Teddy Wilson's laid-back piano playing, and Gene Krupa's driving drums, and I kind of kept them working together. With the pickup bands that I assembled myself, I paid attention to balance among the musicians and had more chance to go off on a solo when I wanted to.

Gladys eventually negotiated a four-year recording contract with RCA, and while this gave me more money, it also gave me less freedom. I didn't think about long-term things, like royalties or anything. What I was thinking about was having some cash in my pocket, since Gladys was so tight with the purse strings. A bunch of us would be on Fifty-second Street and a guy from Victor would say, "Can you do a record date tomorrow?" I'd say, "Yeah, but you got to give me three hundred dollars in advance." The guy would give it to me, and the guys and I'd start drinking up the money so Gladys couldn't get it. We'd run around. We'd go off uptown to the after-hours spots, still drinking up the three hundred dollars. I'd be spending money like it's going out of style. I'd buy everybody a drink because I was big-time, yessir.

The next day, we'd go and do the record date. Gladys is there, sitting there knitting, making sure everything goes all right. We get through, and the guy, the producer, pays the other musicians, and he gives some money to Gladys.

Gladys says, "Where's the rest of the money?"

The guy says, "I gave it to Hamp last night."

Then all heck would break loose. Gladys spent half her time going around telling people not to give me any money. "Don't give him any money, don't give it to him," she was always saying. I was crazy with money. We were all crazy, staying out late and drinking and doing all kinds of fool things, As many chicks as we could run into . . . We didn't know when to go home.

I give Gladys credit, though. She made sure I had something to show for those recording sessions. The other guys usually didn't have any kind of contract, just got paid and never received any royalties. They didn't care, though—they were young and just wanted to play music, just like I did. Like Milt Hinton says—he recorded some sides with me in those days—"We don't get a nickel. That's our fault because we didn't take care of business." I didn't take care of business, either. It was Gladys who thought about the future. I know that a lot of the guys didn't understand how I could let a woman be in the lead, but today I'm a lot better off than many of them, because of Gladys.

*   *   *

I was having a good time playing with Benny Goodman, but he was not the easiest guy to work with. He was a perfectionist. He believed that every audience deserved the best we could give. They were paying for it, and we owed it to them. His motto was: Hit one false note and you're off the stage. He meant it, too. You made a mistake, and you had one more chance. You made two mistakes, and you were fired on the spot. But he always paid you.

He had a way of looking at you over the top of his glasses, really nailing you down with his eyes. The guys called it the "ray," and they were scared of it. I remember one time Ziggy Elman wasn't fast enough picking up his mute. Later he said, "The old man gave me the ray, and it stayed with me four days. I couldn't sleep."

Now, Benny wasn't that old, but he had an air about him that was like a college professor. And with those business suits and those granny glasses, he just didn't look like a jazz artist. He didn't fool around like most jazz artists, either. No boozing or dope for Benny, and nobody in his band better be caught drinking or smoking reefer. You had to have a clear head to play with Benny. He treated rehearsals like performances—you had to be there an hour ahead of time with your instrument ready.

There was another way that Benny acted like a professor—he was real absentminded. When he was concentrating on his music, a building could have burned down around him and he wouldn't even notice. I remember once we were on the road, traveling by train, and the waiter handed him a pad to write his breakfast order on, and he signed his autograph. Hours later, he couldn't figure out why he hadn't had any breakfast.

Touring with Benny was an experience. We went out on tour after a few months in New York, after that first engagement at the Paramount. We traveled in style. Gladys traveled with us. She was the only woman that Benny would let travel with the orchestra. Other than the girl singers, I mean. When I joined Benny, his singer was Peggy Lee. Benny let Gladys come along because he wanted her to keep an eye on me, because I was a wild man. Plus, I sometimes had trouble keeping the schedule straight. This one joke has been told on me so many times that I might just as well tell it on myself. One time Gladys wasn't with us. I don't remember why. I showed up for a gig in Indianapolis only to find that I was supposed to be in *Minn*eapolis!

Traveling with Benny Goodman was a lot different from traveling with my own band. We used to cram into a couple of cars. With Benny, we traveled by train. Benny would have a drawing room, and we would have a drawing room. But when I had my own band, we were all black and we knew what to expect, and the audiences knew what to expect. With Benny, touring with two black musicians was a pioneering effort. Nobody had ever traveled with an integrated band before, and even though Teddy Wilson and I were only part of the Benny Goodman Quartet, not the whole orchestra, that was still too much for some white folks.

I don't know how many times Teddy and I were mistaken for servants—Mr. Goodman's valet or the water boy for the Benny Goodman Orchestra. We learned to take it in stride. There wasn't anything else we could do. We knew what society was like.

Benny didn't have to have us in his band, and he put up with a lot. Theater managers would tell him they were getting a lot of mail protesting Teddy and me, but Benny wouldn't back down. He once bopped a guy in the head with his clarinet when the guy told him he should "get those niggers off his show." Meanwhile, he was getting flack from some critics in the black community who accused him of using blacks. That was nonsense. He didn't have to hire Teddy or me; he hired us because we made his kind of music. And this was in the North. Benny knew he was going to have to make some serious advance plans when we went south.

Benny was invited to perform at the Pan American Casino at the Dallas Exposition in the late summer of 1937. We had just finished up some gigs in Hollywood, including the film *Hollywood Hotel*, and were working our way back east, so it fit in with the schedule. But Benny knew that was going to be a rough gig for an integrated band, because no integrated orchestra had ever played in the Deep South before. So Benny took precautions. In fact, he planned that visit like a military campaign.

First, he made it a part of the orchestra's contract that Teddy and I would be able to stay with the rest of the band in the Statler Hotel in downtown Dallas and that we would also be able to use the same entrance and elevators. (You had to dot every *i* and cross every *t* in those days. If he hadn't made that a specific part of the contract, the hotel would have let us stay there but probably in the basement next to the boiler, and they would have made us come through the service entrance.) The hotel people and the centennial committee weren't too happy about signing that contract, but they wanted Benny Goodman. He was the King of Swing, the biggest name in music in the country, and if they wanted him, they would have to take him on his terms.

But Benny went further than that. He had his own car, a Packard, sent down to Dallas by train so Teddy and I wouldn't have to worry about taxi drivers refusing to pick us up. He also hired a guy just to escort us from the hotel entrance to our rooms and back so we wouldn't be exposed to any unpleasantness.

I knew about all these precautions, so I wasn't worried about going south with Benny. People said to me, "Why you goin' down south? Those white folks will kill you." And I'd say, "They'll have to kill Benny Goodman first."

As it turned out, all these precautions except the car weren't necessary most of the time. Both Teddy and I wound up staying with family a good portion of the trip because we felt more comfortable. Teddy had been born and raised in a town about thirty miles outside Dallas, and he hardly ever used the hotel room. And Gladys had her brother, Dr. Riddle, in Dennison, and we preferred to stay with him.

But you can only take so many precautions against unpleasantness. Teddy and I got insulted anyway, once, and then Teddy got really insulted.

The case involving Teddy and me was minor. We had a drink from a water fountain marked "White." I don't remember why we did it now—maybe we felt protected by the name of Benny Goodman and just wanted to test the limits. A policeman saw us and shouted, "You niggers, don't you ever do that no more!" We walked away, and that was the end of that.

The thing with Teddy happened that night when we were playing at the Pan American Casino. A white man who had known Teddy since he was young tried to bring a bottle of champagne up to him on the bandstand. He was just about to give it to Teddy when a policeman blocked his way. The cop knocked the bottle out of the man's hand and said, "No champagne for niggers," he said. When the man protested, the cop called him a nigger lover. Teddy witnessed this, and he got real depressed. The next morning he didn't show up for rehearsal, and Benny went to his room to find out why. Teddy had stayed in the hotel that night, and he was in his room, brooding. He didn't want to tell Benny why, but Benny considered it a capital crime to miss rehearsal and Teddy had to tell him to save his job.

Benny was furious when he found out what happened. I think he called Marcus of Neiman-Marcus. Anyway, somebody who knew an important local police official got the word out about the cop who had insulted Teddy. He came to the hall, grabbed the guy by the shoulder, and told him to get the hell out.

That night, the police commissioner himself sent a bottle of champagne to the bandstand, with a card that read, "To Teddy Wilson, the great son of Texas."

We were probably lucky that that's all that happened. There

had been predictions of real trouble. But as John Hammond later wrote on the front page of *Down Beat*: "All along I had the suspicion that if the Trio and Quartet made excellent music the crowd would swallow its prejudices and acclaim the artists."

Benny Goodman was no civil rights activist. He didn't talk much about racism. His whole concentration was on music, but it galled him that something as petty as race prejudice could mess up the music he wanted to hear and play. He realized that America was poorer in music than it should be, because of racism. He understood that a guy like Teddy couldn't concentrate on his music when he had to deal with hate. So Benny saw to it that his musicians were protected. And he also saw to it that a lot of talented black musicians and singers got a chance to show their talent to the white public. Benny had a weekly radio show, and he started featuring black artists on it. The first one was Ella Fitzgerald, who'd just had her first big hit, "A-Tisket, A-Tasket." Benny would always say, "I am selling music, not prejudice," and in his no-nonsense way he did a lot more for black artists and blacks in general than most people give him credit for.

It was in the fall of that same year, 1937, that one of the biggest tragedies that ever happened to my family took place. Bessie Smith was killed in a car accident, and my uncle Richard was driving the car. Richard and Bessie had had their ups and downs over the years, but they were still together, and things were looking up for Bessie's career.

We were going to make records. I told everybody in the Benny Goodman band about Bessie being tight with my uncle, and Benny said, "Oh, man, we gotta make some records with her." Meanwhile, I had just signed a contract with Victor to do some small-band recordings with people like Johnny Hodges, Nat King Cole, and guys like that. Eli Oberstein of Victor said, "Be sure to get Bessie," and I was going to get in touch with Richard to see if we could get together on some sides. The way she sang was so relaxed, and the stories rang so true. She always adapted the "now" sound, whatever it was, but we never got around to recording it.

That September, she and Richard and her show were in Memphis. They finished up her last show on Saturday night, September 25. She and the rest of her troupe were supposed to spend the night in Memphis and then drive down to Darling, Mississippi, for a show the next afternoon. But after that Saturday night show, Bessie was restless and wanted to get on the road right away. She wanted to drive down to Clarksdale and spend the night there. Richard was supposed to be in a card game with some of the guys, and he didn't want to leave. They argued, and he gave in, and they set off. They weren't talking to each other. Richard was tired.

They were heading down Route 61, and it was after one in the morning. About seventy miles south of Memphis a big truck suddenly appeared in the beams of the headlights of the car Richard was driving. He thought it was moving along at about sixty miles an hour, like he was. Too late, he realized it was moving slow. He tried to go to the left to miss the truck, but at the same time he put his foot on the brakes. The car went into a skid, hit the truck at an angle, and flipped over. The whole wooden top of the old Packard was sheared off.

Richard was dazed, but otherwise okay. He looked around for Bessie. She was lying in the middle of the road, moaning in pain. She had sideswipe injuries, and her right elbow, which she'd been resting on the bottom of the open window of the car, was crushed. Just then a car approached, and Richard started waving his arms frantically for help. In the car was a white doctor named Hugh Smith, who was on his way to Mississippi to go fishing with his friend, Henry Broughton.

The two men moved Bessie to the side of the road and covered her arm with a handkerchief. Broughton went to a nearby house to call an ambulance. Back at the scene, Dr. Smith and Broughton were taking the fishing tackle out of their car so they could put Bessie in it, when another car came along, and hit the rear end of the Smith car head-on and drove it into Bessie's car.

Dr. Smith was checking on the injuries of the couple in the third car when an ambulance drove up, along with a sheriff and several officers. The ambulance took Bessie and Richard to the colored hospital in Clarksdale, where Bessie's arm was amputated. But she'd lost a lot of blood, and she died later that same morning.

Later on there was a big scandal about how Bessie had first been taken to a white hospital and they wouldn't admit her. John Hammond wrote that in a story for *Down Beat*. But it later turned out that she was taken directly to the colored hospital. By the time they got her it was too late to save her. No reporter ever asked Richard what really happened, or if anybody did, they never wrote the story.

Richard never forgave himself for Bessie's death. He kept saying he should have avoided that truck. He couldn't even say Bessie's name without crying. He was never the same after that. He got real old real fast, and he died just a few years later. I believe that he grieved himself to death over Bessie.

* * *

I got a chance to visit the family in Chicago quite a lot when I was traveling with Benny Goodman. Benny's orchestra was in demand everywhere, and he could have booked a gig 365 nights a year, with a lot of afternoon matinees on top of it. Plus, we were recording a lot whenever we happened to be in a place that had studios. Looking back, it's all kind of a blur, which may explain why I wound up in Indianapolis instead of Minneapolis that time that everybody jokes about.

We had some good times, and we met a lot of good people in our travels. Indianapolis was one of Gladys's and my favorite cities after we met the McMurrays. We were playing the Indiana Theater with Benny, and Frank Sinatra was with us, and there was this guy, a postman who loved jazz but couldn't afford to buy tickets to the show. So he got the idea of pretending that he had special-delivery letters for Benny or Sinatra. He'd put his wife in the trunk of the car and smuggle her into the back of the Indiana Theater to deliver those special deliveries.

Everybody thought this was a pretty clever thing to do, and so we invited him to bring his wife and his daughter backstage for the next show. The daughter was in her early teens, and she was hearing-impaired, because she'd had spinal meningitis and scarlet fever when she was younger. I'll never forget how Sinatra turned sideways so the girl could read his lips as she stood in the wings.

Gladys and I became real tight with that family. We'd stay with them when we played Indianapolis, and Freda McMurray would cook greens and beans and fried chicken and barbecued pig's feet. Freda liked to sew, and she and Gladys would go shopping together and sew together. And then Freda gave birth to another daughter, Patricia, and Gladys and I became like her aunt and uncle.

Gladys and I never had children. So Patricia McMurray became like Gladys's baby. We were playing Indianapolis around Christmas just after Patricia was born, and Gladys decides to buy a crib for the baby. She goes down to L. S. Ayres, which was the Saks Fifth Avenue, Gimbel's, and Macy's of Indianapolis all rolled into one, and she picks out this crib and mattress. Then she says she wants them delivered right away. It's Christmas Eve, and you know they didn't want to be making any deliveries. But Gladys was a strong woman, and they made the delivery. And then Gladys took some of Freda's sheets and cut them down to make crib sheets for the bed, and no baby of a Rockefeller ever had a nicer bed to sleep in.

I guess Gladys had enough to do just taking care of me. But she didn't just follow me around. All the time she was learning about the music business. She learned a lot from Benny Goodman, who was a real tightwad, although he paid us well. Not long after I joined him, he raised my salary from $550 a week to $650, and then later on it was $750. Just the Benny Goodman Quartet cost him most of his profits. But he was willing to pay whatever was necessary to get the kind of music he wanted.

I had some memorable times with Benny. One of the best was when I composed "Flying Home," which later became my theme song. It was around 1939. We were in Los Angeles, and we had to fly to Atlantic City. It was the first time I'd ever been on a plane. We had always traveled by train or bus. I wasn't the only one who wasn't used to flying. Benny had to explain to the whole band that the only way we could make the gig was to fly. We had to leave Los Angeles that morning to get there that evening and do a concert at the Steel Pier.

So we got on the plane, and I started amusing myself. I started singing, and Benny said, "What is that you're humming?"

I said, "I don't know. We can call it 'Flying Home,' I guess."

We were on the West Coast, coming to the East Coast, see. So we got to jammin' it that night. And we played it with the quartet. Later on, we made a recording of it. After I went out on my own, my band always played that song. We still do.

Another memorable experience with Benny was the famous Carnegie Hall concert on January 16, 1938. Benny didn't even want to do the concert, but one of his publicity men, Win Nathanson, talked him into it. Benny didn't think jazz was exactly the right sound for the regular audience at Carnegie Hall. He was right about that. The Carnegie Hall regulars were used to classical. But Win and the other publicity guys brought Benny's fans to the concert, and Carnegie Hall was swinging that night. The audience danced in the aisles just like they did at the Paramount Theater.

When we finished that concert, we were flying high, so we all went up to the Savoy in Harlem to hear the cutting contest between Count Basie's and Chick Webb's bands. What a night that was! Basie, with Jimmy Rushing and Billie Holiday, against Webb, with Ella Fitzgerald. People shouted, stomped, and waved handkerchiefs. Chick won at the end, with one of his brilliant drum solos, but everybody knew that Basie, the newcomer on the jazz scene, was a force to be reckoned with. I didn't sleep at all that night and was still so hyped up the next day that I couldn't sleep all the next day, either.

That happened a lot of times when we were in New York. There was so much going on, you didn't want to miss anything. We used to go to a place called the Black Cat, on West Broadway between Third and Bleecker in Greenwich Village. It was run by the mob, and it had the greatest musicians—drummer Kenny Clarke and his brother Frank Clarke, a bass player. Freddie Green was on guitar. Even Benny would go there to jam sometimes, and Benny was very particular about whom he played with. I also liked the place because the guy, whose name was Frankel, had a set of vibes for me to play.

During my time with Benny, I saw the Benny Goodman Quartet turn into the Benny Goodman Quintet and then into the Benny Goodman Sextet. The Quintet was formed when Gene Krupa left and Benny added John Kirby on bass and Buddy Schutz on drums. Later, it had Fletcher Henderson on piano, Nick Fatool on drums, Artie Bernstein on bass, Benny, and me. It became a sextet when we were out in Los Angeles and Charlie Christian arrived.

John Hammond was the cause. He was always the matchmaker between Benny Goodman and his black musicians—he'd connected Benny up with Teddy Wilson first, then me. Now he wanted to get Benny together with Charlie Christian, a guitarist he'd first heard in Oklahoma City after Mary Lou Williams, the great piano player, starting hyping him. Hammond talked up Charlie to Benny, but Benny wasn't interested. So Hammond brought Charlie to Los Angeles himself.

Charlie walked in, and he was a sight to see. He had on a ten-gallon hat, pointy-toed yellow shoes, a bright green suit, a purple shirt, and a string bow tie. Benny took one look at him and left.

Now, Artie Bernstein and I didn't think Benny had given the kid a fair shot. So we decided to play a little trick on Benny. That night, when Benny was offstage, we moved Charlie's amplifier onto the bandstand. When Benny came on to play with the quintet, there was Charlie. Benny didn't like it, but he was too much of a professional to order Charlie and his amplifier off the bandstand. He announced the number, "Rose Room," as originally planned, and we went into it, and we played that number for almost an hour! Charlie brought out stuff in Benny that even Benny didn't know he had. Benny probably thought he'd get Charlie off the stage quick by choosing a number that was a West Coast song and not in the usual repertoire of black bands. But Charlie had the ear. He picked right up on it.

Benny would play a couple of choruses. I'd answer him. And then Charlie would go crazy improvising. Which meant Benny would have to answer him. That was some night.

The Benny Goodman Sextet recorded "Rose Room" not long after that, for Columbia. I also remember that recording session and that disc, because "Rose Room" was backed by "Flying Home," the piece I wrote. After I left Benny, it became my signature song, but Benny helped make it popular.

Benny never really approved of Charlie, and they never got along personally. But musically they inspired each other, and Charlie stayed with the band until he died, much too young, in 1942. Charlie helped Benny make the transition from swing to bop.

Gene Krupa left Benny in early 1938, not long after the Carnegie Hall concert. They had different ideas about how to play music. Benny didn't like all the crazy antics and sensationalism that he felt were overshadowing the real music. Gene thought that the craziness was just basic showmanship. Although I tended to agree with Gene, I stayed out of it. We were playing a one-week engagement at the Earle Theater in Philadelphia when the feud between them really got hot and heavy—they were going at it right on stage. When the gig was over, Gene left. We went into the Madhattan Room at the Pennsylvania Hotel the next day, with me on drums for the dances and the next recording session. Jo Jones took over on drums for the radio broadcasts. About a week later Davey Tough joined Benny as Gene's replacement, and I went back to vibes. When he left, I filled in for him. I filled in on drums several times after Gene left.

I kept on doing independent recordings throughout my time with Benny. I did a lot of recording in 1939, with all kinds of talented guys. One of the best recording sessions was in September of that year. I had Benny Carter on alto sax, Coleman Hawkins, Chu Berry, and Ben Webster on tenor sax, Clyde Hart on piano, Charlie Christian on guitar, Milt Hinton on bass, and Cozy Cole on drums. I also had Dizzy Gillespie on trumpet. Diz was just coming up then. I'd heard him for the first time at the Apollo Theater a few days before. I went to the Apollo a lot—we all did. That was where you heard real black music. I was sitting behind the stage, and I heard this guy playing trumpet in a different style than I or anyone else had ever heard before. It was the new bebop style, and I said, "Man, I got to get this guy on my next recording session." Some say that it was on those recordings we made, especially "Hot Mallets," which I wrote, that early bebop was first recorded.

Anyway, when you're playing with that kind of talent, you play at the top of your form. Our recording of "When Lights Are Low" was included in the Smithsonian Collection of Classic Jazz in the 1970s, and the guy who selected the pieces wrote in the liner notes that my swing "is as impeccable as Ella Fitzgerald's," which to me is the highest praise.

In the summer of 1940 I invited the King Cole Trio to record with me for Victor. Nat, Oscar Moore, and Wesley Prince played on six or eight sides with me. At the time, the trio was working pretty steadily, but they didn't have any big hits. Nat was doing some of my arranging. By this time I was talking about leaving Benny and going out on my own. Nat wanted to come with me and be my piano player. I said, "Man, you stay out there and you sing, 'cause you got a style all your own." It was just that he wasn't appreciated.

When I went to RCA Victor with the idea of recording with the King Cole Trio, Eli Oberstein said, "Oh, don't nobody want to hear this stuff." But I insisted, and—save the date—we went into the Victor studios in Hollywood and did "Jack the Bellboy"/"Central Avenue Breakdown," "Dough-Re-Me"/"Ghost of a Chance," and "Jivin' with Jarvis"/"Because of You." These were some of my biggest-selling hits that year, and they also helped Nat. Ralph Watkins, the manager of Kelly's Stable on Fifty-second Street, heard "Jack the Bellboy" and made it his business to find the King Cole Trio and book them.

Leonard Feather was writing for *Down Beat* at that time. He picked up and reported the rumor that I was going to incorporate the King Cole Trio into my new band, but it was never more than a rumor. I had plans for a band that did not include Nat's kind of sound. Besides, I wasn't planning on a featured singer, and I knew that's where Nat's real popularity was going to come.

About two or three years later, Capitol Records was just forming, and I went and told one of the founders, a guy who owned a record store called Music City, about Nat. The trio was playing at the Radio Bar, about half a block away, and I told the guy, whose name was Glen Wallichs, that he should go and hear Nat. He wasn't enthusiastic, but they recorded Nat singing his song "Straighten Up and Fly Right," mostly to appease me. And the thing was a hit, and Nat *made* Capitol Records.

I left Benny Goodman not long after I recorded those sides with Nat in the summer of 1940. Benny didn't mind. In fact, Benny lent me some money to start up. In return, he received a percentage of my gross earnings, because he was a businessman.

The years with Benny were some of the best. I became famous with the Benny Goodman Quartet. But it was time to move on.

6

ON OUR OWN

G *ladys* always believed that if you could find a way to do it, you should work for yourself. Even while I was with Benny, she was thinking about the possibilities of forming another Lionel Hampton Orchestra. After I'd been with Benny about four years, she said it was time to try again.

This time, she wanted us to have some seed money, so she went to Benny and to Joe Glaser of Associated Booking Corporation, and she had them to put up the money to get us started. Then we went back to Los Angeles to get the band together.

We liked New York all right, and there's no question that New York was where the jazz was happening. But Los Angeles was our home base, and we decided we could do better getting a bunch of young guys together out there. There was less competition. In New York, you had to compete with Duke Ellington and Cab Calloway and Count Basie. Plus, guys from Benny's outfit were trying to get bands of their own together. Teddy Wilson was trying to put a band together, and he was having problems. He wanted Milt Hinton to join him, but Teddy could only pay $75 a week, and Milt was getting $175 to $200 with Cab. So that's what I would have run into. Teddy wound up with a great group—Al Hall on bass, Ben Webster, Doc Cheatham—but Gladys and I decided we'd be better off in L.A.

We started calling guys and forming the group, and we arranged to rehearse at the Club Alabam on Central Avenue, and the guys started dribbling in. This is the late fall of 1940. Marshall Royal, who'd played alto with me over in Oakland when he was still a kid in high school and I had my first band, was grown up now, and he was playing with different groups. He had a brother named Ernie, who's a great trumpet player, great high-note trumpet player. So I called up Marshall, and I told him I wanted him and Ernie in the band.

I had Vernon Alley, a young guy out of San Franciso, on bass, Eddie Barefield, another young cat from San Francisco, on tenor sax and bass clarinet—but he stayed with me only a couple of months. I had Ray Perry, a young guy who played jazz violin. I had even had a guy whose name was Young—Lee Young, Lester Young's brother, on drums. What I'm saying is that all these guys were young, some of them teenagers.

Karl George and Jack Trainer were on trumpet. Sonny Craven was on trombone. So were Fred Beckett from Kansas City and Harry Sloan from Houston. Sir Charles Thompson was on piano—that was his real name. They came in over the space of several weeks—one would come in one day, and two guys would come in the next—and the group kept getting bigger and bigger until finally I had a full orchestra.

The last place I filled was the guitar player, and Gladys found out about Irving Ashby from a musician friend out of Boston who we'd met in New York. Ashby was just out of high school, working with a trio in a little club in Provincetown, Massachusetts, and Gladys got on the phone to the club and told Ashby I wanted him in my orchestra. Gladys said she'd send him a train ticket, and he and Ray Perry traveled from Boston to Los Angeles together.

Oh, we also had a girl singer, the wife of Bumps Myers, the tenor sax player, though Bumps wasn't in my group. Her name was Evelyn Myers, and she'd been with Les Hite's band at one time, and she sang ballads at the good supper clubs.

We started rehearsing, and meanwhile the guys were being measured for uniforms and Gladys was buying music racks. Gladys was also negotiating with the instrument companies. In those days, if a band used a lot of instruments made by one company, then the company would pay for advertising. A lot of our guys were using Conn instruments, and the Conn Company agreed to pay for advertising. So we had a bunch of photo sessions with me posing with different sections of the band and their Conn instruments. We were organizing a big band from the ground up.

We did a lot of rehearsing. We had a bunch of young people in the band who didn't have much experience, and the older guys like Marshall Royal helped out by rehearsing the different sections. We played our first gig at the Casa Mañana in Los Angeles—and clicked. After that, we went into the Los Angeles Orpheum Theater. We broke all the box-office records there, except for the one held by Ted Lewis. Of course, everybody wanted to come and see how we were doing —there were a lot of fellow musicians in that audience.

Ready or not, we went out on our first out-of-town booking that Joe Glaser had arranged for us. It was at the Trianon Ballroom in Seattle. We really hadn't gelled yet. I was following the pattern set by Benny Goodman. I had Marshall Royal on clarinet out in front with me and the other guys playing some whole-note chords behind us. Marshall later complained that I wanted him to be a black Benny Goodman. I was just trying to go with what worked. And our sound worked enough to get us booked for an eleven-week return engagement at the Trianon Ballroom.

On to the Sherman in Vancouver, British Columbia. One of the critics there wrote: "One of the most diversified treats this city has ever known. . . . The band differs from the average all-Negro outfit in that it features both sweet and swing. . . . A new trend in popular music."

We traveled by bus. Gladys was trying to economize, and she rented a small bus that we all just barely fit into, with our instruments. It was an All-American Bus Line bus, and it was okay as long as we weren't going on any long trips. But this was a brand-new band, and we had to take our bookings where we could get them, and that meant Texas, Arizona, anywhere.

It took us about three days to get to Fort Worth, Texas, and from there we went to Arizona, and from there to New Mexico. It was winter, and it was cold, and the bus didn't have any insulation or any heat. And about that time the guys staged a mutiny. A guy named Jack Lee was our road manager, and the fellows told him, "Get a real bus. We can't ride in our overcoats." So we switched to a Greyhound bus, which was bigger and which was insulated and had heat. Gladys worried about the cost, but we had to keep the guys comfortable.

We played at all-white hotels and at all-black dances—mostly one-nighters. We got better as we continued working together. We lost a couple of guys early on, but I replaced them with guys who were just as talented, if not more. By the time we went into the Grand

Terrace in Chicago about three months later, I had Karl George on trumpet in place of Jack Trainer.

I also had Shadow Wilson on drums in place of Lee Young by that time. I had trouble with Shadow from time to time. I liked my drummers to play backbeat, and that was not how Shadow wanted to play, and he didn't. I almost fired him, but the other guys liked him so much that I ended up keeping him on.

Anyway, that was some experience, playing in my hometown of Chicago with my own big band. I'm just sorry my grandmother didn't live to see it. Uncle Richard was still alive then, and he and my mother and some of my relatives came to see us, and that was one of the proudest times of my life.

After the Grand Terrace, we went into the Hotel Sherman, where we had a guest vocalist named Billie Holiday. She'd just gotten married to Jimmy Monroe, and she spent part of her honeymoon singing with us. I wanted her to stay on and be the band's singer, but Billie wanted to stay a single.

I got Rubel Blakely as my singer instead, and he stayed with me for several years. He was my vocalist when we did our first recordings. We recorded for Victor—and in Chicago, which also made me proud. The instrumentalists were Karl George on trumpet, Marshall Royal on clarinet and alto sax, Ray Perry on violin, Sir Charles Thompson on piano, Irving Ashby on guitar, Vernon Alley on bass, and Shadow Wilson on drums. We did "Give Me Some Skin," "Now That You're Mine," "Chasin' with Chase," and "Three-Quarter Boogie."

I was sorry when we had to leave Chicago. I could have played there for months on end, but the gigs weren't there. We had to keep moving. We played in the South quite a bit, and it was real hard for a black band in the South. In that whole section of the country there weren't more than six black hotels, and that's probably being generous. I remember when they built a new black hotel in Tulsa, Oklahoma, not long after I got my band together. This was the biggest news of the century for black performers. I don't know how many times the bus would pull into a black neighborhood at three o'clock in the morning, and the guys would have to get out and start knocking on doors and ringing doorbells, asking if they could rent a room or if a family could put a couple of guys up for the night.

And meals, we were lucky to get one good meal a day, what with our performing schedule and the way things were in a segregated society.

It was easier for Gladys and me than it was for the guys. There was always some important black family in town who invited us to stay with them and have meals with them. And Gladys always booked us into the black hotels in the towns that had them. Some of the guys wouldn't be able to afford the rates.

I was not in on the business end of things much—Gladys wouldn't even discuss money with me—but I knew what she was paying the guys because they used to complain about it. Ten dollars a night when we were working—if we didn't work, they didn't get paid. After about a year, Gladys agreed to pay $11 a night. Gladys was tight with a dollar. That first time we went into Chicago to the Grand Terrace, she negotiated with the Musicians Union local there to let us go into the Grand Terrace at $38 a week; that was the price for the sidemen. I don't know how much the whole orchestra was getting paid, but Gladys was buying $1,000 war bonds every week that she could. She would tell me that we had to save for a rainy day.

The guys resented Gladys for being so tight, but we had expenses. We had to furnish the uniforms and pay for the cleaning. We were always *dressed*—we were as stylish as Duke Ellington and his band. This was important to both Gladys and me, because it meant we had self-respect and respect for the audiences. We also paid for the bus and the driver. We had to pay Joe Glaser his percentage.

Looking back over some of those early contracts, I can't believe we survived. Joe would book the whole band someplace for $250 for the night, and the next booking wouldn't be for a week, and it would be two states away. Joe Glaser didn't have to worry about taking care of all those guys in between. All he worried about was his percentage.

Gladys was just being a good manager, and she got a lot of advice from one of the most successful managers in the business. Joe Glaser told her, "Buy cheap and sell high. When you get these guys, you've got to hire them as cheap as you can and sell them for as much as you can." Marshall Royal heard Joe tell Gladys that, and that's when Marshall Royal quit. He went into the army. I couldn't blame him.

Gladys said there was always somebody else who was willing to work, and she was right. There were a lot more musicians than there were jobs. There wasn't much the guys could do. One Thanksgiving we were up in Seattle, and we hadn't worked for about a week. Gladys and I were invited to Thanksgiving dinner at the home of some friends, but the other guys were on their own, and they didn't have much money. So a group of them decided to play a trick on Gladys, and they went to a pawn shop and pawned all their instruments and then went out and spent the money on a big Thanksgiving dinner. A couple of days later, Joe Glaser gets us a gig, and the guys say, "But we don't have any instruments."

So we had to get their instruments out of hock, but you could never get the better of Gladys. She charged them double what she had to pay to get their instruments back.

Gladys was really ahead of her time. She was a sharp business-woman back in the days when women stayed home in the kitchen. She was also a gorgeous woman who always looked and dressed beautifully. She was named by the GIs of the 206th Quartermaster Battalion, stationed somewhere in Germany, as their ideal pinup girl and the one they would pick for their ideal wife. And while our papers and scrapbooks are pretty slim until sometime in the early 1950s, we kept parts of a July 1945 magazine with her picture on the cover and a whole article about her.

Gladys was right about socking away as much money as she could in the good times to get us through the lean times. We had some real lean times in those early years. Too much time between bookings and all that, and not enough pay for the bookings we did get. Gladys was consistent. She didn't talk to me about money in the good times, and she didn't talk to me about money in the bad times.

Gladys always told me to concentrate on what I did best, and that was writing and arranging and playing music. That was when I was happiest. I loved performing. Every show I would put in at least a few numbers on drums. I'd juggle the sticks, jump on the drums, and do all that stuff. But my trump card was the vibes—that was my finale. I always let the other guys have their turn. I'd feature them on solos. They couldn't complain about not being given a chance. That's how a band gets its reputation, from the soloists.

Of course I lost one guy, Howard McGhee, because he was afraid I was gonna blow his lip out. He said he didn't want to be hitting high F's and G's at the end of every song, and besides, he wasn't being paid enough. So he left after about a month. That was in the summer of 1941.

It was around that time that Herschel Evans joined the band. He played tenor saxophone. He was up from Texas, and he had a whole lot of *soul* in his horn. He had a unique way of playing. He had a great big body on his horn, and when he started playing, he swung like mad. To me, he was one of the greatest men who ever played the horn. I said to him, "Boy, when the public gets hold and hears this tenor saxophone, tenor saxophone will be it." I could see the tenor saxophone coming into prominence. I said, "That's the horn that people are gonna be listening to," and they did.

A lot of guys made big names for themselves. After Herschel left, I started talking a lot of young guys into playing tenor sax—including Dexter Gordon and Illinois Jacquet.

I think it was that summer that we first played the Michigan State Fair. And then we went into the Greystone Ballroom in Detroit. Every Monday night was big-band night, and it cost something like $1.25 to get in. The teenagers all came to dance, but one young cat named Milt Jackson came just to listen and learn. He'd come up in gospel guitar and had just switched over to jazz a couple of years earlier. He later told me that seeing me at the Greystone was what inspired him to lay down the guitar and take up the vibraharp.

Because we both played the same instrument, Milt and I never recorded together. You could with two trumpets or two saxes, but not with two vibraharps. But in the last few years we've talked about making some recordings together, for posterity. Maybe we'll get to it one of these days.

Our big gig for that year came at the end when we played the Apollo Theater in Harlem in December, on the bill with Billie Holiday. Back then, playing the Apollo was the big-time for black musicians. I was luckier than most, because I'd played the white big-time places with Benny Goodman, but there was something about the Apollo. If you were a black entertainer of any kind—musician, singer, comedian—being a headliner at the Apollo was your proudest achievement.

I brought sixteen pieces into the Apollo, and the crowd went crazy. No wonder. I had some incredible talent in the band then. By the time we came into the Apollo, I had Dexter Gordon and Illinois Jacquet on tenor sax and Joe Newman on trumpet.

Dexter was out of L.A., only about seventeen or eighteen years old. His instrument was the clarinet, and he came with his clarinet wrapped in a newspaper. He came in just before we left to go on the road, and he never even had a chance to rehearse with us before we left. I was the one who talked him into playing the tenor sax, because that's what I needed at the time—and that's the instrument he made his fame on.

Illinois Jacquet was a little young guy that Marshall and Ernie Royal recommended, an alto sax player before I put him on tenor. He cried when I did that—"Oh, you're taking me from my horn. I like my alto." But he made his name on tenor. Illinois played Texas-style tenor, like Herschel Evans.

I found out about Joe Newman when we were playing a gig in

Birmingham, Alabama. Some of Joe's friends came to see us, and when they found out I needed a trumpet player, they told me about Joe. So I sent word to him to come to Atlanta, Georgia, the next night. I found out later that Joe didn't have any money, and his friends pawned some of their clothes to get him the train fare. So he played for me, and I took him on, and he stayed with me until the end of 1943, when he went with Basie.

These were young cats, not known, but as it later turned out, I had some of the best talent in the business when I went into that first Apollo gig. The Apollo audience was famous for booing folks off the stage—and throwing eggs and tomatoes and whatever else was handy. But with my guys, they wouldn't let us off the stage. Our sets went looooong, because I was letting the guys solo as much as they wanted.

We had that audience in a frenzy, and that brought out every bit of my showmanship. I used to do a bit where I jumped up and down on my drums, and I made an arrangement with Bob Hall, the Apollo electrician, to let loose with his smudge pot so it would look like the stage was blowing up. The first time he did that, everybody ran out of the theater. But word got around that it was just a special effect, so the next time everybody stayed in the seats.

Some funny things happened at the old Apollo. There was a time when a guy in the second balcony was high on too much reefer. When we were playing "Flying Home," he got inspired. He climbed up on the rail and starting shouting, "I'm flying, I'm flying." And then he jumped. It was a miracle that no one was hurt. They say that Jerry Valentine wrote "Second Balcony Jump" for Earl Hines on the inspiration of that incident.

We went over so big at the Apollo Theater that every time we appeared there, the crowds lined up around the block for tickets. Gladys saw this and made a deal with Jack Schiffman, who owned the Apollo. Instead of a straight salary, we would play for a percentage of the gross. We would also play as many shows a day as we could fit in. There were times when we played nine or ten shows a day, and still people were turned away at the ticket booth.

I first met Sammy Davis, Jr., when we were playing the Apollo. He was a young kid then—about sixteen—and performing with his father and uncle in the Will Mastin Trio. He was dancing and doing imitations. I taught Sammy how to play the drums, and Gladys and I really took a liking to him and his family. Later on, I toured with them. And Gladys wasn't above telling a club or theater manager that if he wanted Lionel Hampton and His Orchestra, then he'd also have to take the Will Mastin Trio. I'm the one who urged Sammy to sing. I told him, "You've got a good voice. Why don't you go out there and sing? Just go ahead and try it."

The band did our first recordings while we were playing that first engagement at the Apollo in December 1941. It was the day before Christmas. My contract with Victor had run out, and Gladys decided to sign on with Decca. We did "Just for You" and "My Wish" and "Southern Echoes" and "Nola." We played like we did in our shows—we played off each other, one soloist answering another. We were a disciplined band by this time, and we were good, and we just kept getting better.

We did another southern tour in early 1942. We would do two a year, sometimes three. In those early years, a lot of times we got bookings because the managers thought I was white. I'd played with Benny Goodman and got all that publicity, but they clearly hadn't seen any pictures of the Benny Goodman Quartet. But once they heard my music, everything was okay. We even used to get invited out to their homes. In Greenville, South Carolina, Jesse Jackson's town, the whites even gave me a party in one of the nightclubs after our concert.

But we did have our share of troubles down south. Dexter Gordon likes to tell about the time we were in Mississippi and getting our food out of the back doors of restaurants. Something was wrong with the bus, and we pulled into a filling station, and the filling station guy started to work on the bus. There was a diner attached to the filling station, and Dexter and Joe Newman decided to go get some food.

Everybody else figured they'd be back out in a few minutes with their takeout food, and when they didn't come back, we started worrying. Seems that they'd gone in and stood at the counter to order their food, and then one of the waitresses said, "Where would you like to sit?" They were surprised, but they took her up on it and sat down and started eating.

Meanwhile, the rest of the guys got curious, and they started getting off the bus, and yawning and stretching, and then they started moseying over to look in the windows of the diner. When they saw Dexter and Joe sitting down, their eyes popped out. Then they started going in and sitting down, too. Pretty soon, this Mississippi diner is filled with black guys ordering and eating.

The attendant finished repairing the bus and realized that everybody who was on the bus was in the diner! He rushed in and started hollering and carrying on—"Where's my gun?" His face was all red, and he looked like he was going to pop a valve. The guys started leaving fast, and Jack Lee came in and tried to calm him down, explaining that we were from New York and Hollywood and didn't know the local customs. He kept talking until all the guys were back on the bus, and then he made a quick exit, and the bus laid rubber getting out of there.

It wasn't long after that tour that Joe Newman and Dexter Gordon left the band. I don't remember if that experience in the South had anything to do with it.

We did some more sides for Decca in May 1942. At the time I had Karl George, Ernie Royal, and Joe Newman on trumpet; Fred Beckett, Sonny Craven, and Harry Sloan on trombone; Marshall Royal, Ray Perry, Illinois Jacquet, Dexter Gordon, and Jack McVea on sax; Milt Buckner on piano; Irving Ashby on guitar; Vernon Alley on bass; and Shadow Wilson on drums. We recorded "Flying Home" and about seven other sides, and one of them was a piece that Charlie Christian had written. I remember that session because we were right in the middle of recording Charlie's number when the engineer just cut us off. He came out of the booth and took me off to the side and told me he'd just got word that Charlie had passed. And there we were, right in the middle of his piece.

We were getting longer and better engagements now, and playing more often in the big cities. Our reputation was only enhanced when we beat Basie in one of the famous Sunday-night cutting contests at the Savoy Ballroom. Basie's band was good. He had Don Byas, who used to play tenor for me, Al Killian, Buck Clayton, Jo Jones, and a bunch of other talented guys.

Later, Basie and I had different recollections about who won that contest. He agreed that when my guys and I went into "Flying Home," we went at least fifteen minutes, and that was a hard act to follow. He said in his autobiography that the contest ended in a draw, because he got the edge for musicianship and I got the edge for showmanship.

As I remember it, we won. It was touch and go until we went into "Flying Home." Illinois and I both played sustained solos, and yeah, we did go for fifteen minutes, and the audience went crazy. When we finished, they gave us a standing ovation. To my mind, we won, and I could cite some independent sources that agree.

But I'll take the credit for showmanship. We had the crowds lined up to see us everywhere—at the Earle in Philadelphia and the Capital in New York. I had Earl Bostic with me by that time, and Arnett Cobb. Arnett was a real showman. He and Johnny Griffin came up with a routine where they would throw their coats down when they really started into it. I encouraged this kind of showmanship. When I was just starting out, somebody told me, "When you get on that stage, you're in show business. You be kind to your audience. Try to make communication with them. Give them what they want." The audiences wanted good music, but they also wanted a show. I gave it to them.

Dexter Gordon was a real showman, and I was sorry when he left. He was always late, just barely made it onto the bandstand when we started to play. One time at the Paradise in Detroit, he still wasn't there when we started, and we were doing a number that he was supposed to solo on. Just as we got to his solo, he walked out of the wings blowing his horn. The crowd went wild. So did the guys and I. I couldn't even be angry with him, because you couldn't believe the effect he had on that audience.

Dexter wanted to be with Prez—Lester Young—so he started wandering around. I went back to California, and he wanted to stay in the East, so he did. He was going into new styles, and I was willing to go as far as he wanted to go. But I had a thing where I was going good in boogie-woogie, and I was staying in that groove. I was playing modern things, too, but when you ran a band, especially in that era, you had a lot of people who had a lot of ideas, and you had to have a strong person to keep you on track. I'm glad I had a strong person like Gladys to say, "No, you go this way, and when this runs out then you can go another way. You get all you can out of this one first." Gladys understood that a band had to have a reputation for a particular sound and couldn't run all over the musical map. So I lost some good guys over the years because they wanted to experiment, but the band was successful because we didn't experiment too much. And we never forgot that we were supposed to be entertaining an audience, not just playing a jam session in front of a bunch of strange people.

After World War II broke out, audiences needed a good show more than ever, to take their minds off what was going on overseas. I remember we were playing the Strand Theater in Brooklyn the night President Franklin Roosevelt went on the radio and told the nation about Pearl Harbor. Maxine Sullivan was on the bill with us. At the time, I was thinking about the big Apollo engagement we had coming up. I wasn't thinking about how the war would affect the band.

I had a lot of young guys, and young guys were always getting drafted. Some of the older ones enlisted, like Marshall Royal. We had many changes in personnel because of the war. I got Bobby Plater after he got out of the army in 1942. He replaced Herbie Fields on alto, and a couple of years later, after Arnett Cobb left, Bobby became my straw boss, which was like the unofficial leader of the band. Bobby stayed with me eighteen years—the longest a guy ever stayed with me, except for Billy Mackel, a guitar player from Baltimore, who was first with me in the forties and then came back around 1950 after Wes Montgomery left.

It was also during the war years that I hired my first female musician. Her name was Elsie Smith and she played a mean tenor saxophone. We were playing in Los Angeles, and she came backstage to tell me she played saxophone. I said, "Can you read my arrangements?" She said, "I can read anything that's put in front of me." I said, "Well, come to rehearsal." So she came and she read everything I asked her to, and we taught her how to play jazz. She was good for the show, because female jazz musicians were pretty rare, except for piano players. She stayed with a me a long time, about four or five years, traveled all around with us. She got a lot of publicity playing with me, and eventually she hooked up with a chick in an act where she played and the other gal sang—they did the USO circuit. She was at some army camp and got in the wrong car, and it smashed up and crippled her for life.

It also became even harder for us to travel. It was never easy—not the way Joe Glaser booked us. But now we had to watch gas, because of rationing. For long trips, we couldn't use the bus. We had to travel by train. Joe Newman used to talk about how we'd have to get off in some "chitlin' switch town" and have to wait four to six hours for our connection. But we managed, and we still crisscrossed the country. We went all through the South, the Midwest, the West, the East, the North—Boise, Idaho; Spokane, Washington; North Dakota; South Dakota. Joe Glaser said that we could make more money in four weeks in four different cities than we could playing a month in the same place. He was right, but he never stopped to consider that the gigs he set up with a phone call meant miles and miles of travel for us.

I can't say I minded the traveling, because just about all the other musicians were traveling, too, and we'd meet up together in the various cities and towns. They'd come to hear us and we'd go to their shows, and then we'd all wind up at some after-hours joint together, jamming away or drinking and winding down after a performance. And then we'd go our separate ways and say, "See you in Chicago, or Kansas City," because we'd compare itineraries and know when we'd be playing in the same town again.

And then there were the good friends we made who were not in the music business. Leo Moore was one of them, although later he turned out to be not a good friend. He was sixteen years old when we met him in Cleveland, when we were playing some dates in the

Midwest. He was hanging around the theater or the hotel, and the first thing he did for us was to walk Gladys's dogs. Gladys took a liking to him, and he idolized Gladys—the way she dressed and carried herself. He was a fey little cat. Anyway, he became a kind of all-around errand runner, and we put him on the payroll as secretary and baggage manager, and he was on the payroll until shortly after Gladys died in 1971.

Our best nonmusician friends were the McMurray family in Indianapolis, whom we'd met when I was with Benny Goodman. Their second daughter, Patricia, says one of her earliest memories is of being dumped into the car so the family could drive three, four hours to hear me play. Whenever we played Cincinnati, Louisville, or any city within a few hours' radius, the McMurrays were there.

Little Patricia was a doll. Gladys really took to her. They both loved animals. Gladys was a great animal lover—birds and poodles were her favorite pets. I don't know how many times one of the pets would get loose and we'd be running up and down the halls of hotels looking for them. She had a lot of poodles over the years. The one I remember best was an African gray poodle named Mr. Gates.

Patricia was a little girl when her parents bought her a cocker spaniel, and she was about twelve when it died. She was so upset, because that dog had grown up with her. So Gladys went right out and bought her a black cocker spaniel, and we called it Bop's Last Beep. Then the McMurrays came to visit us in New York, and they put Bop's Last Beep in a kennel, and when they got back, they found out it had caught distemper and died. So the next time we were out there, Gladys went to the pet shop and bought a huge Indian Hill mynah bird for Patricia. It was the most expensive bird in the place. The cage was so big it took up the whole backseat of the car. So Gladys drove over to the McMurray house with this huge bird cage and talking bird in the back, and then she got cold feet. Gladys, who never got cold feet, suddenly got to worrying about how Patricia's parents would react to this huge talking bird. I guess they weren't mad and they liked the bird, because they kept it for years and years until it died.

We had good friends all over the country, but the McMurrays were our best friends on the road, and so the Midwest was our favorite place to play when we were out on tour. It was because of them that we got to know the city of Indianapolis pretty well and to care about what went on there. We were there one time around 1945 when I heard that a small Catholic church, St. Rita's, was in trouble. The roof was leaking, and the parish, which was mostly poor and black, couldn't afford to fix it. The priest, Father Joseph Ritter, had a good reputation in the black community. He was promoting integration when most people didn't say that word. So I went to see him and I said, "I'm going to raise ten thousand dollars for you, Father," and I canceled my other bookings and played a whole week of free concerts and dances. I raised the ten thousand dollars, and Father Ritter used it to repair the roof and to do a lot of other good things. Later, he became Joseph Cardinal Ritter, and Gladys and I went to Rome just to see him get his hat.

My least favorite area of the country was the South, because of the segregation. In the South, we played a lot of military bases. First, we'd give a show for the white troops, and then we'd give a second show for the black soldiers. That was the way things were in those days—the armed forces were completely segregated. We couldn't do anything about it—those were the rules. But we'd always put a little extra into our playing when we performed for our own.

We were traveling with a big show by 1942. In addition to all the musicians, I had two singers, one guy and one gal, Rubel Blakely and Madeline Green, who used to sing with Earl Hines's band. I also had a comedy act called the Two Zephyrs, and one of the two was Slappy White. They didn't travel with me all the time—like the singers, I had them for the bigger dates. But by this time in the big-band era, you had to have a lot of variety in your show to compete.

In December 1942 we were playing the Regal Theater in Chicago, with Billie Holiday singing. Boy, when she sang, she just kicked the band off and made it fly. We tore the roof off the Regal on New Year's Eve. I was still thinking about how I'd like Billie to be my singer, and I was thinking that I should have a regular girl singer, which I didn't have at the time.

Joe Glaser kept telling me I should have a regular girl singer, and he was the one who set me up to hear Dinah Washington, before she was Dinah Washington. He came to Chicago because Joe Sherman, the owner of Garrick's Show Bar, told him about this girl singer that he should hear. Garrick's was a place that a lot of sailors went to when they came off the ships on the Great Lakes. Walter Fuller's Sextet was playing at Garrick's, and the ladies' powder room was right next to the bandstand, and when they'd play some piece that Dinah knew, she would stick her head out the door and start singing with the band.

So one night Joe Glaser went to hear her, along with a couple of guys from my band—Clark Terry and Snooky Young—and when they heard her sing "Sweet Georgia Brown," they knew she was something. So Joe Glaser said I should go to Garrick's to hear her.

I was playing four or five shows a day at the Regal Theater, including two matinees, but I went the next night to hear Dinah sing at Garrick's Show Bar. She sang "Sweet Georgia Brown" for me, and after listening to a few bars, I knew she was the girl I was looking for. She could make herself heard, even with my blazing band in the background, and she had that gutty style that they would later call rhythm and blues. So I invited her to sing at the matinee at the Regal Theater the next day.

She came out to the Regal Theater, and she walked out on that stage like she owned it. I said, "Ladies and Gentlemen, here's Ruth Jones, Chicago girl Ruth Jones," and she went over great.

Afterward I said, "I like your singing. Would you like to go with my band?"

She said, "Yes."

I said, "What was your name again?"

She said, "Ruth Jones."

I said, "Gee, I don't like that name. Can I change it?"

She said, "I don't care what you call me as long as you give me the job."

So I said, "Well from now on your name is Dinah Washington." It came to me right out of the clear blue sky. Now, other people claim to have given Dinah her name, including Joe Glaser and Joe Sherman, but I'm the one who gave it to her, backstage at the Regal Theater.

A guy was standing next to her backstage, and he heard us, and heard me offer her the job, and he said, "Gee, there goes my chance. I wanted to join the band."

I said, "You can sing the next show." So he sang, and I liked his singing, and I gave him a job. His name was Joe Williams. So right there the same day, I got Dinah Washington and Joe Williams.

Joe joined us in Boston a couple of weeks later. He stayed with me about two or three months, but we didn't get to record because the record ban was still on. James Petrillo, the head of the American Federation of Musicians, had called a strike back on August 1, 1942, and none of the musicians in the union could make any new records. The strike lasted until late October 1943, so nobody did any recordings for over a year. Even without the record ban, I don't know if I would have featured a singer on my records. My contract with Decca was for big-band instrumentals, not as a backup band for a singer, no matter how good.

Of all the male singers I ever had working with me, Joe Williams was my favorite. He was Gladys's favorite, too. A quiet man, a nice man. He was born in Georgia but grew up in Chicago, and he was only nineteen when he started singing with Jimmy Noone's band in 1937. He sang with Coleman Hawkins's and Andy Kirk's bands in the 1940s, along with mine, but it was when he joined Basie in 1950 that he really took off.

Dinah Washington was Gladys's and my favorite girl singer. Dinah really brought out the mother instinct in Gladys. She was only about nineteen or twenty. That girl was so poor she was raggedy. She was dark—the light-skinned girls got all the attention in those days. She wasn't pretty, and that was hard for a girl singer traveling with a bunch of guys. The guys were not kind to her. The story has been told many times, and it's true, that the first time they saw her, they covered their heads. All but Slappy White. He was nice to her, made sure she had a room, showed her the ropes.

Gladys made it her business to make Dinah look as good as she could. She managed to remake some of her own evening gowns for Dinah, though I don't know how she did it, because Dinah was top-heavy, with a chest big enough for the big sounds that came out of her. And Gladys noticed that Dinah had nice legs and pretty feet, and she would give Dinah some of her old shoes, which were still good because Gladys had a thing about shoes and spent a lot of money on them even in those days. What was interesting was that after Gladys went to work, the guys in the band started noticing Dinah's legs and feet, and they nicknamed her Legs, and that made Dinah feel better about the way she looked.

When Dinah joined us, we were really getting hot. The money was coming in good, and now Gladys was buying real estate. She'd get a big check, like when she signed a new recording contract, and go out and make a down payment on a building. I remember she bought a building on Adams Street in Los Angeles for twenty-seven thousand dollars around that time, because she had Slappy White to go with her to take the money to the bank. We had a good bunch of guys—Joe Morris, Lammar Wright, Joe Wilder on trumpet; Milt Buckner was playing piano and doing some arranging. I had Arnett Cobb on tenor, Eric Miller on guitar, and George Jenkins on drums. Our big numbers were "Hey Bobarebop" and "Hamp's Boogie-Woogie," and we were smoking.

But Dinah alone could stop a show. I started her out at the Paradise in Detroit, and by the time we got to Boston, where Joe Williams joined us, I had to put her down next to closing, because nobody and no one could follow her. She had a background in gospel, and she put something new into the popular songs I had her sing. Dinah made her debut at the Apollo Theater with my band that December, and we blew that place apart.

The record ban was over by this time, and I was making plans to record, but we hadn't gotten together on a date or a repertoire yet. Meanwhile, this young guy named Leonard Feather, a songwriter and agent who I knew, came to see us at the Apollo. Afterward he came backstage and wanted me to introduce him to Dinah. Leonard was really impressed with her voice. She wasn't singing blues, but he said he thought she had a great voice for blues. He had written some blues songs, and he wanted her to record them. He even had a record company in mind—Keynote, a small independent label in New York.

He wanted to back her with a sextet of my guys, and that was okay with me. In fact, I went to that recording session, too, and played on all four sides. The sextet was Joe Morris on trumpet, Rudy Rutherford on clarinet, Arnett Cobb on tenor, Vernon King on bass, and Fred Radcliffe on drums. After we got through at the Apollo around midnight, we all went down to this little RKO studio in Radio City Center and recorded "Homeward Bound," "Salty Papa Blues," "Evil Gal Blues," and "I Know How to Do It." I played vibes on "Evil Gal Blues" and "Salty Papa Blues." I played drums on "I Know How to Do It," and I even played my two-fingered piano on "Homeward Bound." I was having a good time, and we jammed until about four-thirty in the morning. At one point, Feather said to me, "You sure this is okay, Lionel?" and I said, "Oh yeah, don't worry about it."

I couldn't see that this recording session was any conflict of interest with my contract with Decca. That contract was for big-band instrumentals. With Dinah, we were backing up a singer. I didn't realize that the whole thing was contractually illegal.

Needless to say, Gladys didn't know anything about it. I didn't bother to mention it to her, and she was busy with the holidays—the recording session took place between Christmas and New Year's. If she'd known, she never would have let me do it.

The main problem was that the records were released as Lionel Hampton Sextet with Dinah Washington, and my contract with Decca included all rights to my name. To make matters worse, the records were hits, and Decca was going to sue Keynote, and sue me, and Keynote had to change all the labels so they read "Sextet with Dinah Washington." Gladys was furious. She had to go through all kinds of trouble over that, and she didn't let me forget it for a long time. I can't blame her. We were in a real legal mess with Decca, and I didn't record for that label again until the spring of 1944.

I didn't have any problems finding a way to get recorded on other labels. For a time I went over to Radiola. The first recording

I did with them was with the Esquire All-American Jazz Stars. Me, trumpet player Roy Eldridge, trombone player Jack Teagarden, clarinet player Barney Bigard, tenor sax player Coleman Hawkins, piano player Art Tatum, guitar player Al Casey, bassist Oscar Pettiford, and drummer Sid Catlett recorded at the Metropolitan Opera House in January 1944. We did "Tea for Two," "Flying Home, Parts I and II," "Jammin' the Blues," and "National Anthem." The other guys did "Esquire Bounce," but all I did on that was a two-bar break. Then Sid Catlett and I got together on "Drums for Two." This was an important milestone in my career. Not only had *Esquire* named me as a jazz all-star, but this was the first LP I ever recorded. All my earlier recordings had been 78-rpm discs. The record business was changing.

In the spring of 1944 I signed on with a label called Black Jack and did my first LP with my own band. I had Cat Anderson, Lamar Wright, Jr., Roy McCoy, and Joe Morris on trumpet; Al Hayse, Mitchell "Booty" Wood, and Fred Beckett on trombone; Earl Bostic and Gus Evans on alto sax; Al Sears and Arnett Cobb on tenor sax; Charles Fowlkes on bars; Milt Buckner on piano; Eric Miller on guitar; Vernon King on bass; and Fred Radcliffe on drums.

Dinah still wanted to record, and the people at Black Jack agreed that she could. She had a great voice, but the changeover to LPs probably helped. On an LP you had a lot of cuts and could afford a few vocals mixed in with the instrumentals. We did an LP with fourteen cuts, and Dinah sang on "Jubilee," "No Love, No Nothing," and "Evil Gal Blues." Rubel Blakely was also featured on a couple of cuts.

In May–June 1944, I did an LP for the Joyce label. Dinah was featured on "Million Dollar Smile," a cut on another LP. Madeline Green was also featured on one cut on that one. And then in June, when we were playing at the Trianon Ballroom in South Gate, California, the Joyce and Sandy Hook labels recorded a live broadcast we did, and put it on an LP, and Dinah sang "There'll Be a Jubilee" and "No Love, No Nothing." In other words, Dinah did more and more recording with my orchestra.

In 1945, Decca finally came around, and the different legal problems were resolved. Decca recorded a big Carnegie Hall concert I did in April, and when it came time for Dinah to sing "Evil Gal Blues," I had Leonard Feather to take Milt Buckner's place at the piano. A month or so later, Dinah sang with a septet from my band—Wendell Culley on trumpet, Herbie Fields on alto sax, Arnett Cobb on tenor sax, Johnny Mehegan on piano, Billy Mackel on guitar, Charles Harris on bass, and George Jones on drums. Decca recorded her on

"Blow Top Blues." But we had some misunderstandings about who was to have publishing rights to "Blow Top Blues," which Leonard Feather wrote and which was one of the songs we did in that session, and release of the record was held up for several months.

Dinah still wasn't happy about the amount of recording opportunities she was getting, but that's about all she could complain about. I paid her well. I started her at $75 a week, and by the time she left me more than two years later, I was paying her $125. But Dinah wanted to make records, and there was no way she was going to be able to do that with my band. So Dinah left in the fall of 1945.

That year, 1945, saw a lot of changes in the music business. Records were becoming more popular, and *Billboard* magazine started its first pop chart, called "The Honor Roll of Hits." A lot more people were buying record players, and so more records were being produced to meet the demand. Guys were coming out of the army and back into the bands. Herbie Fields had come out a couple of years earlier and tried to head up his own band, but that didn't go. He joined me in 1945. Herbie Fields was white, the first white cat I had in my band. When we performed onstage, he wore makeup to darken his face so he didn't stand out so much. It was still unusual to have an integrated band.

Herbie played alto sax and tenor sax, and he really wanted to have his own band. He'd hang around Fifty-second Street and jam with guys, and he did some recording for small, independent labels, like Signature. I played on one of those recording sessions, for Savoy. The group was called Herbie Fields's Band, and I played drums. I don't remember how I got away with it. I don't even remember if my name was on it, or whether it was legal and Gladys knew about it, or if I kind of did it on the sly. As I remember, also in on that session was a young student at Juilliard School named Miles Davis, on trumpet, but Miles played quietly, and from that session you never would have known what he could do.

Miles hung around Fifty-second Street a lot. We jammed together. He never was a paid member of my band, but he used to come around and jam with me all the time. I admired his playing. He was just kind of a roaming cat in those days. He had to heed the call of his feel, his sound. Miles always figured that he was an individualist and he had something individually to say. He started hanging around with Prez and they recorded together for Savoy that same year.

I tried a new direction in the middle 1940s. In January 1946 I recorded a rock and roll album for Decca called *Rock and Roll*

Rhythm. But they never released it; they said it was too "cacophonous." I was ahead of my time on that. Rock and roll wouldn't be big for another ten years. In the forties it was still a black thing, which is why I was into it. Later on, Elvis Presley got all his stuff from Bo Diddley.

I stayed in the black groove. You'd know my band was black just from listening to it. The crossover to the white audience hadn't happened yet. That came later.

7

THE POSTWAR YEARS

*B*lack music started getting more attention at the end of the 1940s. It was in 1949 that *Billboard* magazine started its rhythm and blues chart. "R and B" meant black—only black records were on it—but it was a better-sounding title than "race records," which is what they used to be called. The year before that, my old friend Nat King Cole had a number-one hit with "Nature Boy" and managed a complete crossover to the white audience. I always told him he should concentrate on his singing, and it finally paid off. Billy Eckstine was also making records that white audiences were buying.

I like to think that I helped bring black music to white audiences. I know I exposed thousands and thousands of white people to some of the most talented black musicians who ever lived. For a while in 1948, for example, I had a band that included both Wes Montgomery on guitar and Charlie Mingus on bass. I brought Mingus from California when nobody wanted him to play. I brought him to New York. I found Wes Montgomery playing in Indianapolis with a little hometown band, and he turned out to be one of the greatest. At the same time I had Teddy Buckner on trumpet. Teddy Buckner had one of the most beautiful tones on trumpet you'd ever want to hear. He played so well that Louis Armstrong gave him a horn and said, "Man, you're a real trumpet player." Between our concerts and our recordings and our live radio broadcasts, we were getting the word out about black music. We helped a lot of other people make the crossover.

One of my greatest honors was being invited to play at President Harry S. Truman's inaugural gala on January 19, 1949. We opened up the show with a boogie-woogie arrangement of "Missouri Waltz," and the president like to went crazy! He was jumping, clapping his hands. He got the whole house rocking. Not only did I play for him, but after our performance, he came up and shook my hand. Truman made a real effort to increase integration during his time in office, and he started the ball rolling by having Lena Horne and me perform at his inaugural gala, along with Abbott and Costello, Edgar Bergen and Charlie McCarthy, George Jessel, Dick Haymes, Gene Kelly, and a bunch of other white performers. Truman was also the first president to tell the Hollywood studios to hire more blacks and to order the armed forces to start integrating. I liked Truman, and after playing at the gala, I started paying attention to the difference one man can make, provided that he's president.

I can't remember for sure, but I don't think there were any black guests at that inaugural gala. At the Capitol, and out in the rest of the country, there still wasn't any crossover when it came to live performances. We played for either white audiences or black audiences, although sometimes at the white concerts there would be some blacks up in the balcony. My band was doing great. We were grossing a million a year and doing one-nighters fifty-one weeks out of the year. We were also branching out in the music business. We had formed a music publishing company, Swing and Tempo Music, which mostly published my compositions. We also had a record label, Hampton Records. Gladys was manager of both. It was around the same time that Ahmet Ertegun was forming Atlantic Records, and he approached Gladys and me about going into partnership with him. He wanted an investment of something like ten thousand dollars. Gladys said to me, "We have our own label. We don't need partners." Looking back, that may have been the only wrong business decision Gladys ever made. We could have afforded to make the investment.

Gladys was wearing diamonds and fur coats and driving a little sports car to meet us, or flying in to meet us. In 1949 she was named "Most Outstanding Woman of 1948" by Mary McLeod Bethune, commander-in-chief of the Woman's Army of National Defense (the WANDS). She was honored "as an example of the leadership among women which is coming more and more into its own" and "for unusual proficiency exhibited in business and managerial capacities as the only woman manager of a band in America."

For me, the money we were making meant that I could have several singers at a time for the engagements where it was good to have singers. I had Jimmy Scott, Jackie Paris, and a couple of girl singers, Jeannette Franklin and Irma Curry. I didn't usually use singers when I played dances. But it was when we were playing a dance at the Forest Club in Detroit that I first had Betty Carter sing with me.

That was 1948. She was at the dance with her friends, and hanging around the bandstand. All her friends knew she wanted to be a singer, and someone asked me if she could sing, and I said okay. She was good, and about two weeks later I sent for her. I sent a telegram to her agent in Detroit, and she joined me in Toledo, Ohio. Betty was into bebop. She'd already sat in with Dizzy Gillespie and Charlie Parker. I was into swing, but I wanted some of that bebop sound in my performances. I'm the one who gave her the nickname "Betty Bebop." Betty did "The Hucklebuck," which was one of my big numbers at the time, and she also recorded that with me and the band. But most of the time she scatted. She was a young girl, about eighteen, trying to get started. She was with me as long as Dinah had been—about two and a half years.

Gladys was nice to Betty, too. She taught her a lot about dressing and would pass some of her clothes on to Betty. She also taught her a lot about being a woman in the music world. Betty says that the main reason the guys didn't like her was because she was a female. She also says that the one thing she had in her favor was that Gladys controlled the band. Betty did not like it when I called her Betty Bebop, but Gladys told her to just go with it, and when Betty had the experience she needed and could leave the band, she could call herself anything she wanted to. Of course, she's still known as Betty Bebop. Betty finally left me because she wanted a chance to sing lyrics, and I encouraged her to move on. Young people had to get experience, and that meant playing with a lot of different bands. Over the years, I'd seen a lot of young people come and go.

The same year I hired Betty Carter, I tried to hire a really young cat named Quincy Jones. We were in Seattle, and this fifteen-year-old kid came backstage at the theater and showed me a suite he had written called "The Four Winds." I played it, and it was really good. In the meantime, I found out that he'd been born in Chicago and he also played trumpet. I offered him a job, and he accepted, and he played third trumpet for a little while. It must have been the summertime, when he wasn't in school. He wrote a piece called "King-fish," and we recorded it. I wanted him to stay with the band, and he wanted to stay with me, but Gladys overruled us both. She was not going to take a kid out of school. So I left him with an open invitation to join me after he graduated.

Jerome Richardson came on around that time. He was the kid who'd played with my band in Oakland about fifteen years before. I'd offered him a job, too, but his father said he had to finish school first. He joined me in San Francisco, and here he was with me at last, playing second alto, flute, singing sometimes. He was featured on that recording of "Kingfish."

Gladys took a particular liking to Jerome Richardson. When he asked her if he could borrow money, she'd give it to him. She wouldn't do that for most of the guys. She was a businesswoman, but the people she liked could get by with little things. The guys were making twenty-three to twenty-five dollars a night by then, but only when they played. We were playing most of the time, though. We were playing almost all one-nighters in big theaters, clubs, concert halls. Traveling by bus across the country and up and down the country. We were very popular, and no matter how tired we got sometimes, we always gave a good show.

Al Grey was with me then. He was a trombone player who had been with Jimmie Lunceford and Lucky Millinder. He told Stanley Dance in *The World of Count Basie* that when he got with me it was a whole different atmosphere. " 'The fellows would sit up and clap their hands and pop their fingers, and Lionel would say, "Gate, eh-eh-eh . . . pop your fingers, Gate!" I couldn't see it at first, but it developed a different feeling, a stronger rhythmic feeling. It taught me the more human side of life, to be more jolly in music. . . . I think everyone should have that experience, to be around someone who has as much rhythm as Hamp.' "

I had a great group of guys then: Clifford Brown, Fats Navarro, Jimmy Cleveland, Benny Powell, Ellis Bartee, Billy Mitchell, Jerome Richardson. They could really shake down, and they understood that you had to entertain, not just play music. I found Clifford Brown in Wilmington, Delaware, at the YMCA. He was playing around with little local bands. I had Sonny Parker singing with me then, and he used to really like to holler the blues, and Al Grey would jump in and play along with him, and the crowd loved that. Billy Mitchell was a young kid who played tenor sax. One time we were playing the Oakland Auditorium—I forget if it was an accident or not—he was dancing around and he fell over backward right into the audience. The crowd pushed him back up onstage, and he kept playing the whole time, and they loved it. So that became part of the act. Then he got busted for drugs. So I had Gene Morris do a Russian deep-knee dance playing saxophone. We had him doing all kinds of things out there on that stage.

Jerome Richardson reminds me of the time we were playing the Brooklyn Armory. It was supposed to be a dance hall, but when we were playing, the people didn't dance. We got off for intermission, and there was this Latin band that came on, and everybody started dancing. Jerome says I start walking around the edges of the crowd, just looking and watching, and I don't like it that everybody is dancing when this band plays and nobody dances when my band is playing. So when we get back onstage, I say to Jerome, "Can you play 'Begin the Beguine'?"

He says, "Yeah."

I say, "Play it on your flute, Latin style."

I had the rhythm section go into a Latin beat, and Jerome starts in on the flute, and then everybody starts dancing. For the rest of the evening we played most of the arrangements in Latin style. I always played to the people. That's why I was in such great demand to play at political fund-raisers.

From the time I was a youngster, I've always been interested in politics. My family used to read the papers and discuss politics, and then after I became a newsboy for the *Chicago Defender*, I would read the paper and follow the news. I kept up with the news even after I went into the music world. A lot of musicians are so tied up in their music that they don't know what's going on in the world around them. But if you're a band leader and trying to be a good businessman, you have to keep up with the times, see the trends. Gladys and I made friends with a lot of important people, and we knew how politics impacted on business, real estate, and all that. But I didn't become active in politics until the middle 1940s when I helped Richard Nixon get elected to Congress.

Nixon was a lawyer in Whittier, California, which is right across the line from Los Angeles, the black section of Los Angeles. He had been appointed to fill out the term of a congressman who died. Now, he was running for the seat on his own, and he decided he needed some black votes. So he came over on Central Avenue, and we met, and I wanted to get into politics, so I decided to help him.

I introduced him to Norman Houston, who was just starting his Golden Gate Insurance Company at that time, and then I introduced him to the head of the Elks, and the head of the Masons, and all the different leaders in the black community. And they all decided they didn't have enough registered black voters, so Nixon started a voter registration drive. I would take my band and play up and down Central Avenue, and we'd play at the Elks Home and give free dances, and Nixon would make an appearance and ask everybody to register. We got twenty thousand blacks to register as Republicans, and Nixon and I got pretty tight, and he made me his assistant campaign manager. Came the night before the voting, we had a big rally, and he won the election. He got something like twelve thousand black votes, and that was enough to put him over.

Next, he decided to run for the Senate against Helen Gahagan Douglas. I was assistant campaign manager again. Kenny Washington, the ex–football player, was also working for him. We signed up some more black voters for him and held rallies and all that. He must have decided Central Avenue was lucky for him, because the night of the election he was sitting in a little bar there, called the Last Word, drinking beer.

Then, a couple of years later, Nixon was nominated to be vice president on the ticket with General Eisenhower. I was at the Waldorf Astoria Hotel in New York with my band, when lo and behold, in walked Nixon with his family. He asked me to get on the Eisenhower bandwagon. I was glad to help out.

They had a private plane for us, donated by an industrialist in Cleveland. We had a private jet plane and pilot, and depending on the occasion I'd break down the band to five, six, or seven, eight pieces and we'd fly off to play at a rally somewhere. We'd go to different cities—Cleveland, Detroit, Indianapolis—and play for the General. I remember in Cincinnati we played around noontime, and there must have been a hundred thousand people there.

So they won, and my band played the inaugural ball. And when he was in office, President Eisenhower did some good things for blacks. He signed that first Civil Rights bill. A lot of people said it was a weak bill, but it was still a law that hadn't been on the books before. He was the one who put those black kids in that white school in Little Rock, Arkansas, by backing them up with the whole United States Army. He did what was right.

I remember one time Walter White, head of the NAACP, stood right next to me in the dressing room at the Apollo Theater and told me about what led up to the Supreme Court decision in the school desegregation case in 1954. Walter told me he had gone to Roosevelt about school desegregation; he had gone to Truman about school desegregation. Truman told him, "Well, Walter, I'd like to help you, but you know the southern senators won't go for it. I'm sorry I can't help you." So when Eisenhower came in, Walter decided that time was running out and that he was going to take a chance on Eisenhower.

He phoned Eisenhower and requested an appointment. He said he went there and he listed all the reasons why school segregation was wrong. He said that if the Supreme Court agreed to hear the case *Brown v. Board of Education* and ruled against desegregation, it would break the back of segregation in American society. He said, "Mr. President, this is the last chance for you to help us." Eisenhower listened, didn't say a word. But then he picked up the telephone, and said, "Get me Chief Justice Earl Warren." And he got on the phone with Warren, and he said he knew the president was not supposed to put pressure on the Supreme Court, but he was going to send Walter White over to talk to him about the case. And the Supreme Court decided to hear the case and ruled in favor of the NAACP lawyers and desegregation. The only thing that Walter White was sorry about was that Charles Houston, the Dean of Howard University Law School, didn't get to present the case to the Supreme Court. He'd worked on that case so long, but Thurgood Marshall ended up carrying the papers to the court. Thurgood Marshall got all the credit.

It was Walter White who suggested that I take an integrated band down south. This was earlier—about 1951. He thought it would be a good thing to show whites—because I was doing a lot of concerts at white halls and clubs—that black and white can get along together. So I took a band down that was half white and half black. I even took a white girl singer with me, Janet Thurlow. When we got to Macon, Georgia, on the front page of the newspaper was a picture of this white girl and the headline, "Come Hear Janet Thurlow Sing with Lionel Hampton." She married a trombone player in the band, James Cleveland.

Duke and Cab stopped performing in the South, but I felt it was my duty to go because the people didn't have any entertainment. Down south, they had ropes to separate the black and white dancers. I cut the ropes down on the dance floor more than once—they weren't going to have segregated dancing where I was playing. I think we helped soften them up through the years.

By the time the *Brown* case went to the Supreme Court, I was in Europe a lot. We made our first trip over to Europe in the fall of 1953. It was Gladys's idea. She decided that if jazz was hot there, I would be, too. Joe Glaser told her she wouldn't be able to get enough bookings, but she got three months' worth.

Looking over the letters that Gladys kept between herself and Joe Glaser, I realize that Europe was also a place where we didn't have any lawsuits pending or axes to grind. Looking back, maybe Europe and Africa were the logical places to go. We had legal problems in California and in Chicago at the time.

I don't remember much about the problem in California. But Gladys wrote a letter to Joe Glaser in 1954 that referred to a contract she'd signed for a California tour, on Joe's advice, but which she'd signed against her better judgment because it had only one name on it, Brisk Enterprises. For some reason, there was a lawsuit that was still going on in 1954, and Gladys said she was afraid her home might be attached because of it. She also says in that 1954 letter that we couldn't work in California because of that lawsuit.

Gladys kept a copy of a telegram she sent to Joe Glaser in April 1954, and in it she says that we had stayed out of Chicago for four years because we couldn't get the terms we wanted. Looking back, I remember that we did refuse to play Chicago because there was a deal that paired the Regal Theater with the Chicago Theater and we didn't feel we were getting paid enough for both bookings. Gladys said in her telegram to Joe Glaser: "If I must live without Regal I will but think it unfair for Mr. Platt not to give top attraction like Lionel the same money we get at Apollo Theater plus giving him Chicago Theater. I took him at his word that we would play it and I hate to think he would renege on Lionel Hampton." In that same telegram, Gladys brought up the fact that the last time we had played the Regal we were knee-deep in snow. I remember that. We could barely get across town to play our gigs. But it was Gladys's business to remind Joe Glaser about that four years later. It was my business to keep the band going.

But even if we'd had no problems in the United States, it was still time to go abroad. After the war, the most popular jazz in the U.S. was small-combo jazz. It was more for listening than for dancing. Funny how those things go. When Nat King Cole tried to get work for his small combo back in the late thirties–early forties, nobody wanted small groups. Now everybody wanted small groups, and few people wanted big bands. Gladys and I tried to follow new trends, but we weren't about to break up the band and try a small combo. So we just went to other audiences. Jazz was hot outside the United States, especially in Europe. It had been brought over by Americans during World War II (I should say "brought over again," because Europeans first got turned on to jazz during World War I). Anyway, over in Europe there was a big outcry for American big bands, and our first tour there in the fall of 1953 was a great success. We were booked for four weeks and held over for fifteen. Gladys even had Christian Dior design a whole wardrobe for her as a publicity stunt.

The members of the band who accompanied me on that trip included: Clifford Brown, Art Farmer, and Walter Williams on trumpet; Jimmy Cleveland, George "Buster" Cooper, and Al Hayse on trombone; Gigi Gryce and Anthony Ortega on alto sax; Clifford Solomon and Clifford Scott on tenor sax; Oscar Estell on baritone sax; George Wallington on piano; Billy Mackel on guitar; Monk Montgomery on bass; Alan Dawson and Curley Hamner on drums (Curley also did a dance act); and Sonny Parker and Annie Ross on vocals.

I also took Quincy Jones along on that trip. He was the kid who I'd met in Seattle back in 1948 when he was fifteen years old. Well, in the intervening years, Quincy had gone to the Berklee College of Music in Boston and then arrived in New York to become a record producer and arranger. We kept in touch, and whenever I was on the West Coast, he'd try to sit in with me. He played trumpet when we recorded in Los Angeles in 1951. I took him to Europe with me in 1953 as both a trumpet player and an arranger. He stayed over there for a while to study music some more. After he came back, he did some work with Dinah Washington—arranged a number of recordings for her in 1955. Later, he became the first black music director at Mercury Records, and the rest is history.

We played Sweden, Norway, Denmark, Germany, Holland, Switzerland, and France. And then we went to Algiers and Oran and Casablanca. In some of the Scandinavian towns, the people had never seen a black person. They danced in the aisles, showered us with flowers, went crazy over our music, demanded encore after encore. It was some experience. The crowds went wild. But I was especially happy to play in Algiers and other places in Africa and to find out that the people there were really jazz conscious, too.

We did a number of recordings on that trip—several sessions in Paris, one in Copenhagen. It was only later that I found out that some of my guys were doing some "moonlight recording" on their own. Like in Paris, we did a session on September 28 with the band, and then later—must have been in the wee hours—some of the guys did some more recordings as "Gigi Gryce and His Orchestra." Now, the press says I was annoyed when I found out about it later on, and maybe I was at the time (I *know* Gladys must have been). After all, we were paying for their travel and hotel rooms and everything. But looking back, I realize that they were just trying to get over, make a name for themselves, just like I did when I was playing with Benny Goodman and making all those small-band sides. I don't harbor any grudges about it.

That was quite a trip. After I got back, my press agent, Mike

Hall, and I counted up the concerts, and we'd played eighty-seven in fifteen weeks. I knew we'd been working, but I didn't know we'd been working *that* hard. It was an exhilarating experience.

We caught up with Josephine Baker over in Paris—she and Gladys were calling each other "Sis" in a minute. Josephine was touring all over the place then, trying to make money for her Rainbow Tribe and her dream of an international hotel and school at her villa, Les Milandes. All that was just getting started. She wrote to Gladys the following April—1954—and Gladys kept the letter.

Dimanche le 11 Avril

Dear Gladys

I just arrived in Paris from Scandinavia and they are still talking about Lionel. I am so proud dear because this is what will give our people confidence in themselves. I ran down home for a day everybody is well and happy all but Jo [Bouillon, Josephine's husband] he just lost his mother, tonight I take the plane for Tokio—I will be there three weeks—I am bringing back our adopted baby—you know we have five in all—a *Jewish* baby—a *Japonise*—an *Indian*—a *South Africain* and a *Parisien* —you know these children have been adopted as a symbole of democracy well I will not go into that you know how I feel—yes I have my visa—and expect to be in N.Y. at the end of June— and as usuale I am in a fighting spirite for our people—and for *all* defendless *people* all my love your big sis Jos.
    Kiss Maria.
    I will be playing in Paris from the 14th of May until the end. I arrive in Paris on the 7th of May. When you come to Paris on the first of May I will arrive the 7th so we will surely see each other—yes the Power [?] Hotel is good and too . . . you must start living like the French do the Claridge is only for tourists it is too expensive for Frenchmen. Love Jos.

That successful trip to Europe also gave me more substance back home. It was after that tour abroad that I got written up for the first time in *The New Yorker* magazine. Mike Hall got that publicity, but he wouldn't have been able to get it if we didn't have knee-deep piles of clippings from European newspapers to prove our success. I even had a whole album of clippings, with a big picture of me cut out and glued on the front cover, compliments of the travel agency that had booked us in France.

I realize now that that's when Gladys and the people who were working with me on press started keeping clippings on me. I never paid much attention to all that. Now, I wish we'd kept scrapbooks of the articles that were written about the band. We didn't in the early years. Suddenly, for the years 1953 and 1954, we've got papers in Swedish and French and German in the files. I guess in my organization, at least—and that includes Gladys—going to Europe meant that I had really made it.

I should add that the European tour was not a financial success for us. Eight months after we got back, we still owed Joe money for commissions. Three months of bookings and nothing to show for it except newspaper clippings. But it was worth a lot in prestige.

After we got back, I reorganized the band. I was always trying to keep up with new trends, and modern jazz was in, so I wanted to have some modern jazz musicians in my orchestra. I got three guys who had been making names for themselves in modern jazz in Boston—Herb Pomeroy on trumpet, Dick Twardzick on piano, and Jackie Crown on trombone. It was the most integrated band I'd ever had. In fact, from the group I formed the UN Sextet, which had musicians from six different nations in it—A. Greenstein (Israel) on bass, Wallace Davenport (French Morocco) on trumpet, Floyd "Floogie" Williams on drums (Jamaica), Retney "Ricky" Brauer (Germany) on tenor sax, Jackie Crown (Norway), Herb Pomeroy (England), and Dick Twardzick (Poland). At the time, I thought I had the best band ever. But none of those guys lasted very long. I don't think they could relate to my style of showmanship, which was always to give the audience what it wanted to hear, not what the musicians wanted it to hear.

Maybe they couldn't take the steady string of one-nighters. We were all over the map that late winter–early spring. We did a big southern tour between late February and early April. Somebody saved the half-page spread that we did to promote it. "Triumphant Tour of Dixie"; "First Tour Since His *Mad* Return from Europe." Pictures of Gladys, me, singer Sonny Parker, drummer and dancer Curley Hamner. It was a big show. We had Cook and Brown on comedy, a girl singer, and a guy singer. I even had "Hamp, Jr.," along. He was a four-year-old drummer from Nashville. I'm sorry to say I don't remember his real name. He was a big hit with audiences. This was the schedule: February 26, Norfolk; February 27, Charleston, West Virginia; February 28, Richmond; March 1, Roanoke; March 2,

Raleigh; March 3, Columbia, South Carolina; March 4, Spartanburg; March 5, Charlotte; March 6, Fayetteville; March 10, Bradenton, Florida; March 11, Orlando; March 12, Jacksonville; March 13, West Palm Beach; March 14, Miami; March 15, Ft. Lauderdale; March 16, Tampa; March 18, Pensacola; March 19–20, Kessler Air Field, Biloxi, Mississippi; March 21, New Orleans; March 22, Jackson, Mississippi; March 24, Houston; March 25, Austin; March 26, Oklahoma City; March 27, Tulsa; March 28, Ft. Worth; March 29, Dallas; April 1, University of Mississippi, Oxford; April 2, Tennessee State University, Nashville.

I especially remember Mississippi because we played at the University of Mississippi in Oxford, and at the time I had a white piano player, Twardzick, and a Japanese guy named James Araki on alto sax. But we didn't have any trouble at all-white Ole Miss. In fact, it was one of the high spots of our season. The auditorium was jammed to the rafters, and when we finished, we got twelve standing ovations. After the concert, the students crowded around the bandstand and shared their liquor with us, and we all drank from the same bottles and danced for about an hour.

We were due in Nashville the next day, so we piled back onto the bus, and a motorcade of about fifty cars full of students accompanied us to Nashville. A whole bunch of them came to our gig in Nashville, even though it was at a black place—Tennessee State University—and whites weren't supposed to be there. They must have had influential parents or some kind of connections.

The next year, I went back to Oxford with an even more integrated band, and this time we got thirteen standing ovations. Of course, that was the same year that Nat King Cole was attacked in Birmingham by some White Citizens Council guys, so I'm not saying the South was free of danger. All I'm saying is that as a rule we were very well received.

That was around the time that Martin Luther King was getting his movement going. I talked to him by telephone and told him I was going to Europe, but if he needed me, I would be at his call. He said, "Okay, if I need you, I'm gonna call you." But he never did.

Back to Twardzick and Pomeroy and Crown—like I said, they didn't stay around long. Maybe they didn't like it that the first recordings I did after they joined up weren't with the band but with a "Lionel Hampton Quartet" that included Oscar Peterson on piano, Ray Brown on piano, and Buddy Rich on drums, and a "Lionel Hampton Quintet" that added Buddy De Franco on clarinet. Whatever the reason or reasons, around the time I did those recordings in New York, Herb Pomeroy had gone back to Boston. I'm not sure if Dick Twardzick and Jackie Crown stayed that long.

We did those pickup recordings in New York for Norman Granz. We started doing a lot of recording for Norman Granz, a jazz impresario who really knew his jazz, and his marketing. He'd started collecting jazz records when he was a student at UCLA, and soon after he'd graduated college, he'd started arranging and recording jam sessions. He took advantage of a Musicians Union rule guaranteeing musicians who were employed on a regular basis one night off a week, and he got them all together on their night off and had them jamming at Billy Berg's club in Los Angeles. He also had them open to everyone, black and white, which wasn't the rule in L.A. clubs then.

I didn't connect up with Norman until a few years later, because at the time I was with Benny Goodman and arranging my own jam sessions with the musicians I met on Fifty-second Street in New York City. And then later I went with Decca. But all the time I was tuned in to what Norman Granz was doing, and he was doing things right. He recorded a lot of black musicians when they wouldn't have been recorded elsewhere. He had Nat King Cole as his "house pianist" before Nat was discovered. He also recorded a lot of established bands, like Duke Ellington's and Jimmie Lunceford's, because he recognized that a lot of these guys just lived for playing and recording and didn't much care where or when they did it. He must have paid them okay, too, because he got a lot of them to record for him.

He had an understanding with Mercury Records at first, and then he started forming his own labels. And then after World War II he moved into Europe, and after a while, if you were in the United States or Europe, if you were a jazz musician, you thought first about recording for Norman Granz.

What I liked about him was that he'd go out on a limb and work with different combinations. It was with Norman Granz that I was able to continue my habit of recording with pickup groups made up of the best musicians. I recorded with the Lionel Hampton Quartet (Oscar Peterson on piano, Ray Brown on bass, Buddy Rich on drums, and me on vibes); the Lionel Hampton Quintet (add Buddy De Franco on clarinet or Herb Ellis on guitar); and the Lionel Hampton Sextet (Peterson, Rich, Brown, Ellis, and De Franco). I recorded with the whole orchestra at the Trianon Ballroom in Chicago in July 1954. My personnel at the time were: Julius "Billy" Brooks, Ed Mullens, Wallace Davenport, and Roy Slaughter on trumpet; Al Hayse, Buster Cooper, and Harold Roberts on trombone; Elwyn

Frazier and Jay Peters on tenor sax; Emmett J. Dennis and Bobby Plater on tenor sax; Oscar Estell on bass; Dwike Mitchell on piano (more on Dwike later); Bobby Mackel on guitar; Peter Badie on fiddle bass; and Wilfred Eddleton on standby.

I lost Jay Dennis (as Emmett J. Dennis preferred to be called) not long after that. We were playing in Wildwood, New Jersey, and Jay and some other guys decided to take a shortcut through the kitchen of the Club Fracas. The owner of the club, Oscar Garrighaus, objected, and there was a fracas in the Club Fracas. Jay Dennis pulled a knife and cut a gash in the owner's forehead, and we had to leave him behind.

Once Gladys started keeping book on Europe, she also started keeping information about my U.S. gigs, including her correspondence with Joe Glaser. I'm glad she did, because it helps me to recall what went on during those years. It also helps me separate one year from another, because it's hard looking back thirty-plus years.

Reading the copies of letters Gladys wrote to Joe, I am reminded that it was a tough job for Gladys to keep ahead of Joe and his bookings. He'd make deals and not tell us about them, and then we'd arrive, and Gladys would have to deal with Joe's deals. She saved a letter that she wrote on August 15, 1954. She wrote it from Wildwood, New Jersey, on stationery from the Fort Garry Hotel in Winnepeg, Manitoba, which gives an idea of our road schedule in those days:

Dear Joe,

I am writing you because I cannot get a chance to see you and
tell you just how Lionel and I feel about what has happened here
on this job. When you talked to me on the phone from
Winnipeg, as you know I wanted to cancel this job after I saw in
the contract TWO matinees each week end. You told me in exact
words, Go ahead and sign the contract, Gladys, it can't be over
2.00 a man, if it is I will pay it myself. I only took it as a joke at
the time and as you know I have never wanted you to pay
anything for our band. But I did expect . . . that you would split
commissions with me, because out of this job Lionel has
not made for himself nearly as much as the commission for the
office is.

In that same letter, Gladys chided Joe for not paying as much attention to us as he did to Louis Armstrong:

Both Lionel and I do not think you have given us much
cooperation the last two years. You never come to any of
Lionel's openings as you do Louie's. We opened at Dude Ranch
for the first time and no one from the office showed up to see if
they could be of any help, and believe me we needed plenty
there, but I managed to argue thru it.

Joe Glaser booked just about all the big black entertainers, including Dinah Washington and Louis Armstrong. Louis wasn't doing
so well then, and Joe wanted to give his career a boost. At first it
was just paying more attention to Louis, at our expense. We didn't
mind all that much, because we were doing well. And there were
things that Joe Glaser could help us with. He had a good relationship
with the Musicians Union and could usually put in a word for us
when we needed it. Around the same time as we were playing in
Wildwood, we had to fire a drummer because he was on drugs. A
hypodermic needle was found on his seat on the bus, and we fired
him on the spot because we didn't think it was good for the rest of
the band to be around him. But the guy took us to the union and
said we had fired him unjustly. We didn't want to go on record as
putting the finger on anyone for narcotics use. Joe was good at dealing
with the union on things like that.

We returned to Europe in the fall of 1954 for a shorter tour,
sailing out of New York on the *Nieuw Amsterdam* on October 18.
A short tour was just as much of a headache for Gladys, though. I
still have her lists of personnel, with their dates and places of birth
and their passport numbers. She had to make sure everybody had a
passport, and every time we went, there were some new guys who
didn't have them, so she'd have to see to that. We had a nineteen-
piece band, I think, plus there were two singers—Bertice Reading
and Sonny Parker (whose real name was Willis Benny, according to
the passport list). And then there were George Hart, our road manager; Leroy Thomas, our property man; and Leo Moore, who we
listed as "Secretary and Baggage." And finally, there were Gladys's
pets: Gates, the African Gray parrot, and Curley, the Gray cockatiel.
I guess she was between poodles at that time.

I left all that up to Gladys and concentrated on the music
and the entertainment. We had Nat Adderley, Ed Mullens, Billy
Brooks, and Wallace Davenport on trumpet; Leon Comegys, Buster
Cooper, and Harold Roberts on trombone; Bobby Plater on flute
and alto sax; Jay Dennis on alto sax; Elwyn Frazier and Jay Peters
on tenor sax; Joe Evans on bass; Peter Badie on flute and bass; Billy

Mackel on guitar; and Rufus Jones on drums. We also had Dwike Mitchell as our pianist, and he was one of the best.

I first heard him play back in the late 1940s when I went to a concert at Lockbourne Army Base in Columbus, Ohio. They had a great band at the base, and Dwike was something on the piano. I told him that when he got out of the army to get in touch with me, because I wanted him as my piano player. I didn't hear from him. Then, one time in late 1953 or early 1954, we were playing an engagement in Jacksonville, Florida, and Dwike was visiting his mother in Jacksonville and he came to hear us. He came backstage and said, "Hello, Lionel," kind of shy. He didn't know if I'd remember him. I remembered him all right.

"You're the man I want to see," I said. "I want you to go with me." He joined me two weeks later in Baton Rouge and stayed about two years.

He says he learned a lot from touring with me, especially about pacing and programming to different audiences. He says I was "the rock 'n' roller of jazz," and that the audiences at rock concerts never acted as wild as the people did at one of my concerts.

Ten days after we set sail for Europe, we played in Amsterdam and recorded "Stardust" there. From Amsterdam, we went on to Germany, where we played Kaiserlautern and Mannheim, Frankfurt am Main, Berlin, Hannover, Munich, Stuttgart, Düsseldorf (we recorded at the Apollo Hall there, too), Dortmund, Kiel, and Hamburg.

Then we went to Switzerland and Belgium and on to France. I had a dancer named Curley who was a big hit with Hughes Panassie and the crowd at the Hot Club de France. From France, we went to Italy. It was one-nighters, just like in the United States, but the only casualty during that trip was Elwyn Frazier. I forget why he left. If we'd been back in the States, we would have lost more. Playing on the road—playing all those one-nighters—was hard for musicians, and the only reason why we didn't lose more on those European trips was that they didn't have anywhere else to go.

After we went to Italy, we went on to Israel. I was, and still am, a great fan of Israel, and we took that side trip to help that new country. We gave all our profits to the State of Israel. I don't know what that amounted to, because we had to pay the guys and the bookers, but Gladys and I didn't take a thing from that side trip. We played three weeks in Israel—in Tel Aviv, Haifa, and back to Tel Aviv. All told, we did forty concerts in Israel, and the papers said that 170,000 Israelis attended our concerts. And we were invited back again the following year.

After Israel, we returned to France and played in Marseille,

Toulouse, Bordeaux, Limoges. Benny Bailey came over to join us in France for our last gigs, because I needed a trumpet player for our concerts, plus for the recordings we were scheduled to do in Paris.

Back in Paris, we recorded as Lionel Hampton and His New French Sound. We had Bernard Hulin, Benny Bailey, and Nat Adderley on trumpet; Dave Amram on French horn; Maurice Meunier on clarinet and tenor sax; William Boucaya on bass; Rene Urtreger on piano; Sacha Distel on guitar; Guy Pedersen on bass; and Mac Kec on drums. A couple of weeks later, we did some sides as the Lionel Hampton Quartet with Michel Attenoux on clarinet, Raymond Fol on piano, Guy Pedersen on bass, Moustache Galepides on drums, and me on vibes.

We were a great success on that trip, too. We killed 'em, everywhere we went. We played one of the grandest halls in Vienna and had the crowd screaming and tearing up the seats. Another time we were playing in Copenhagen, and the people were jumping so hard that the floor gave way. The stage slid, and we almost slid off it, with all our instruments.

The only real mishap we had on that trip was when my male singer, Sonny Parker, suffered a cerebral hemorrhage at a concert in Valenciennes, France. We stayed on in France because of him, wanting to stay with him and make sure he was all right. We delayed our departure several days.

We returned to the United States at the end of March and started out on a midwestern tour. Jay Peters, one of the tenor sax players, left us in Chicago, and I think that's when Retney Brauer came back. After that, we played some dates back east, and then played a week at the Apollo in New York in late May—early June. It was during that week that I recorded with Mahalia Jackson. We did "No Room at the Inn," "The Holy Babe," "Joy to the World," "Oh Come All Ye Faithful," and "Sweet Little Jesus Boy." I had a good time doing that. Nobody has ever had a voice to match Mahalia Jackson's.

Eddie Preston, who played trumpet, joined me in New York. Then we went out to Cincinnati and Toronto, and from June 29 to July 10 we were at the Blue Note in Chicago. That's when Eddie Chamblee came on. He was a native of Chicago and had known Dinah Washington in high school, but the two of them hadn't kept in touch since graduation. Dinah was also playing in Chicago and the Midwest then, and we appeared on the same bill with her in a couple of places, and lo and behold, Dinah and Eddie got back together. At first, it was just reliving old times, but pretty soon they were writing and calling back and forth. Eddie was married to his second wife at the time, but it wasn't too long after he and Dinah got together that he was in the process of getting his second divorce. Dinah, by this time, had already had a couple of husbands herself.

In July, Gladys and I headed west without the band. I think we still couldn't perform with the orchestra because of our legal problems, but this was work of a different kind. I went back to appear in *The Benny Goodman Story*. Steve Allen played Benny, but Benny worked closely with the director as a consultant. They hired Sol Yaged to teach Steve Allen the fingering on the clarinet, and he did a good job playing Benny. Gene Krupa and Teddy Wilson and I had a nice reunion with Benny, and we had a good time making the picture. I even had to learn some lines. Sammy Davis, Jr., was in the picture, too. So were Harry James and Ziggy Elman and Buck Clayton, although he'd never played with Benny. The director, Val Davies, said what he was after was good musicians. We made some great music for that picture, but they cut a lot of it out so they could show more scenes of Benny and his love life. But it was fun jamming with all those guys from the old days.

By the way, that same year I got a little play from Hollywood. It wasn't any major motion picture or anything, but Universal Pictures put out a short titled *Lionel Hampton and Herb Jeffries*, and I got permissions payments for their use of "Universal Stomp," "International Boogie-Woogie," and "Baby Don't Love Me No More" (which I shared credit for with Robert Mosely).

The other musicians who were involved in *The Benny Goodman Story* and I also did a bunch of recordings out there that month. For Norman Granz, it was a gold mine to have all those musicians who had played with Benny together in one place. I recorded with the Gene Krupa Quartet, with Stan Getz, and with the Art Tatum Trio, all for Granz's labels. The band joined me in early August, and I did a session with a Lionel Hampton Quintet featuring Billy Mackel on guitar, Peter Badie on flute and bass, Rufus Jones on drums, Isodore Hernandez on conga, Dwike Mitchell on piano, and Willie Ruff on trumpet. Willie Ruff was a good friend of Dwike Mitchell's, and the two of them later teamed up together. As far as I know, they are still together today, playing colleges and high schools and really making a contribution by educating young people about jazz.

The whole band recorded a big-band album the same day, and then we did a concert in Oakland, so by that time the legal problems must have been ironed out. From California, we went into Las Vegas and played three weeks at the Moulin Rouge, which was practically a record stay for my band.

We stayed on the West Coast for September. During that time

Dwike Mitchell left and I got Oscar Dennard to replace him. Dwike was suddenly called away because of a "domestic emergency." He never came back. He sent our attorney in New York a wire saying, "The extent of my domestic emergency did not permit my return to the band before two weeks' notice expired. Kindly forward pay from Las Vegas and Cleff [sic] Records." That was great timing for him. If he'd stayed with me another couple of weeks, he could have been hurt in the bus accident we had.

8

TROUBLE ON
THE ROAD

*O*n October 3, 1955, we were on our way from El Paso, Texas, to Denver, Colorado, and were just south of Socorro, New Mexico, when our chartered bus blew a tire and plunged down an embankment. When we came to rest at the bottom, the bus was practically totaled, and there was so much moaning and crying that I knew some of the guys had been seriously hurt. I had searing pains in my right ankle and was shaken up pretty badly, but otherwise I was all right.

Some of the guys weren't hurt at all. Three had minor injuries, like I did. Rufus Jones, the drummer, and Frank Holt, the singer, had body lacerations. Billy Brooks and Eddie Preston, trumpet players, had minor injuries. But three were seriously injured. Alvin Hayse, my trombone player, had a broken neck. Larry Wilson, slide trombone player, lost all the toes on his right foot. George Hart, our road manager, had compound fractures in both legs. The doctors had to put a plate in one of his knees, and for a time they thought they were going to have to amputate the leg. And George Alliston, the driver, was pinned against the dashboard and had his leg almost severed. The doctors had to amputate it, and later on he died.

I was taken to the hospital in Truth or Consequences, New Mexico. Those of us who had been injured were taken to three different hospitals in the area. The doctors decided to rebreak my ankle, so I was there about two months. I got telegrams from all over. Sammy Davis, Jr., said I was just jealous of him; I don't remember why he said that, but he must have been in the hospital recently himself. Steve Allen, Count Basie, the George Shearing Quintet, Duke Ellington, the whole Jazz at the Philharmonic Gang (Norman Granz, Ella Fitzgerald, Buddy Rich, Oscar Peterson, Illinois Jacquet, Dizzy Gillespie, Lester Young, and a bunch of others). The orchestra and I received a telegram from the inmates at Central Prison, Raleigh, North Carolina, where we had played a concert a couple of months before.

Benny Goodman sent two telegrams. The first was a sorry to hear about the accident message. In the second, he said he'd been contacted by the Israeli people about substituting for me. But he couldn't because he was still in Hollywood tying up odds an ends on *The Benny Goodman Story*, which hadn't been released yet. He was referring to our planned trip to Europe and Israel in early 1955. The Israel bookings had been set up back in the spring, and I guess the guy in Tel Aviv, who called himself "M. Wallin, Impressario," was worried.

Gladys sent a telegram of her own—a hot one to Mike Hall, our publicity agent. She'd heard that Walter Winchell had said on his radio program that my condition was worse. She demanded that Mike retract that statement, and said, "There are enough good things to tell about Lionel without trying to pretend he is half dead." Mike must have got on the phone with Winchell, because Gladys kept a clipping of Winchell's column in the *Daily Mirror* of October 21, 1955, saying, "Lionel Hampton and his crew are much improved at the hospitals after that bus wreck. They tour Yurrop in Jan."

It was a frustrating time for Gladys, stuck in a hotel in Albuquerque. She took the opportunity to put herself into the hospital for a minor operation—had some corns removed from her foot or something. They were so painful that she couldn't walk right. She had to attend to all the business of canceling engagements.

I was doing fine but worrying about the engagements we had to cancel. We had bookings in Omaha, October 5; at Purdue University in Lafayette, Indiana, October 7; in Cincinnati, October 8; New Bedford, October 12; Bangor, October 13; Holyoke, October 14; Carnegie Hall, October 15; Bridgeport, October 16; Blacksburg, October 17; Camp LeJeune, North Carolina, October 18; Wilmington, North Carolina, October 19; Knoxville, October 22; Memphis,

October 23; at Jackson College in Jackson, Tennessee, October 24; at the Aluhaje Hotel in Atlanta, October 25; in Charlotte, October 27; Roanoke, October 28; Charleston, West Virginia, October 29; Columbia, South Carolina, October 31; and Fayetteville, North Carolina, November 1. When you did as many one-nighters as we did, a month in the hospital meant about 25 to 30 bookings we had to cancel. I was going stir crazy. I was used to life on the road. So one night some of the guys and I had a jam session at the home of one of the doctors. I thought that was harmless enough, but a couple of days later Gladys got a letter from our attorney in New York, Louis P. Randall, calling her attention to the fact that "if the boys are able to work, you will not be eligible to receive certain insurance benefits, nor will the boys be able to receive Workmen's Compensation Insurance. . . . If the boys are able to play an instrument for free, they certainly are not entitled to be paid for sitting around."

Next, I decided to reorganize my band. Those guys who were not injured had gone off to get other jobs, and I couldn't blame them. If they didn't work, they didn't get paid. I got on the phone to a bunch of guys and started lining up some new personnel. I also started planning my comeback. I wanted to do it up big, at the Apollo Theater.

> St. Joseph's Hospital
> Albuquerque, N.M. Oct. 28

Mr. Frank Schiffman
Apollo Theater
New York City

Dear Mr. Schiffman:

I recently received your very nice letter. Don't worry about the flowers—I would much rather hear from you. I read it to my boys and it really lifted our spirits. There are about six of us still in the hospital and we expect to be here for at least four or five more weeks.

You know, Mr. Schiffman, you could easily be the one to start a "Let's Bring Hamp Back" campaign. This is something I haven't spoken to Joe or Gladys about as yet because it will be strictly up to me to decide where and when to start. You know I have a score to settle and I can think of nothing better than to walk into the Apollo Theater and shake hands with you and say

"I'm back—on with the show!" Discuss this with my friend Ralph Cooper and see how much steam he can gather in the community on "Let's Bring Hamp Back."

My ideas are this—Ralph could produce and emcee the first half of the show with about five current race and blues artists that have hot records and the last part I could perform for about one half hour on stage with just my band and vocalist, starting one week Dec. 27th to go over New Year's, after which I will be sailing to Europe. If we can get enough steam to "bring Hamp back," the Apollo will be the place to let America know I am back better than ever.

Here is a funny coincidence. Before receiving your letter a few days ago, I was dreaming of this incident when my nurse woke me and gave me this letter from you, so God works in mysterious ways and sometime for our betterment.

Do give my love to your family, Mr. Frankco, all the backstage gang and all the good employees of the Apollo Theater and patrons likewise. Thank you again and do write. God Bless you.

Most sincerely,
Lionel Hampton

Mr. Schiffman wrote a letter to Joe Glaser and enclosed my letter, because he said he wanted to get Joe's approval first. Joe wrote to tell Gladys. Joe didn't think I was going to be up to a European tour and said I wouldn't be able to jump around onstage as I usually did. He thought I should stay in the United States. But we weren't paying too much attention to Joe by that time. We went ahead with our plans for the European tour.

I didn't get the Apollo gig that I wanted. But I got the next best thing—I staged my "comeback" at Café Society. It was a seventeen-day booking, and Barney Josephson's club was an integrated club. In fact, it leaned toward a white clientele. Barney was a real white pioneer when it came to attracting white audiences to hear jazz in an integrated setting.

Meanwhile, Gladys was busy making arrangements for Europe, not just to perform but also to record. We now had an exclusive arrangement with Norman Granz. In a letter Gladys wrote at the end of December to Felix Marouani, who had a theatrical agency in Paris and was doing most of the booking for that tour, she said: "Norman and I have an agreement that I am not to record for anyone here or over there because he will give me all the record sessions both here and in [Europe] that I want and will give me dollars, so I wanted you to know of this deal before I come over there because there is no commission that any of the booking offices get on my record sessions over there because it is my own booking and Norman will send records all over the world for publicity for me for free."

In that same letter, Gladys talked about not mentioning prices to Joe Glaser. We were trying to move away from him.

We sailed for Europe on the *USS United States* on January 11, 1956, and arrived at Le Havre on January 16. This was going to be our longest tour yet—over 300 concerts in thirteen countries. I think we were away seven months. I had no trouble doing my usual antics on stage—jumped around all over the place. I was completely healed from the accident.

What was also nice about that tour was that I had some official business to do as well.

As a way of thanking me for campaigning for him and playing at his inaugural galas, President Eisenhower gave me a certificate as a goodwill ambassador. It was the same kind of certificate that regular ambassadors received, and every town I went to, they'd roll out the red carpet for me. Over in Europe, I was billed as America's "Ambassador of Goodwill."

My personnel were as follows: Julius "Billy" Brooks, Dave Gonsalves, Ed Mullens, and Ed Preston on trumpet; Al Hayse, Walter "Phatz" Morris, and Larry Wilson on trombone; Scoville Brown on clarinet and alto sax; Bobby Plater on alto sax and flute; Eddie Chamblee and Retney Brauer on tenor sax; Curtis Lowe on bass; Oscar Dennard on piano; Billy Mackel on guitar; Peter Badie on fiddle bass; and Albert "June" Gardner on drums. We played a one-nighter at Versailles and then went on to Paris, where we played the Olympia for three weeks, every day except for Wednesdays. On one of those Wednesdays, we did a one-nighter in Rouen.

We recorded twice while we were in Paris, for the Versailles label. Then we set out for points east. We played Switzerland, then more than a week of one-nighters in Stuttgart, Munich, Mannheim, Dortmund, Hamburg, Berlin, and Frankfurt. We went back to France at the end of February and played Lille, Valenciennes, and Narbonne.

From France we went to Spain. We had wanted to go to Spain. In that late-December letter to the booker in Paris, Gladys said: "Felix, please see if you can send us to Spain, I understand Louis Armstrong went to Spain. . . ." So Felix had got us bookings in Barcelona and Madrid. Then we went to Scandinavia—one-nighters in Oslo, Gothenburg, Stockholm, Boras, Copenhagen, Odense, Aarhus. Then France again—Bordeaux, Bayonne, Pau, Clermont-Ferrand—and to Belgium.

Back in Paris in early May, we recorded with both the orchestra and with a group we called "Lionel Hampton and His Rhythm." That group included Oscar Dennard on piano, Billy Mackel on guitar, Peter Badie on bass, June Gardner on drums, and me on vibes, and almost all the pieces were either French or German. We did that for the Harmony label. For the orchestra recordings we had some European cats, including Guy Lafitte on tenor sax and Claude Bolling on piano. We also recorded as Lionel Hampton and His Sextette, and this group included Ed Mullens on trumpet, Eddie Chamblee on tenor sax, Robert Mosely on piano, Billy Mackel on guitar, Paul Rovere on bass, and June Gardner on drums. I did vibes, piano, and vocal on those sides. A couple of French musicians sat in on a couple of sides—Jean-Claude Telletier on piano and Benoit Quersin on bass.

After that we went to Israel for about a month. Gladys had a hard time with that booking, because the Israeli booker didn't like the idea that the Paris booker was trying to handle everything. Gladys wound up dealing with the Israeli booker directly, and whether he and the Paris booker ended up suing each other, I don't know. I do know that a suit was threatened, but Gladys and I always had enough legal problems of our own without worrying about those that we weren't directly involved in. I do know that a couple years later we sued Moishe Wallin because he refused to pay the band's hotel bill. I don't remember how that all came out.

We returned to the United States on the French ship *Liberté* in the early part of August and rested up a couple of weeks before playing at a jazz festival in New York, in Las Vegas, and at Basin Street, back in New York. Then, in October, we set off for our first tour of the British Isles.

There was one big reason why we hadn't played there before, and that was the British Musicians Union. It had convinced the Ministry of Labor that if American musicians were allowed to perform there, then British musicians would be deprived of work. The union wanted an arrangement under which every time American musicians played in Britain, an equal number of British musicians would play in the United States. But the American Federation of Musicians didn't like that and wouldn't agree to it. By 1956 rock and roll had hit Great Britain, and American records were being played there, and the kids had put so much pressure on the Ministry of Labor that they started allowing in a few American groups.

I wasn't on any official goodwill mission, although I had a letter in my pocket from Secretary of State John Foster Dulles, wishing me well on my "goodwill mission abroad." But I was hoping to increase

Wife, Gladys, about 1971

Mother, Gertrude Morgan
Hampton

Father, Charles Edward Hampton

Grandmother, Louvenia Morgan

High school graduation picture
of his brother, Samuel Davis,
Jr., 1948

*Sharing with my mother the joy of being
able to realize her expectations of me.*
Devotedly, your son,
Samuel
"48"

Family reunion—Lionel about
6 years old (*see arrow*)

ROYAL FESTIVAL HALL

(General Manager : T. E. BEAN)

CHRISTIAN ACTION

presents

HUMPHREY LYTTELTON
and his Band

JOHNNY DANKWORTH
and his Orchestra

and as guest artist

LIONEL HAMPTON

at a

MIDNIGHT JAZZ MATINEE

TUESDAY, 15th OCTOBER, 1957

in aid of the

CHRISTIAN ACTION DEFENCE AND AID FUND
in connection with the 156 accused in the
SOUTH AFRICAN TREASON TRIAL

Management: DENNIS H. MATTHEWS
SECRETARY, VISITING ORCHESTRAS APPRECIATION SOCIETY
(JAZZ MUSICIANS)

Royal Festival Hall Program Benefit for Nelson Mandela, 1957

Les Hite Group, featuring Louis Armstrong

Audience with President Nixon. Bill Titone, executive vice-president of Lionel Hampton Enterprises, is standing beside Lionel Hampton. Others are presidential aides.

Front row from the left: Count Basie, Lionel Hampton, Artie Shaw, Les Paul; (*rear*) Illinois Jacquet, Tommy Dorsey, Ziggy Ellman, Buddy Rich

Dr. Arthur Logan, A. Philip Randolph, Lionel Hampton, Governor
Nelson Rockefeller, Jackie Robinson at New York State Awards
Ceremony

Left to right: Benny Goodman,
Teddy Wilson, Lionel Hampton,
and Gene Krupa

Birthday party for Gladys

Lionel and Gladys at private
audience with Pope Paul

At nightclub (*standing
left to right*): Lionel
Hampton, Johnny
Mathis, Nat King Cole;
(*seated*) Dorothy
Dandridge, Leon
Washington, founder
and owner of *L.A.
Sentinel*, Mrs. Nat King
Cole

Performance of *The King
David Suite* with conductor
Dimitri Mitropoulus at
Town Hall

Lionel Hampton playing at the Savoy Ballroom, 1944.
Playing tenor sax is Dexter Gordon (*standing*).

At nightclub (*left to right*): Norman O. Houston, founder of Golden State
Insurance Company, Dinah Washington, Lionel Hampton, Leon Washington
of the *L.A. Sentinel*

Lionel Hampton in Paris

In front of Lionel
Hampton School of
Music at the University
of Idaho in Moscow,
Idaho

British-American understanding. That's how I felt about all my trips abroad. Jazz is the only art America has produced. If Europe could come to appreciate our music, then it could appreciate us a little better, too.

I took my regular band over to Britain. I had Dave Gonsalves, Ed Mullens, Eddie Williams, and Richard Williams on trumpet; Larry Wilson, Julian Priester, and Locksley "Slide" Hampton (no relation) on trombone; Bob Plater and Scoville Brown on alto sax and clarinet; Eddie Chamblee and Retney Brauer on tenor sax; Curtis Lowe on bass; Oscar Dennard on piano; Billy Mackel on guitar; Richard Evans on fiddle bass; Wilbert Hogan and Curley Hamner on drums. I also took along two vocalists, Mamie Watts and Robert Moseley, and we made arrangements for a British vocalist named Tommy Whitle to play about fifteen dates as guest soloist.

We arrived in London and played our first gig at Empress Hall there. Then we went out to Preston, Leicester, Birmingham. A lot of people asked us to play some of our old stuff, so we featured blues numbers like "Smack Dab in the Middle" and "Baby Don't Love Me No More." Most of our material was stuff we'd been doing for years. I just jumped up the melody a little. "Midnight Sun" is a tune I wrote and that Sonny Burke arranged. It tells a story, and it has lots of rhythm. It has a camp-meeting beat, a backbeat, that's traditional. People thought it was rock and roll, but it wasn't. Rock and roll is just a few minor riffs over a few simple chords. My band had the camp-meeting beat when Bill Haley, the first famous white rock-and-roll bandleader, was in diapers. But people thought "Midnight Sun" was rock and roll.

Same thing with "Shake, Rattle and Roll." That was blues put on record several years before by Joe Turner, one of the greatest blues singers. People thought that was rock and roll, too.

So there we were giving concerts of music in a program I had worked out that was supposed to include pretty well everything, a kind of history of jazz. Meanwhile, people think it's mostly rock and roll. Some people were happy as can be. Others were getting madder and madder. Some guys who wrote for *Melody Maker*, the big British music newspaper, started complaining in print that we weren't playing enough jazz. I didn't pay much attention. I knew what I was playing.

We spent most of our time in Britain playing outside London. We did Kliburn and Bristol, Bournemouth and Hanely, York and Manchester and Sheffield. We gave two concerts in Lewisham, and that's where Eddie Williams left me to return to the States. I replaced him with a British trumpeter, Jimmy Deuchar. Jimmy came in the band reading everything right down. Pretty soon I had him doing solos.

We'd been in Britain about a month when we went into Royal Festival Hall for a midnight concert titled "Jazz for Jazz Lovers." This was a special all-American jazz concert arranged by a three-year-old organization that called itself Visiting Orchestras Appreciation Society. It was a group of jazz musicians and fans who wanted to broaden the outlook of jazz lovers in Britain. The all-American jazz concert was their first big affair.

The place was packed, and a lot of British musicians were there, including Johnny Dankworth, a bandleader who was a big deal in the Musicians Union. I don't know what possessed him to start letting out cat calls from the gallery. He later said that the only reason the Musicians Union relaxed their barriers to letting American musicians into the country was on "cultural" grounds, and that since we weren't playing jazz, we didn't deserve to be let in. Anyway, there came a break between numbers, and suddenly, as clear as a bell, comes this shout, "Why don't you play some jazz?" I was stunned. It was embarrassing. The whole audience had heard it, and everyone was shouting at each other. I couldn't get that concert back under control after that, which is a shame, because I'd planned to feature Jimmy Deuchar on a number. Anyway, I think that was one of my worst experiences ever at a concert. It's a big thing when one musician criticizes another in public, and especially right in the middle of a concert.

A lot of other British musicians were embarrassed by Dankworth's outburst. Thirty-three of them sent a letter to *Melody Maker* stating:

> As British musicians representative of many schools, we wish to dissociate ourselves from Johnny Dankworth's views and actions . . . and from the severe criticisms of Hampton shows which have been aired by the *Melody Maker*. Whether at the Festival Hall or on other occasions, we heartily enjoyed the show—full of solid jazz content—put on by this swinging band. And we are prepared to accept and enjoy supreme artists like Lionel Hampton and Louis Armstrong on their own terms.

From a business point of view, all this controversy was good. We were a front-page item, and after reading about the incident, a lot of people who might not have come to the concerts decided they wanted to see for themselves what all the fuss was about. But personally, I didn't like it. It was against my sense of professionalism.

I was glad when we left for Sweden about a week after the Festival Hall concert.

There weren't any further incidents in Europe, and we got home in time for Christmas, and thinking that all in all, it had been a pretty good tour.

Back home, we played at the second inaugural gala of President Eisenhower. Then we did the college circuit for about six weeks. Meanwhile, I was putting the finishing touches on my *King David Suite*, which was based on my experiences playing in Israel. We had done some sightseeing, because after all, there we were in the cradle of Christianity. I have always been very religious. I carry my Bible with me, and I read a bit every day, so it meant a lot to me to be able to visit some of the places that are in the Bible. One of the places we went to was King David's tomb.

Now, I knew from the Bible about David the shepherd boy. When he would go into the temple to pray, he would take a band with him. I remember I walked into the tomb and looked around for a few minutes, and I was thinking about David and his harp, and a chant just came to me. And then I was talking to the chief rabbi of Israel, Dr. Jacob Herzog. He told me that David would take fifty-four musicians into the temple, and in the temple he sang and sang. Then David would leave the temple followed by the musicians, playing. I told the rabbi about tailgating in New Orleans—the second line, you know, following the lead musician—and Rabbi Herzog, who was a hip rabbi, said that David had the first jam session. I told the rabbi, "Man, I just play music like David played."

Anyway, I wrote the whole suite based on that chant. It is an eighteen-minute, symphonic jazz suite with five movements: David's Prayer to God, David at the Wailing Wall, David's Deliverance of the Children of Israel, Israel Today, and Israel Tomorrow. It starts out with a harp playing about the trials and tribulations of the Jews. Then there's a blast of brass blowing down the Wailing Wall. There's a vibraphone dance and then a full orchestra finale. We debuted it at Town Hall in New York City as part of Negro History Week. Dimitri Mitropoulos conducted it. Since then, it's been performed a number of times—by the Boston Pops, by the symphony orchestras of Milwaukee, Cincinnati, Toronto, San Diego, Dayton, others.

Meanwhile, we played weekends at Basin Street because we were doing a lot of recording.

We played a week at the Howard Theater in Washington, D.C., and then a few gigs in the Middle West before our first tour in Australia, which lasted about three weeks. After that, we played a bunch of one-nighters through the South in June.

We were traveling by Greyhound bus at that time, and we had a driver whom we called Wild Bill. He was a white man, and I have never had a better driver. He would pull into a southern truck stop and walk in and announce that he had a band in his bus, and it was a black band, and if the guys weren't served, then Greyhound would never stop there again. He'd say, "I am a Greyhound bus driver, and out there is a Greyhound bus, and you will serve the people on that bus." We never had any trouble in the South when Bill was driving.

In July we went up into New England before opening a four-week stint at the Waldorf-Astoria in New York. Richard Nixon and his family came to see me there. I told him, "Tell Ike that I'll only be here for about two weeks more." I don't think the president had a chance to see me on that gig, but about a month later I interrupted my stint at the Jazz Under the Stars festival in Central Park to go up to Newport, Rhode Island, to play a one-nighter for him.

I got to talk to him about my European and Australian tours and about some ideas I had for increasing goodwill between the States and other parts of the world. As a goodwill ambassador, I thought that was part of my responsibility.

That fall I did a bit of personal goodwill ambassadorship when I went to London for one concert, and a benefit concert at that. It was held to raise money for the defense of the 156 opponents of South African apartheid who had been arrested and imprisoned in December 1956.

All those arrested were leaders or active members of the African National Congress. The most famous one was Nelson Mandela. The South African government charged them under the Suppression of Communism Act and said that the liberation movement was part of an international Communist-inspired effort to overthrow the government. They were all charged with high treason. Everybody else knew that was ridiculous, but the government didn't.

Anyway, Father Trevor Huddleston, the precentor of St. Paul's Cathedral over there in London, got a group of people together and formed the Christian Action Defence and Aid Fund for the 156 accused and their families and dependents. They wanted to raise money to help in the legal defense and also to aid the families of all those people in prison. Somebody in the Visiting Orchestras Appreciation Society had the idea of a benefit concert. They also decided that, "in view of the tremendous influence made on the jazz scene by coloured musicians we feel that we are showing our appreciation by helping their friends in South Africa." Father Huddleston contacted me, and I went. I had to cancel about five thousand dollars' worth of concerts. Gladys came, too. She always said her home was her suitcase. We wanted to show our support for the South Africans, because they'd been so mistreated and oppressed. A lot of Americans didn't know much about apartheid back then. It's sad that more than thirty years later, it's even worse. And Nelson Mandela has been in prison for more than twenty-five years for trying to help his people. But you can't keep hitting a wall without it falling someday. That wall's going to fall at some point.

We circled London for three hours because of fog, which I didn't like at all. I wasn't much for planes. I still prefer going by boat, but I didn't have time to do so for this gig.

The concert was at Festival Hall, the same place where the incident with Johnny Dankworth took place, and it was also a midnight matinee, same as before. And the funny thing is, Dankworth and his orchestra were also on the program. So was Humphrey Lyttelton and his band—he's one of the guys who wrote to *Melody Maker* to criticize Dankworth. Cleo Laine was on the bill, too (she didn't have anything to do with the controversy).

I have an idea that the Visiting Orchestras Appreciation Society decided that this benefit concert for the South African Treason Trial Defense Fund was a good opportunity to get me and Johnny Dankworth together and kind of smooth over the unpleasantness of a few months before. I didn't mind going along with it. I don't carry grudges.

I went over there by myself. Gladys was with me, but none of my musicians. The L. W. Hunt Drum Co., Ltd., supplied me with a Premier vibraphone. I played vibes, drums, and piano, accompanied by groups taken from the Lyttelton and Dankworth orchestras. I also was spotlighted in some of my own band arrangements, which were played by the Johnny Dankworth Orchestra. Needless to say, I got more out of that night than just playing for a good cause.

We jammed for more than three hours. In fact, we were still going strong when the manager said we either had to stop or he had to be paid another hundred pounds. Somebody gave him the money and we kept going. We raised a lot of money that night, and I got a nice writeup in *Melody Maker*: "The grip that Hampton got and held on his audience was almost uncanny. Only a select few of the great jazz players could have matched this feat, I'm sure. That Hamp accomplished it after a night in the air and long, tiring day on the ground, using a borrowed instrument and working with two strange bands on a minimum rehearsal, is further proof of his remarkable personality, energy and talent."

We saved another writeup from that trip. This was from the *News Chronicle* and it's funny because it has me talking jive to Canon

L. John Collins, the precentor of St. Paul's Cathedral, who organized the concert. Here's how part of the article goes: " 'I am here,' said Mr. Lionel Hampton, 'to hip you.' Quivering like a coffee blancmange, he added: 'The world has become so grooved to jazz that even the miles aren't square any more.' . . . I detected a flutter of the eyelids from Canon Collins. 'I do not understand jive talk but I am learning,' he murmured bravely."

Joe Glaser helped to arrange my appearance at that concert, although it must have killed him. Joe wasn't much on giving services away, except when he decided it was good for PR. Personally, I enjoyed doing benefits and would have done a lot more if it wasn't for Joe. Back home, I signed on with the Hampden-Harvard Brewery, Inc., in Massachusetts, to do a bunch of charity concerts. I also accepted the chairmanship of the Elks' Scholarship Campaign for Heroes, which meant I was to arrange big benefit shows. I had to hand most of the responsibility over to other people, though, because I was about to leave on a ninety-six–city tour as an official goodwill representative of the United States government.

I had Ed Mullens, Art Hoyle, and Ed Williams on trumpet; Larry Wilson, Louis Blackburn, and Wade Marcus on trombone; Bobby Plater and Leon Zachary on alto sax; Andrew McGhee on tenor sax; Lonnie Shaw on bass; Oscar Dennard on piano; Julius Browne on fiddle bass; Billy Mackel on guitar; Wilbert Hogan on drums; Curley Hamner on drums and vocals; and Cornelius James on vocals. We piled onto the Holland-American line's *Ryndam* along with a huge shipment of gifts for the children of the different countries we were going to visit. What a trip. We were jamming before the ship even left the dock.

This was probably the first trip to Europe that Gladys brought Caroline Carruthers along. Caroline could speak French, Spanish, and German, and Gladys was getting a little leery about hitting the European trail without someone along who really knew some of the languages. She was a good friend of ours, and also of Archbishop Fulton J. Sheen. She had been a school teacher and worked for the Port Authority in New York when she wasn't helping us out.

Practically the first thing we did when we reached Hamburg was to record for Bertelsmann, a German label. We did a couple other recording dates during that trip. But mostly we just performed. We had a real tight schedule. I remember we played Zurich, Baden, and Luzern all in the same day. Gladys joked that she was even too busy to shop, which for Gladys meant busy with a capital *B*. One reason why we were so busy in Germany was that we played a lot of U.S. armed forces bases. That was part of my job as goodwill ambassador.

We had a very embarrassing experience in Germany. It all started a couple of years before when we were in England and a German woman named Madame Gunderlach booked us for five days in Germany. Gladys had it written into the contract that this woman would provide four first-class tickets, by plane or train—whatever Gladys wanted. When we got to Copenhagen, Madame Gunderlach's lawyer tried to convince Gladys to go by train, but she wanted to fly. Finally, a travel agency sent Gladys three plane tickets, and we flew to Germany. Then about six months later, Gladys got a letter from the travel agency asking her to pay for the tickets because Madame Gunderlach had refused and said she'd never ordered them. Gladys wouldn't pay for the tickets.

Anyway, about a year had passed, and there we were in late January 1958 playing different cities in Germany. I was traveling by train with the band, but Gladys decided to fly. They ran into bad weather and she was grounded in Gutenburg airport and didn't arrive at wherever we were playing until the concert was over.

The next afternoon, we were rehearsing for that night's concert when here come about five local officers of the law and they attached my instruments for nonpayment of that travel agency bill. Our local representative, a Mr. Stangerup, had to pay the equivalent of $450 to get my instruments back so the concert could go on. That was very embarrassing. Gladys wrote a hot letter to Joe Glaser, and I guess the matter was straightened out eventually.

We played in France and Belgium in February, and then in March we went on to Ghana. We were part of the celebration of Ghana's first anniversary as an independent nation, and that was quite an experience. I was proud to see an African country independent at last. I even wrote a special composition, "21 Ghana Salute." We wound up the tour in Israel to celebrate the tenth anniversary of its founding. I soloed with the Israel Symphony Orchestra and made an official presentation of gifts sent by the State Department for the children of Israel.

That was my last official trip in that position. And it didn't have anything at all to do with the fact that in 1960 John Kennedy beat Richard Nixon in the presidential election. It was all the doing of Joe Glaser, who decided that there was somebody who needed that goodwill ambassador certificate more than me.

He asked Gladys for the certificate, and she gave it to him, and he took that certificate and changed it and put Louis's name on it and never gave it back to Gladys. And then the State Department wanted a goodwill ambassador to go to Africa, and they got in contact with Joe. He said Louis was available. He gave it to Louis. That was supposed to have been my project. Like a fool, I never notified the State Department about what happened. That was my fault. The whole thing kept going backward and backward until it went out of existence.

The thing is, Joe Glaser had been trying for years to get Louis named a goodwill ambassador. Back in 1957 when I was given that honor by President Eisenhower, Joe let the State Department know more than once that Louis was available. But then Louis told a reporter that President Eisenhower didn't have any guts in handling the school integration crisis in Little Rock, Arkansas, and that the government could "go to hell." That put a crimp in Joe Glaser's campaign. The band and Gladys and I were in Europe when all that happened, but a press agent in London sent us a copy of his piece, where he quoted the Dorothy Kilgallen column in the *New York Journal-American*: "Reaction from the State Department to the availability of Louis Armstrong for friend-winning chores abroad (following his blast at the Government over Little Rock) has been extremely cool. Washington's biggies have let it be known they'd much prefer to throw the top 'good will ambassador' jobs to Lionel Hampton, who combines giant entertainer appeal with infallible diplomacy."

That's not the only thing I lost to Louis. The song "Hello Dolly" was supposed to have been mine. Jerry Herman wanted me to have that song. Joe gave it to Louis. I have never revealed this before.

Joe Glaser didn't do all that for Louis; he did it for himself. He was building up receipts, because he was getting 50 to 75 percent of whatever Louis made. It was a dirty thing to do, and that was when it became clear to us that we were going to have to leave Joe Glaser one day. He was the biggest booker in the business, and we had signed contracts—six- or seven-year contracts—and we had to stay on for a few more years, like it or not. But we knew that eventually we were going to move out on our own.

Back in the United States, we played in Chicago for a week and then some one-nighters until the summertime, which was jazz festival time. We played a bunch of jazz festivals in New Jersey, the Berkshires, Chicago. I had in my band that summer Art Hoyle, Dave Gonsalves, Eddie Williams, and Ed Mullens on trumpet; Wade Marcus, Louis Blackburn, and Clarence Watson on trombone; Bobby Plater and Leon Zachary on alto sax; Eddie Pazant and Andrew McGhee on tenor sax; Lonnie Shaw on bass; Oscar Dennard on piano; Billy Mackel on guitar; Julius Browne on fiddle bass; Wilbert Hogan on drums; and Cornelius James on vocals.

We were doing quite a bit of television—CBS, NBC. We played Las Vegas a lot. I was glad to get back on the road in my own country and to have a chance to visit all my friends in the far-flung cities and towns of America. Good friends, like the McMurray family in Indianapolis, would drive three or four hours to one of my concerts. Their younger daughter, Patricia, was a young lady by then, and she would spend at least one holiday a year with us. Whenever we were playing somewhere in the Midwest, she would get a chance to ride on the bus with the band—she and her girlfriends. We'd arrange it so that the bus would drive me right to the McMurray home, and I'd go in and get some of that good home cooking while the bus took the rest of the guys to the hotel, and Patricia would ride to the hotel and back with the bus to her house. The neighbors got used to seeing a big Greyhound bus parked out front. And then when we played the University of Illinois and the other colleges around, Patricia and one of her girlfriends would ride along and dance at the dances.

I remember visiting the McMurrays once not long before Christmas, and I said to Patricia's parents, "She's going to be eighteen. I'm going to take her to Las Vegas with me." And so right before we left, we got her a plane ticket, and after we were gone, her Daddy handed it to her in an envelope. She flew out to join us in Vegas—her first plane ride.

Our driver, Bill Bergac, used to always know where to find me when I was anywhere near Indianapolis. I was always at the McMurray place. I'd tell him I'd meet him somewhere, and then I'd get to laughing and talking, and I wouldn't show up, and he'd drive that big Greyhound up and park it on the street outside and come in fuming, "The only reason I have to bring this bus all the way out here is you." Freda McMurray would put on a pot of coffee and calm him down, or she'd offer him some food. There was always a pot of something going on the stove in that house.

I was beginning to pay more attention to ways to give back some of my good fortune. Those benefits for the beer company in Massachusetts and being chairman of the Elks Scholarship Fund were fun, and I liked the idea of helping children.

We were playing in New York one time, and somebody invited me to see a little nine-year-old boy playing drums. He was fantastic, and so I nicknamed him "Little Hamp" and had him to play with me a few times. That got me thinking about how important a musical education could be for kids. I know how important it was for me.

Most children love music, but they aren't taught properly, and so they lose their appreciation for it. So it was my idea to start a correspondence course in music for kids and maybe later a whole chain of music schools across the country. I got a toy company in the East to make child-size drums and vibraharps, and I got working on an instruction sheet to go along with the instruments. It displayed the scales and chords and used numbers to help the kids find the right chords. I had the idea that once kids completed the primary course, the parents could send away for the advanced course.

That idea didn't pan out the way I wanted it to. I guess I didn't have enough time to devote to it as I needed. I had to put it on the back burner, and without me it just didn't fly.

But I was doing a lot of other good things for kids and people in need. And in 1959 I was voted "Man of the Year" in Harlem. That honor was more important to me than most of the others I was used to getting. Oh, I liked being voted a member of the ideal band in the *Playboy* polls, which started in the late fifties. I was proud to receive honorary Doctor of Music degrees from Allen University and from the University of Liège in Belgium. But being chosen "Man of the Year" in Harlem meant that my people still considered me one of them and didn't think I had turned my back on them just because I was rich and famous. They appreciated the fact that Gladys and I had remained in Harlem and hadn't moved downtown like a lot of other black stars.

No, Gladys and I were still in Harlem. So were Langston Hughes, the writer, and Duke Ellington and Dinah Washington. The people of Harlem, cultural center of black America, knew that a lot of other "cultural leaders" had moved on. Gladys and I didn't feel the need to move away from our roots.

Of course, for Gladys, part of the reason was that a place downtown was a lot more expensive than what we were paying uptown. We were still in the same small apartment we'd moved into back in 1936. It was very small, and since Gladys was a professional shopper it was jam packed with stuff. There was a hallway that was lined on both sides with boxes and steamer trunks. The steamer trunks were for our frequent trips to Europe. Her room was lined with mirrors, and the closets were stuffed with clothes. And shoes! Imelda Marcos had nothing on Gladys when it came to shoes. In my room, I had a couple of steamer trunks, plus my drum set and piles of record albums. My vibes and piano were in the living room. That place was coming apart at the seams. But Gladys didn't want to move—she wanted to save that money.

She was still getting all the checks, too. I can probably count on one hand the number of checks I actually saw after Gladys took over. She had arrangements with Joe Glaser and all the managers of the places where we played—the check was to be sent directly to her. I got "spending money." She'd leave me a few dollars on the dresser every day. That was it. She knew I could go through a fortune in a minute, and so she didn't give me the chance. Or, rather, she gave me as few chances as possible. I had my ways of getting money, and Gladys knew that, but she controlled the money as much as she could.

But anyway, we stayed in Harlem, and with the money we saved by staying in that little place, we were able to build a lot of housing in Harlem for the people.

9

END OF
AN ERA

Nineteen sixty marked our twentieth year out on our own as a big band, and thanks to Gladys's business savvy and my showmanship we were rich. We owned something like twenty-two houses in Los Angeles, property in Las Vegas, land in Texas where they'd struck oil, so we had oil royalties coming in. I didn't like to talk about it in public—one word and those taxation hound dogs were after you—but we were rich. For our twenty-fifth wedding anniversary in 1961, I gave Gladys a seven-thousand-dollar diamond ring. I didn't need to work anymore. I could have sat back and watched the money from investments come in. But I wanted to work. I hadn't done anything but play hundreds of one-nighters a year since I was a teenager. We had kept our big band going way past the time when big bands went out of style. The big-band era had really ended with the 1940s. But the 1950s were especially hard on the bands.

The big problem was rock and roll. Everybody wanted to listen to rock and roll. Where did it come from? Black musicians. But it was white musicians who became famous for it. They took rhythm and blues and turned it around and called it rock and roll. They took songs from B.B. King and Bo Diddley and got black guys to go into the studios and play behind them and write arrangements for them. They were thieving. Most of those white rock stars only knew about three songs, but they imitated blacks and got to front place in white society.

Another problem was television. People didn't go out as much anymore, because they could stay home and be entertained in their living rooms. There were lots of musical variety shows on TV—I appeared on most of them—and people thought they were hearing the real thing when they watched musicians on TV. Or listened to records at home. But what they were missing was the excitement of being right there when the music was being made. Especially with jazz, you never know what kind of sound is going to come out, because you're always improvising. I couldn't understand why the general public didn't see that.

It used to be that all the major hotels had big bands playing every week. That stopped. A lot of the jazz clubs closed. In New York, most of the jazz places had stripteasers in them, and most of the clubs had to book three groups into the same place at one time in order to attract an audience. One reason why we went to Europe so much was that we could still get a bunch of one-nighters in the big concert halls there. And also because jazz was so popular in Europe.

But I couldn't complain. I was lucky enough to keep my big band going for a few more years. In the summertime, we always had a lot of work because of the jazz festivals, which were a godsend for jazz musicians. My name was still out there. I was still winning the annual polls as the best vibraharpist. For 1960 I won both the *Playboy* and *Jet* polls. Milt Hinton was winning his share by then, and there were some up-and-coming vibraharpists, like Cal Tjader and Terry Gibbs. But they all had their own styles, and there was room for every one of us.

There was a magazine for men called *Nugget* published at that time, and there was a comment in its December issue attacking jazz polls. I am not one for writing "Letters to the Editor" very often, but I really felt I had to say something positive about jazz polls. This is part of the letter I wrote and that was published in the June 1961 issue:

> When I was a kid, just starting out in the music business, the polls were a kind of inspiration to me, just as, I'm sure, the Academy Awards are a source of inspiration to young actors. All of us young musicians had an idol, and he was usually a poll

winner. We all dreamed about one day being handed an award and being recognized by the public for the work we had put in on our instruments. I recognize the drawbacks to these contests as well as any other creative jazz artist, but the emotional satisfaction derived by the winning musicians and the intense interest stirred up about jazz far outweighs the bad points. I suppose you might call me prejudiced since I've won many polls over the years, but they never seem to lose their thrill for me.

Another thing that marks 1960 for me is that it's the year that I was "rediscovered."

Anyway, that's what a Las Vegas paper headline read that August when I was playing the Riviera there. What the writer meant was, I was being discovered by a whole new generation. I was making the kind of records I wanted, put out by my own company, and the kids were beginning to groove on my sound.

Gladys and I had started another record company. This one was called Glad Records, and the symbol was a parrot, because Gladys loved birds. We started it along with a guy named Kip Walton, a music director for CBS, and we had an office in L.A. and an office at 165 West Forty-sixth Street, corner of Broadway, in Manhattan. All the big black stars had offices in that building at one time or another—Bill Robinson, Sissle and Blake, Cab Calloway. Right across the street was a building where a bunch of white musicians had offices. They called our building Uncle Tom's Cabin.

We'd tried to have our own company back in the forties, but we had trouble with distribution and a few other things. Anyway, it didn't go. By 1960 we'd been out on our own for twenty years, and we were a lot wiser. We still did recordings with the big labels. At the time, we were with Columbia Records. But having Glad gave us a chance to do some things we wanted to do that the big labels weren't willing to risk. What I mean is, with Columbia we recorded an album like "Silver Vibes," which was full of romantic standards like "Skylark" and "What's New." But we made our first rock and roll records on the Glad label—"Wild Bill" and "Shimmy." In no time at all they'd sold about half a million, and that was before we even got them distributed in the West.

Next, we did "Exodus" with me singing. It also featured a young Israeli mezzo-soprano named Regina Ben Amittay, who sang "Song of the Cowboy" on the flip side. We'd met her on one of our trips there—she was married to an attorney in Israel. She wanted to come to America to study music, and we helped her. We hadn't planned to put her on a record, but when she came to New York, she dropped in, and we took her along to the recording session. She started singing, and pretty soon we had her on the record.

Anyway, the record sold like hotcakes, and I made plans to do an album with her. It would have six Negro spirituals and six Israeli spirituals, but the twist would be that I would sing the Israeli songs in Hebrew and Regina would sing the Negro songs in English. All the proceeds would go to the Children's Foundation in Israel, which was sponsored by the national chapter of Hadassah. (By the way, I had recently been named an honorary member of Hadassah by the West Coast chapter in Los Angeles.)

Regina and I did a concert at Town Hall that fall, and we also did some TV and radio appearances together.

Anyway, Glad records had a short life. Seems there was already a label called Glad, and the guy sued us. Now, this other label was really small, and the guy was a real estate agent. But he claimed that our releases were hurting his sales. We were going to fight for the name at first, but as I recall, we decided we didn't want to be saddled with a long, expensive suit, so we changed the name. That's how the Glad-Hamp label was born, and I'm still recording on that label today. We kept the parrot symbol.

We were still doing a lot of traveling. We flew down to Buenos Aires to play a three-day auto show in May. Transportation alone cost eighteen thousand dollars. It was a big deal because it was the celebration of Argentina's 150th year of independence, and they weren't sparing any expense. What a time we had. That huge stadium was filled to capacity with shouting, foot-stamping Argentinians. The reviewer for *La Prensa* wrote: "Let's say, to close this commentary, that Lionel Hampton shows no signs of declining with the years whatsoever, he is still tops in his field, with the same great inventiveness, dynamism, ardor and magnetism. Throughout the years, this great musician maintains his leadership by combining all of these things along with his own personal and tremendous talents on the vibes."

They were right. I had never felt better, and it was like rediscovering myself. Of course, I had a great band, the best band I'd had in a number of years. I still had Bobby Plater on alto sax, Oscar Dennard on piano, Slide Hampton on trombone, Andy McGhee on tenor sax, and Dave Gonsalves on trumpet. But I had some new guys who were really great: Floyd Jones, who was out of Detroit, and Vergil Jones from Indianapolis on trumpet; Vincente Prudente and Haleem Rasheed on trombone; Harold Mayburn on piano; Roland

Faulkner on guitar; Lawrence "Skinny" Burgan on bass; Wayne Robinson on drums. I also had a great vocalist named Pinocchio James who could wail the blues.

Of course I spent quite a bit of time during 1960 playing for Richard Nixon's campaign when he was running against Kennedy. I thought Kennedy was a nice guy, but Nixon and I went way back. Whenever Nixon called, or his campaign manager called, I'd drop whatever I was doing to play for his campaign. I felt bad for Nixon when Kennedy won the election. It was going to be the first inaugural celebration I hadn't played at in years.

We went into the Metropole in New York for the Christmas holidays. The club was known for showcasing small combos, and this was the first time they'd ever had a big band. We had to make some adjustments. There was no room for us to assemble the way we were used to doing. We had to line up single-file behind the long bar. This made it hard for us to hear each other, but we got around that by watching each other in the mirror on the opposite wall. We didn't mind—it made us pay attention. There also wasn't enough room for our usual stage antics, but we adjusted to that as well. My friend Charlie Mack reminds me that one night I marched the band across the bar, out the door, and across Seventh Avenue and back. We stopped traffic, and picked up a bunch of people from the street in the process.

Playing there opened us up to a whole new group of kids. One reviewer pointed out the kids there were grooving to the band and they were young—too young to have more than about three dollars each to spend. But they didn't come to eat and drink, they came to listen and dance. And I gave them what they came for. I was always looking forward where musical tastes were concerned.

Meanwhile, I was also looking backward. One of my big projects around that time was arranging a reunion of the Benny Goodman Quartet.

The occasion was a ten-day TV and music festival sponsored by Macy's department store, and they really did it up right. They contacted me about performing, and after they told me all they planned to do, I got excited and suggested that we have the reunion of the old Benny Goodman group. So the Macy's people asked me to arrange it, and I got on the phone, and on February 8, 1961, the Benny Goodman Quartet lived again.

Benny was fifty-two and graying at the temples. Gene Krupa was also fifty-two. He'd suffered a heart attack the previous November. He used to have a mop of black hair; now he had a salt-and-pepper crew cut. Teddy Wilson was forty-nine and had gone completely gray, and I was fifty-two and didn't have a gray hair in my head (it's in the genes). But when we got together to play, all those years just melted away. I felt like I was eighteen again—the Macy's people had to keep rushing fresh shirts to me because I was working up such a sweat. Plus, it was hot in there. We were playing on a small bandstand in a cleared-away spot on the fifth floor, and there must have been a thousand people at any one time crowded around us. I wasn't the only one who worked out. Benny started twirling his clarinet like a drum major. Gene couldn't let go because of his condition—he had his pills with him, just in case—but he pounded those skins like in the old days. And Teddy never was one to engage in public displays.

Anyway, the players may have been older, but the sound we made was the same. When we launched into our classics, like "Stompin' at the Savoy" and "Avalon," the older folks in the crowd clapped and smiled. The young kids liked it, too, and there were quite a few who had skipped school just to see and hear us.

There were a lot of other great music makers at Macy's that day—Jimmy Rushing, Milt Hinton, Buddy Rich, Dave Brubeck, Larry Elgart, Gerry Mulligan, J.J. Johnson, Andre Previn, Cannonball Adderley, Dizzy Gillespie. And all of us were working for union scale—$17.50.

What was great was that Macy's made sure that the world would hear us. The whole thing was taped for Radio Free Europe, Voice of America, and Armed Forces Radio. By the time I got to Europe for my next tour, everybody we met had heard the concert.

I also recorded the theme song, "Cry of the Blues," composed especially for the Macy's Jazz Festival. It was backed by "Forbidden," which was written by a senior vice president at Macy's, and the disk was released by MGM Records and on sale at the festival.

I made a short trip to Europe in January, before the festival. We went there on the occasion of the elevation to cardinal of Archbishop Joseph Ritter of St. Louis. We went with a group of Catholics from Indianapolis. I admired Archbishop Ritter. He'd done a lot for integration and in the educational field, and I'd helped him in my way by playing a lot of benefits for him. I was proud to kiss his ring after he became Cardinal Ritter. Thanks to him, Gladys and I also had a private audience with the pope, which was one of the most memorable experiences of my life.

That was a short trip, but not too short for Gladys to do some shopping. She bought a black sable that cost me about five hundred one-nighters. Gladys loved fur coats. When she died, she had thirteen of them—everything from Russian sable down to raccoon. She had a green mink one time, red fox, beaver, ranch mink, Blackglama mink.

Back in the United States, we went into the Metropole again. In between shows, I started teaching Sammy Davis, Jr., the vibes. I taught him drums way back in the 1940s at the Apollo when he was just a teenager. Sammy had the idea of making a movie of my life, to be titled *Mr. Wonderful*. He was going to play me, and he decided he had to learn the vibes to be believable. I don't know what happened with that project. The film never got made.

I also performed my *King David Suite* with the Buffalo Philharmonic at the end of February, and just before we left for our long European tour, I took the train down to Texas to visit Arnett Cobb, my old friend and former tenor sax man. He was in a hospital in Dallas, and I couldn't leave without seeing him. I would have flown down if Gladys had gone with me, but she was busy with preparations for the trip, and I had never liked flying without Gladys.

The night before we left for Europe, they threw a surprise going away party for the band and me at the Metropole. Benny Goodman and Gene Krupa were there. So was Louis Armstrong. That was one of the best surprise parties I've ever had.

This tour was seven weeks, and I took the same guys who usually played with me. The only addition, as I remember, was a girl singer named Bertice Reading, who I discovered in Philadelphia, singing the blues. She was a hefty gal, very light complected, with a blond wig, and she had big eyes and a dimply smile. She really knew how to catch and hold an audience.

We played all over Germany and Switzerland. We flew over to Wiesbaden, and the route from the airport to the hotel was lined with screaming fans. They had police cordons all around so we could get to the hotel without being mobbed. In Berlin we attracted a bunch of fans from the Russian zone. There were minor riots because not everybody could get in, and the police had to be called. They named a little street for me in West Berlin—Hamptonstrasse. In Switzerland, I tried to learn to ski, but I was happier on the drum slopes. I discovered a young female composer named Manouchka in Berne, and I added one of her numbers, "Le Beau Julot," to my repertoire. I wanted her to write more blues songs for me and come back with me to the United States for my Las Vegas opening, but there was too much red tape or something.

One nice thing about that tour was that a lot of the concerts were filmed for TV distribution.

We flew back from Europe and went right into the Flamingo

Hotel in Las Vegas. We were all wearing short leather britches and lederhosen. We'd bought them in Switzerland. The Vegas crowd loved it. We also had another piece of Swiss baggage—a very rich young man from Zurich who had fallen in love with my singer, Bertice Reading. They flew back together and got married somewhere in Pennsylvania. They honeymooned in Vegas, because Bertice was still singing with me.

They gave me a big birthday party at the Flamingo—with a huge cake. The hotel gave me a two-thousand-dollar silver chess set. Joe E. Lewis was the emcee, and Jerry Lewis busted in and clowned around for a while. Dean Martin also appeared and sang a couple of songs. With Dean Martin around, Sammy Davis, Jr., wasn't far away. I gave him some more lessons on the vibes, because he was still trying to get that movie about my life off the ground. Sammy was getting pretty good at the vibes.

Speaking of teaching music to young guys, I taught drums to Gregory Hines. He and his brother, Maurice, and his father had an act called Hines, Hines and Dad. They worked for me in Los Vegas—I hired them. They were there, and the management was going to let them go, and I said, "No, let's keep them." Gregory used to do everything I did on drums at one time, but he didn't keep up with it.

We played six weeks at the Flamingo, and we were such a hit that we signed a contract to play there eighteen weeks a year for the next five years. We went back to New York for another stint at the Metropole with Gene Krupa. In between, we did a one-nighter at Freedomland, an amusement park in the Bronx. The park was going to have a summer jazz series, and I was happy to kick it off. I turned down a Canadian date for a lot more money because I wanted to see if I could get the sort of audience that would be at Freedomland. We drew eighty thousand people in three nights, and a lot of them were preteens and teens. It was a way to reach that new generation with jazz.

In fact, I was thinking seriously of trying to book a series of dollar hops so that the kids could afford to come and hear good jazz. It wasn't their fault that the main music they got to hear was the lowest form of music dished out by record producers just trying to make a buck.

Next we did the annual festival at Tamiment-in-the-Poconos. Then we went back to Freedomland to appear with Julius LaRosa, who got famous with Arthur Godfrey. That's where I first met Julius, when I appeared on Arthur's show. Arthur was a very modest man. When I told him I heard his radio show over in Europe, he was really surprised. He didn't even know his show was aired in Europe.

I think it was at Freedomland that Bertice Reading and I were jitterbugging and we got to swinging a little too hard and fell. She was knocked out and was out of commission for about six weeks.

It was amazing to see how big-band jazz was beginning to come back into popularity. In the fall of 1961 an LP of some of the great sides I recorded for Victor back in the late 1930s was issued—"Ring Dem Bells," "Muskrat Ramble," "When Lights Are Low," "I'm in the Mood for Swing." Those were the days. Benny Carter, Coleman Hawkins, Chu Berry, Ben Webster, Duke Ellington's sidemen like Johnny Hodges and Cootie Williams, Benny Goodman's sidemen—we'd all just get together and jam and make a record. You couldn't do that anymore in the fall of 1961, since the Musicians Union wouldn't let guys jam after hours or record unless they were paid. I understood the economic reasons, and it did cut down on the exploitation of young musicians. But in my opinion it also helped cut down on the flow of young musicians. That's how a lot of us learned, by sitting around and playing with other guys and listening to them. One of the troubles with jazz by the early 1960s was that nobody listened to anybody anymore. A few musicians would go off in a corner and say, We got the best style, and wouldn't pay any attention to anybody. There was a lot more envy in the music business than there used to be.

It seemed to me that some guys who wouldn't touch commercialism with a ten-foot pole were really trying to cover up a lack of musical knowledge and technique. I said so publicly, without naming names. There were a lot of guys who agreed with me but didn't want to be quoted. Anyway, the noncommercial guys had the stage, and so did the jazz critics who were against commercialism. I just went about the business of playing my music and entertaining the public. I rounded out the year by playing in the Macy's Thanksgiving Day parade and then flying out to play a couple of special concerts in Nigeria.

We were honored to be invited to Lagos, Nigeria, for a two-day festival and conference of the arts presented by the American Society of African Culture. The society was celebrating the opening of its new West African Cultural Center in Lagos, and I was celebrating the existence of an independent African state that was really making progress in all areas.

The concert was held in the King George V Stadium, and I

fronted an orchestra that was made up of both American and Nigerian musicians. The Americans were a quintet from my band, plus Randy Weston and His Quartet. The Nigerians included Michael Olatunji, who was very popular in New York and later started a school for African music and dance there, and Bobby Benson. We played about ten choruses of "Flying Home," and then we paraded down off the stage and through the stadium up to where Dr. Nnamdi Azikewe, governor general of Nigeria, was sitting. He stood up to greet us, and first we shook hands and then we hugged. The whole stadium cheered, and so we paraded up into the crowd and then back to the stage.

Other American blacks performed at that concert—Odetta, Brock Peters, and Nina Simone sang; Geoffrey Holder danced. There were a lot of others. Langston Hughes was one of the emcees. He also served on conference sessions between Africans and Americans on drama, music, dance, and art. Hale Woodruff, the artist, was there, and Dr. Horace Mann Bond, who was president of the American Society of African Culture. Wole Soyinka, the playwright, was one of the African panelists. I was really proud to be part of that festival.

By now I'd gotten into the habit of discovering young talent in the various parts of the world where we traveled, and this trip was no exception. I made a bunch of tapes of six Nigerian drummers and hoped to get them a record contract in the States. I also discovered a thirteen-year-old kid who could play trumpet like Miles Davis. I played these tapes on NBC's "Family" TV show after I got back. I wanted to show the American public that there were some exciting musical things going on in Africa.

I met my friend Charlie Mack when I was working in the studio with those tapes I'd brought back from Africa. He was a studio engineer at the Regent Sound Studio in New York. He'd been a musician before becoming an engineer and hadn't been engineering very long. He later said those drum tapes from Africa didn't make much sense to him, but he really tried to understand what I heard in them. We spent about four hours that day going over and over those tapes, and editing them. Too much time, in Gladys's opinion, since in a recording studio time really is money. She called Charlie the next day and told him, "From now on, you're not to let that man in the studio without his office's approval." So that's how Charlie met Gladys.

Charlie says that I was not an engineer's dream to work with. I'd listen to something and say, "That's good," and he'd be waiting for me to tell him to get that chord, or whatever, and I'd say, "Don't stop it." But at least he *acted* like he knew what I was talking about, and we hit it off pretty well.

The next thing we worked on together was music the band recorded at the Metropole. At the time, my trumpet player, Joe James, was acting as my musical director. This was music Charlie had a better understanding of, and he got the idea of what we were after. I later found out that he redid the whole thing after hours.

Gladys had a passion for short records. She was always worried about time, because she was dealing with distributors and disc jockeys, and she knew they didn't like long cuts. In fact, their chief criticism of my recordings was that they were too long. I always seemed to manage to run over the two minutes and thirty seconds that was supposed to be the maximum length of a cut played on the radio. So Charlie would have to cut them down. And he could do it.

Poor Charlie. He reminds me that when we were recording in the studio, I had a habit of starting a new song about three minutes before quitting time—and playing for about fifteen minutes. And then, as I'd be leaving, I'd tell him to send me a two-minute-and-thirty-second record in the morning. But I knew he would do it. I trusted him to eliminate the bad solos and choruses and get the best out of it. Charlie really got an education in editing while working on my stuff.

Gladys liked Charlie's work, too. She saw that he worked on his own time a lot, and then billed us for less time than he'd really spent. She didn't bother actually watching him work. She was interested in the finished product.

Gladys would sometimes come to the studio when we recorded. Usually, it was for a big date, when I recorded with the big band. The Regent Sound Studio was on West Fifty-seventh Street, between Fifth and Sixth Avenues, and there were all those great stores—Henri Bendel, I. Miller. Gladys would have I. Miller send up shoes for her to try on while she was listening to the session. Some of us joked that that's why she chose the Regent Sound Studio, because of its convenient location!

Charlie doesn't feel that I was ever really great in the studio. I admit that I always felt more comfortable on the stage. The studio was inhibiting, a frustrating situation sometimes. The vibes aren't that loud an instrument, and to get it recorded right the microphone really has to be up close, and that inhibits my stick movement because I'm afraid of hitting the mike. And a lot of times I will hit the mike anyway. I even do it sometimes on stage, because I swing those sticks pretty wildly.

Also the technology kept changing. I made hundreds of recordings when the sound was recorded right onto the acetate. Because of that, I learned not to give the initial countdown out loud, because there was no way to edit it off the acetate. But once they started using tape, the engineers wanted a good strong "one, two, three" so the musicians and the engineers would know when to start playing and recording. I couldn't get used to that for a long time. Charlie would say, "Hamp, count off loud and strong."

Charlie was really in my corner in the studio. If we made a bad start—started in on a tune and we didn't all start in one place—and something sounded off to him, he'd stop the tape and announce that he had some technical difficulty and would we start again, please? Musicians in the studio can't always hear this kind of problem, but the engineer can. Rather than say, "You messed up," Charlie would say he had the problem.

Not long after I met Charlie, I got a chance to get to learn more about the new technology and to do even more to get out to the American public the sounds I had discovered in my travels. A new TV station was getting started in Washington, D.C.—WOOK-TV, the first station aimed at the black audience. In June they named me musical director.

Also about this time, we made plans to produce an album that was totally different from what I'd ever done before. It was called "Hampton Plays McHugh," and it was all sentimental tunes written by that great composer Jimmy McHugh. I didn't even use my own orchestra but instead fronted Jack Pleis's all-string orchestra.

Meanwhile, we came out with "Bossa Nova Jazz," with some nice dance cuts like "The Same to You," "Some Day," and "Una Nota Sol." It was just me on vibes backed up by a rhythm section. It was a little late in the Bossa Nova craze, but it was a very fine album, with Bobby Plater on baritone sax and flute and a Brazilian rhythm section.

Charlie Mack says I have a way of throwing ideas out every which way, and that if we started trying to work on every one, everybody would go crazy. Back then I wanted to record every kind of music in the world—every kind of combination. Charlie developed this rule of thumb: when he heard me talk about the same idea twice, he'd get to work on it.

One of those ideas he heard twice was to record some rhythm and blues. We went on a short tour in the South, and I brought back a girl singer I'd discovered named Little Annie, who was a great young blues singer. That inspired me to record six or eight rhythm and blues singles, which were the first live recordings that Charlie Mack worked on for me.

We did five weeks, including Christmas to New Year's Eve 1962, out at the Flamingo in Las Vegas. We racked up the biggest New Year's Eve gross in the history of the hotel, and the owners gave me a five-thousand-dollar bonus. After that, we went on our first tour of Japan, and I loved that country and those people. On our way back, we stopped in Hawaii, and there I discovered a young Japanese jazz singer named Miyoko Hoshino and had her to come over to the United States and perform with me. She was lovely, sang in the style of Billie Holiday, and won me over when she said, "I have no difficulty in grasping the meaning of the songs. Your jazz music, like all great music, is universal and appeals to people of all nations. You don't need to understand English to know when Billie Holiday is singing the blues." She made the front page of *Jet* and was a big crowd-pleaser, singing the blues in her kimono. I was sorry when she went back to Japan because she was homesick. I couldn't stop raving about Japan, after we got back, and Dorothy Kilgallen wrote in her column that the Japanese Chamber of Commerce should give me a public relations prize.

I did get a public relations prize from the Metropolitan Advertising Club of Washington later that spring—the "Performer of the Year" award.

But the performer of the year still wasn't performing enough to suit him. I don't care how many kids were turning on to the big-band jazz, there still weren't enough clubs to play it in. And because I was getting my name in the papers because of engagements at the Flamingo or at Freedomland, that didn't mean that I was working steady. There were lots of days when the phone at the office didn't ring at all. Bill Titone reminds me that he and Gladys would sit there in the office and wait for the phone to ring. They'd get tired of waiting, and Gladys would say, "Let's close the damn office and get out of here. Let's go have some lunch. I'm tired." But Bill would say, "We can't. Maybe something will come through."

We hired Bill in early 1962 to handle the Glad-Hamp label. We wanted it to be a major label, and we decided we needed someone with experience in the record business. Bill had been sales manager for Apollo Records, which put out mostly spirituals, like Mahalia Jackson and James Cleveland. But then Apollo Records sold out and went into the music publishing business, and Bill didn't want to be in publishing. He wanted to produce. Somebody told him that we were trying to really establish our label, and Bill flew to Washington, D.C., where I was appearing, and we sat down and talked all one afternoon. We hired him, and he's been with me ever since.

Now, Bill's job was supposed to be producing records on the Glad-Hamp label and taking care of the record business. But he and Gladys and I became very close, and he started working for our best interests in other areas. It bothered him that the phone didn't ring with offers of bookings. It also bothered him that if Associated Booking didn't call, I didn't work. Oscar Cohen was the guy at Associated Booking who was handling our bookings. Oscar didn't call. Big bands were having a rough time then—there were very few bookings to go around. It was the era of the Beatles.

So Bill started making some discreet inquiries. He called a few contacts in the Catskills and that sort of thing, and started getting some bookings. He reminds me that it was sort of under the table because we still were under exclusive contract with Associated Booking. But they weren't paying much attention to me, except to call up and ask for their commission whenever they heard that I'd worked somewhere.

Bill booked me into the Rainbow Grill for a two-week engagement. A few days later, Oscar Cohen calls and wants to know where the commission is.

Bill said, "I don't owe you any commission, Oscar."

"What are you talking about? We have a contract," Oscar said.

Bill told him, "Oscar, if you check the contract, you'll see that it expired six months ago. You didn't even bother to call about negotiating a new contract. If you thought that much of Lionel, six months prior to its expiration you would have started talking about negotiating a new deal."

So that's how we finally got out from under Joe Glaser and his Associated Booking Corporation. We just waited for the contract to expire.

After that, we free-lanced. We were approached by other agencies. Willard Alexander tried to woo Gladys, because he booked big bands almost exclusively. They had several meetings. But Bill talked Gladys into staying independent. Bill took over the bookings, and we probably got as many bookings that way as we had with Joe Glaser's office booking us. Plus, we didn't have to pay him any commission.

But by this time I'd had to give up my regular band. There just wasn't enough work. Guys like Bobby Plater, who had been with me for eighteen years, had to leave because they weren't making enough to make ends meet. He joined Count Basie and stayed with him for eighteen years, although he did play with me and record with me from time to time. I was sorry to see guys like Bobby and my drummer, Floyd "Floogie" Williams, go. But I couldn't do anything about changing times and changing tastes. We'd done the best we could, and better than most big bands, except maybe Basie's.

My collaborator reminds me that the cabaret scene was dead in New York around that same time, and people like Mabel Mercer couldn't get work. It was hard for a lot of people. At least I could afford not to work. I don't have any explanation about why tastes change. I only know that the middle 1960s were a time of unrest and change, and I guess people needed new music to go along with it.

I haven't said much about the civil rights movement up to now because I wasn't directly involved in it. Gladys and I read the papers and watched the news broadcasts on TV, but we didn't talk about going down to march with Martin Luther King or anything. I have always been interested in politics, but it seemed to me that this was a young people's campaign. And anyway, direct confrontation has never been my style.

That is not to say that we didn't take a few stands against discrimination along the way. I remember one time—must have been in the fifties—when I was playing in a ballroom in Tennessee. Cab Calloway was in town and he came down to hear me play. Somebody came backstage, one of the porters, and told me, "Man, they're giving Cab Calloway a hard time up in front there. They won't let him come in and see you." I went out there and spoke to the manager, and he still refused to let Cab in, so I pulled the band off the bandstand. It was about ten-thirty at night. I refused to play there after that. From then on, I told all the managers that they had to let in mixed audiences to all my concerts.

I've always been happier working in more positive ways, like playing benefits to raise money for worthy causes that help people in need or help bring the races closer together. I played a lot of benefits for the civil rights movement, but I've played a lot of benefits for many causes.

I donated $75,000 to the Israeli Red Cross because Israel was taking in 75,000 black South African refugees and paying all their expenses. I gave a benefit concert in Indianapolis at the annual convention of the Knights of Peter Claver (named after the Spanish Jesuit priest who baptized 250,000 slaves after they were brought to South America from Africa) and raised $25,000 for the diocese of Laurian Cardinal Rugumba of Bukoba, Tanganyika, the first black cardinal in the history of the Roman Catholic Church.

Gladys and I worked together on one of the most enjoyable benefits I did around that time. It was a benefit performance for the Wiltwyck School for Boys in upstate New York. I got the Benny Goodman Quartet back together for a one-night concert at Carnegie Hall. I also got Sammy Davis, Jr., to perform. That same night I conducted a fifty-piece orchestra and a twenty-eight-voice choir. Joan Crawford, Gladys's old client from the Hollywood days, and now one of her good friends, was chairwoman of the event.

By the way, RCA Victor brought the Benny Goodman Quartet together again to record in late 1963. The album was called *Together Again*, and we did cuts like "Seven Come Eleven" and "Say It Isn't So" and "Runnin' Wild." It was always good to play with those guys, but it was even sweeter to know that the sound we made and could still make together was respected so much. And we showed that you *can* relive musical history.

Still, I was shocked and saddened by what was going on down South, like James Meredith not being able to enroll at Ole Miss. I remembered playing Ole Miss back in the middle fifties when I had a white piano player, and we got twelve standing ovations and a student escort to Memphis. But a visiting black band is a lot different from a black guy trying to be a fellow student. Even black musicians sometimes had trouble in the South. I remember back in 1956 when Nat King Cole was attacked in Birmingham—*my* town. That was ugly, just ugly. But I personally had been treated pretty well in the South, and I knew there were good people down there. It's just that the bad people seemed to have the upper hand at the time.

Hate had the upper hand. It was hate that killed President Kennedy. How I mourned that man's death. I was for Richard Nixon in the 1960 election, but Gladys and I both felt that President Kennedy was working to help black people. And we were honored when he and Mrs. Kennedy invited us to a special Lincoln's Birthday celebration at the White House. Sammy Davis, Jr., and Noble Sissle, and a number of civil rights leaders were also invited, and it was an occasion as special as any inaugural event I'd played there. I had the invitation framed and put up on display in our living room.

Looking back, I believe it was President Kennedy's assassination that spurred me to start working for the administration, doing whatever I could to help President Johnson. I may be a Republican, but I'm first of all an American, and I thought that what President Johnson was doing was good for the country. So in 1964, when he ran for election as president, I jumped party lines to support him. I had nothing personally against Barry Goldwater—in fact, we were good friends—but Johnson had signed the 1964 Civil Rights Act and said, "We shall overcome," and he was the man I wanted to support.

When his campaign people asked me to perform at a rally in New Jersey for him in October 1964, I was glad to do it. I had another engagement earlier that same afternoon, but I promised to get there by 5:00 P.M. When I arrived at the Bergen Mall in Paramus, there wasn't much going on. I changed that real quick. I did a takeoff on "When the Saints Go Marching In" called "When LBJ Goes Marching Home," and the crowd went wild. President Johnson was so pleased that he sent a note to me asking if I'd repeat the performance at his rally the next day in Brooklyn.

I didn't get invited to play at LBJ's inaugural gala, but I didn't mind. I was just glad that he won.

10

BEGINNINGS
AND ENDINGS

*E*ven if I'd been asked to perform at President Johnson's inaugural gala, I probably would have had to cancel. Gladys had to have an operation, and in late January 1965 she checked into Memorial Hospital in Los Angeles. We were supposed to go on an Eastern European tour—Yugoslavia, Czechoslovakia, and Russia—plus trips to France and Germany, but I canceled all that.

It was the same time that Nat King Cole was in Saint John's Hospital in Santa Monica, dying of lung cancer. That was really hard to take, because he was younger than me, and such a nice, nice man. I'd smoked a lot of years, too, but a couple of years before, Gladys had started getting me away from that and onto a corncob pipe. Later, after Nat died, reporters called me and reminded me that I was the first one to put Nat Cole on record—way back in the late 1930s in New York when the trio was hanging around Fifty-second Street looking for a break and I had them back me on "Jack the Bellboy."

From childhood, I have not been good at dealing with death, and I didn't want to think about how I would never see my old Chicago buddy again. But I also was spending a lot of time that late winter–early spring worrying about Gladys. She was just about getting over the operation when she was back in the hospital, this time in New York. She came down with hepatitis, which had set in after the operation. I rearranged my schedule again to be with her. I was devoted to Gladys and didn't want to be away from her. I didn't care how many dates I had to miss. Gladys came first.

I had plenty of things to do while I was watching over Gladys. For one thing, I decided to have a movie screen installed in the bus so the band members could have some entertainment while we were traveling. I also worked with Gladys and Bill Titone on our plans for a Glad–Hamp "Gold Label" series featuring all-star jazz groups playing with me. We'd already recorded the first album in April with Coleman Hawkins on tenor sax, Lucky Thompson on soprano, J.J. Johnson on trombone, Hank Jones on piano, Clark Terry on trumpet, Arvell Shaw on bass, and Osie Johnson on drums.

I was a real stickler when it came to my recordings—always have been. For one thing, they had earned me a good piece of money over the years. I think it was in the fall of 1964 that I cashed my thousandth royalty check for "Flying Home" and celebrated by having a thousand silver-plated mallets with my name on them made up to give out at the Metropole, where I was appearing with my band. Sad to say, they arrived all right, but with Duke Ellington's name on them! Record royalties had given me running around money for more years than I cared to remember. Gladys always left five dollars on the dresser in the morning. I liked to carry four, five, six hundred dollars in my pocket. So I'd go visit the recording companies and get an advance on royalties.

But I was also a perfectionist about recording because that was a whole different scene from a live performance. In live performance, you're playing for entertainment, you want the audience to have a good time. You do what you have to do to make that happen. I was often accused of having sloppy bands, and maybe sometimes that was so. But the audience came to be entertained, not to enroll in a conservatory. The patrons always got their money's worth, and there has never been an audience in the world that was made up of only informed jazz lovers. You have to play to the average Joe who hardly knows what jazz is and try real hard to make him know what it is when he leaves.

But records are for listening, and I was always after quality. That's another reason why I liked having my own label. I could control the quality. It was in 1965 that I junked twenty-five hundred dollars' worth of tapes because of a single sour chord.

By 1965, Charlie Mack, my favorite engineer, had left Regent

Sound Studio and gone to work for Peer-Southern, a music publishing company with offices in the Brill Building and with its own small studio. I couldn't do any big band stuff with him because there wasn't room for a big band in that studio. But while Gladys was sick, I wasn't doing that much recording anyway, and so I'd go visit Charlie. He had the idea of my doing demo records for the company—playing the musical background for the songs—and that way Peer-Southern got Lionel Hampton recording for them, and I got to use the studio as long as I wanted to.

While Gladys was recuperating in New York, I also got deep into politics again, this time for John Lindsay in New York. He was a Republican congressman who was running for Mayor of New York, and I thought a lot of him. He really had the black man's best interests at heart, and when he wasn't sure about something, he'd ask me about it, and he would listen to my advice. I recruited a lot of support for Lindsay in the show business world.

I even came up with his official campaign song, a takeoff on "Oh, Johnny, Oh," the song written by Ed Rose and Abe Olman back in 1917, when the World War I doughboys were in the thick of it in France. I got Abe Olman's permission to do a parody. This is how the first stanza went:

> Oh, Johnny, oh, Johnny,
>   who's gonna swing,
>
> Go, Johnny, go, Johnny,
>   ring-a-ding-ding;
>
> When you're mayor of New York Town,
>
> You'll keep the whole place snappy—
>   so very happy,
>
> 'Cause you're the new Johnny,
>   new Johnny, you are the one,
>
> Who's gonna win we know;
>
> You'd be fearless and fair,
>   a real swinger, no square,
>
> 'Cause you're right, Johnny,
>   fight, Johnny, oh!

By the time Gladys was well enough to travel again, the guys in the band had accepted other jobs. So instead of going out with a big band for the next date, I had a septet. This size group fit better into most of the clubs anyway—very few had room for sixteen pieces anymore. I had my longtime guitar man Billy Mackel with me still —he was the only guy who stayed—Roy Burns on drums, Eddie Pazant on alto sax and flute, Ronnie Cuber on baritone sax and soprano sax, Zeke Williams on piano, and Lawrence Burgan on bull fiddle. I called the group "The Jazz Inner Circle, the Power Structure of Music." We kicked off the tour at the London House in Chicago and did very well, but I was pretty much restricted to the vibraharp and couldn't mess around on drums and piano the way I liked. But I liked the way we sounded for a change. I hadn't given up the big band. I was back at it with all sixteen pieces in about a month.

In August 1965 I celebrated my twenty-fifth anniversary as a bandleader. Dorothy Kilgallen was going on vacation, and she invited me to be her guest columnist, and I thought it was a good chance to say a few things about my career and the state of music at that time. Here is the column that appeared in the Tuesday, August 31, 1965, issue of the *New York Journal-American*:

THE VOICE OF BROADWAY
"HAMP" LOOKS AT THE BIG BEAT

BY LIONEL HAMPTON

I just celebrated my 25th anniversary as a band leader and my 35th anniversary as a professional jazz musician. In spite of the "sour grapes" some of my contemporaries have been spouting, I'm sincerely happy with the changes that have taken place in my own career and in music in general. At the very least, I'm proud of the role my music has played in the development of jazz and rock 'n' roll.

When Benny Goodman plucked me off the stage of a Los Angeles ballroom in 1936 to become a member of his famous quartet, Swing was at the height of its popularity and still climbing. Teenagers collected photos of Benny, Gene Krupa, Teddy Wilson and me just as they do of the Beatles today.

And our popularity then was very much like the Liverpool quartet's pop-ularity today. Parents condemned us; critics scorned us; columnists editorialized about the kids' wild antics in the aisles of the Paramount Theatre; and professional writers spouted phrases akin to "What is this country's youth coming to?"

In time we became accepted. Gradually we became respected. Today most of us from that era have won international artistic acclaim and are being held up as examples for the young musicians of today to emulate.

The point is simply this: talent—genuine talent—will eventually be recognized. One European critic, who a couple of decades ago thought I was "too modern," recently revised his opinions and listed me as one of the few all-time Giants of Jazz.

Let's talk about The Big Beat for a

With Benny Goodman sextette: on bass, Artie Bernstein; on drums, Nick
Fatool; on guitar, Charlie Christian; on clarinet, Benny Goodman; and on
piano, Teddy Wilson.

Playing with Dave Brubeck, Illinois Jacquet, Clark Terry, and Ron Carter

At table with Lucille
Armstrong, Louis
Armstrong, and club owner

Lionel Hampton with
Clifford Brown on
European tour

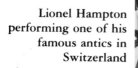

Lionel Hampton
performing one of his
famous antics in
Switzerland

Hampton being visited by
Vice-President and Mrs.
Bush after a performance.
Present also are Mayor
Koch, Audrey Smaltz, and
other government officials.

Lionel Hampton with
Sammy Davis

First publicity photo of
Lionel Hampton as
leader of his own group,
dedicated to his
brother Sam

Lionel Hampton in special performance with Gene Krupa and Buddy Rich

Lionel Hampton performing on the *Ile de France*

Lionel Hampton receiving honorary degree from Pepperdine University. L.A. Mayor Tom Bradley is on the extreme right.

While on tour in Tokyo, Japan, Hamp visits Boys School

Being awarded an honorary doctorate by Dr. Norman Francis at Xavier University

With Dizzy Gillespie in concert

Inaugural Gala

In Honor of the Inauguration of

President Harry S. Truman
Vice-President Alben W. Barkley

WEDNESDAY, JANUARY 19TH

1949

THE ARMORY

Washington, D. C.

LIONEL HAMPTON was a star before he ever thought of starting his own band. He was a "name" when he was a member of Benny Goodman's Trio. He is known as the world's greatest Vibraharp player. He was born in Louisville, Kentucky, in 1914, and was educated in Chicago and Los Angeles. He studied music at the University of Southern California. He was a member of Louis Armstrong's band. Later he joined Benny Goodman and became a stellar attraction. In 1940 he organized his own band and in one year it became one of the most popular orchestras in the country.

Inaugural Gala

41st INAUGURAL
JANUARY 19, 1949
THE ARMORY · WASHINGTON, D. C.

Truman's inauguration

At piano in a mellow mood

moment. It's merely a re-hash of what we used to call rhythm and blues. Back in the late 30s and into the 40s every record company had a subsidiary label that marketed Negro folk music, at that time almost exclusively for the Negro market. Now it's come full circle and the tastemakers of the American Negro sub-culture have provided a mass-marketable item that turned out to be the major attraction in the entire world's Pop culture. That music has made its mark on every young combo performing today.

And instrumentally, I'm proud to say, my work on the vibes has also left its mark on musicians of every age, nationality and origin of playing today. But to those of my contemporaries who complain bitterly about the new music sweeping the country, I can only say that even the best of them lacked the one important thing required to "sell" their music to the world's audiences: showmanship. The best and the worst of today's combos realize the importance of that.

Showmanship is something that I've always stressed on the bandstand, and often been criticized for by the so-called jazz "purist." But close analysis of today's successful jazzmen will reveal that showmanship has helped bring their music to the attention of the entertainment-glutted public.

It was an unconscious thing on the part of Miles Davis, but many a fan of his was won over through curiosity at wanting to see "the trumpet player who turns his back on his audience." And thousands of jazz aficionados became Thelonius Monk fans in spite of themselves; they originally went to see the piano player who wouldn't take his hat off and who wandered off the stand between solo choruses.

Once those people were captive audiences in night clubs or concert halls, they really listened to their music for the first time and discovered that they loved it.

Artists, established performers like Duke Ellington, Count Basie, Stan Getz, Woody Herman and myself don't have to worry about a place to work. Our agents can keep us busy 52 weeks a year, every year, and our records will always sell. But the young jazzmen who seem to resent having to perform, or to communicate with an audience, had better wrap up their horns and try another profession. All art is a communication of the artists' ideas, sounds, thoughts; without that no one will support the artist.

I'm currently having the time of my life fronting a small band which I call Lionel Hampton's Inner Circle. Together only a few months, we've already won accolades in smart hotel rooms and night clubs all over the country, and my audience ranges the entire gamut of public taste, from teenager and college student to married folk in their 30s and 40s who remember me from the old Benny Goodman days. I may bring the big band back for a few club dates, but for the moment I'm enjoying our own version of The Big Beat.

One thing about the current trend does disturb me. Where will we get the musicians of tomorrow from? The small rock 'n' roll combos have a limited instrumentation—no trumpets, saxophones, pianos, etc. And there are no touring big bands to give a youngster the kind of professional training he needs—the kind of roots that produced Dizzy Gillespie and Charlie Parker, Lester Young and Benny Goodman, Milt Jackson and Lionel Hampton.

We all paid our dues in someone else's band before striking out on our own. With only half a dozen bands working steadily, there's no place for the musician of tomorrow to pay his dues. Since American jazz has proved such a great cultural ambassador all over the world, perhaps the Federal government, in co-operation with the musicians union, could do something to rectify that situation.

Let me add one more thing to my airing of these once private thoughts. I love music, perhaps as much as life itself, and it's given me a great deal of happiness as well as a comfortable living. I have fun playing and it's that fun and happiness that I try to communicate to my fans in person and on record. Now that I have my own disc company, Glad-hamp Records, I expect every artist I sign to do the same. It's the very least we can do for the public—and they're the ones paying the bills.

Glad-Hamp Records was still doing mostly Lionel Hampton material. I had more than enough ideas to keep the label busy. I was still enjoying playing beautiful, melodic music, and I came out with a record titled "A Taste of Hamp" around the same time as that column appeared in newspapers across the country. It was mostly slow, sad ballads, like Rodgers and Hart's "Little Girl Blue" and Gershwin's "I Love You, Porgy" and "Prelude to a Kiss." I had Sy Mann on piano and his son, Bob Mann, on guitar. I also had a couple of Brazilian vocalists, Sevuca and Carmen Costa, who each sang two vocals on each side. There was only one traditional "big-band Hamp" cut and that was "Jazzland."

But I hadn't given up on the big-band sound—far from it. While I liked the Inner Circle group and kept it going—and recorded it quite a few times over the next couple of years—I still was most comfortable with a big band. In September I had a fifteen-piece group going again. And there were signs that maybe the big band was coming back. By the end of the year New York had a room that depended completely on name bands—the Mark Twain Riverboat under the Empire State Building, which seated seven hundred people. And outside of New York, too, new locations for big bands were beginning to appear. Plus, a lot of small clubs were trying to cram big bands into their spaces. Needless to say, I was very pleased with this turn of events.

I wasn't waiting around for the U.S.A. to rediscover the big band, though. I had the world as my stage. We went to Bangkok, Thailand, in March 1966, and King Bhumibol Adulyadej joined us in a two-hour jam session at the palace. Later in the year, we went to Spain, where we played Barcelona and Majorca, and then on to Paris and Brussels.

I spent most of the summer in New York. There was a lot of unrest in the black community there and in other parts of the country. Black civil rights workers had gone through a lot trying to get people registered to vote. Stokely Carmichael had been beaten and jailed so much that I'm surprised he could still talk. He was head of SNCC, and he came out with the slogan "Black Power" around that time.

He probably wasn't talking about me or the guy who was trying to get some new housing on St. Nicholas Avenue. I don't know what he was talking about. I did know that I wasn't going to get involved in it. When people asked me what I thought of Stokely Carmichael's "Black Power" theme, I said, "He's got to be excited about it. After all, it's the first hit Carmichael's had since 'Stardust.' "

I don't mean to make light of what was happening. That summer of 1966 was a tense one in New York City, and Mayor John Lindsay decided to hold some big jazz concerts to ease the tension. I played at one of them, in the Wollman Skating Rink in Central Park, and about ten thousand kids jammed in there and went wild over jazz. A good kind of wild.

Lindsay also started the Jazzmobile. Art Blakey, Dave Brubeck, Billy Taylor, Herbie Mann, me, and a bunch of other guys would drive through the streets of New York from 6:00 to 8:00 P.M. in a special musical caravan designed to act as a kind of safety valve to release pent-up tension. In July of 1966, Mayor Lindsay presented me with the city's highest cultural award, the George Frederick Handel Medallion. He also appointed me to serve as the city's goodwill ambassador to the Far East and gave me five solid-gold keys to present to the mayors and governors of Manila, Seoul, Hong Kong, Bangkok, and Tokyo. (We were scheduled for trips to the Far East in December and again in March).

I had kept my schedule open for the fall of 1966, because I had promised to campaign for my friend Nelson Rockefeller. I'd been in on Rockefeller's campaigns from the beginning, since he first ran for Governor in the late 1950s. I was the bandmaster for all his campaigns and always had my campaign group of about six, seven pieces. Sometimes there wouldn't be but two people on the campaign trail —me playing and him speaking.

By 1966, he had already won twice, and he probably thought I was good luck for him. His theme song was "Sweet Georgia Brown," and he'd say, "Hamp, play 'Sweet Georgia Brown' when I'm coming in and then again when I'm going out." I'd give him a warmup before he came in, maybe twenty, twenty-five minutes, and then when they told me he was coming in, I'd change the music to "Sweet Georgia Brown," and he'd come in waving. And then after his speech, he'd give a signal that he was going to leave, and I'd play "Sweet Georgia Brown" until the man gave me the signal that Rockefeller was out of sight.

Anyway, that fall in 1966, between the middle of October and election day in early November, I gave up about forty thousand dollars' worth of bookings to play "Sweet Georgia Brown" all over New York State for Nelson Rockefeller. But it was worth it to see him win. He was going to do some important things for Harlem.

I was so closely associated with Republican politicians in New York that in the spring of 1967 there were rumors that I might be a candidate for the special congressional election that the governor called after Adam Clayton Powell, Jr., was censured by the House of Representatives because of his legal problems. I told reporters that I had no intention of running against my friend Adam Powell. I also told them that for me politics was an avocation and that I intended to stick to my music. Adam ran again and won again. I wasn't involved in the campaign.

At the time I was on my first extended tour with the Inner Circle, which for this trip was an octet. I had Blue Mitchell on trumpet, Al Levit on drums, Lawrence Burgan on bass, Billy Mackel on guitar, Reynolds Mullins on organ, and Eddie Pazant and Pete Yellin on alto sax. I also had Pinocchio James along as vocalist. We played again for the king of Thailand, and then we did a bunch of one-nighters, a combination of hotel gigs, concerts, and performances for servicemen at U.S. bases.

I have to say that it was a lot easier going abroad with an octet than with a fifteen- or sixteen-piece orchestra. You don't know the logistics of traveling with a big group. You have to make sure everybody's got passports and visas; you have to make hotel and travel accommodations for everybody. It is not easy, as Gladys often reminded me.

Still, I jumped at every chance to perform with a big band, and one of the best venues was the annual Newport Jazz Festival, organized by George Wein. The summer 1967 festival was one of the greatest. It was great for me because I got to play with some of the veterans of my bands. George Wein put together a seventeen-piece band for me: Joe Newman, Snooky Young, Jimmy Nottingham, and Wallace Davenport on trumpet; Al Grey, Garnett Brown, Britt Woodman, and Benny Powell on trombone; Eddie Pazant on alto sax, flute, and tenor sax; George Dorsey on alto sax; Dave Young and Frank Foster on tenor sax; Jerome Richardson on baritone sax; John Spruill on piano; Billy Mackel on guitar; George Duvivier on bass; and Steve Little on drums. Some of these guys hadn't played with me for years. Jerome Richardson and Snooky Young hadn't been with me since the forties. Man, it was like old home week. For "Flying Home," none other than Milt Buckner and Illinois Jacquet sat in with my group. Talk about déjà vu! That's what was great about the Newport Jazz Festival—you got to see and play with guys you'd known for years but hadn't played with. And we all fit together like a glove, because those guys knew the music—they had learned it with me. Victor recorded that concert on an LP.

Dan Morgenstern wrote a nice article on the festival, and about me, for *Down Beat*. I give a lot of credit to Dan for reminding the readers of jazz magazines like *Down Beat* that I was a serious musician as well as an entertainer. Beginning in the early 1960s, he wrote a number of articles about me that helped a lot to put me in a position of respect in the music world—as a musician. Here's just a little of what he said in that article about the 1967 Newport Jazz Festival:

> Now it was time for the old master. Lionel Hampton's "How High the Moon" was the last word as far as solo efforts were concerned. Not only did he invent the instrument [vibes] as a jazz voice—he continues to set the pace. His sound has made him the Louis Armstrong of the vibes, and his uncanny sense of rhythm enables him to construct lines that bring constant surprise and delight. Moreover, his melodic imagination is such that the thread of continuity is never lost, no matter how many corners he rounds.

Gladys and I kept that article, and underlined some of the nice things Dan wrote, like "old master" and "last word" and "uncanny sense of rhythm." Some people might think it's strange that we'd be underlining words of praise after all the words of praise that had been written about me over the years. But there had been a time back in the fifties when the only good words about me were put in the columns by my publicists, and those words had to do with my charity work. It was like my music was completely ignored, or else criticized. It was good for the soul to read what Morgenstern wrote. He's now head of the Institute of Jazz Studies at Rutgers, and a good friend. I credit him with doing a lot to shore up my image when I needed it.

You have to understand that you can get all the honors and keys to the city that there are. You can even get named in the jazz polls every year—I'd made the *Playboy* jazz poll for ten years in a row by 1967. But if music critics ignore you or say you're just an entertainer, not a serious musician, not a player of "pure" jazz, you feel hurt.

All that was beginning to change by around 1967, and I give a lot of credit to Dan Morgenstern, since I was still playing the same way I always had. He made people listen to me with new ears. Or maybe he was just the first critic to sense that my sound was really coming back.

I don't chart trends. Gladys was the one who did that. But I do know that 1968 was a big year for me. One of the biggest honors was being the first solo instrumentalist invited to play the San Remo Song Festival in Italy. I was chosen to play backup for each song that was sung at the festival, so that they could vote for the winning song and singer. It was all carried on Euro-Vision TV.

An even bigger honor was that we were invited to a special audience with Pope Paul I. Louis Armstrong was also at the festival, and he and his wife, Lucille, and Gladys and I were invited to meet the pope. Both Louis and I got the Papal Medal for bringing joy and happiness to the world with our music. We gave the pope albums. Then the pope said, "I want you to be my guests this afternoon and go through the Vatican Gardens and the Sistine Chapel." And Louis looked at the pope and said, "Maybe next time, Pops. I have to catch a plane." Louis was a funny cat. Didn't matter who it was, he called everybody Pops. We *all* left after that.

That was in February. In August, because of my success at the San Remo Festival, I was invited to make a tour of Italy, including the Italian Riviera. Then, that same year, I was nominated for the Jazz Hall of Fame.

Meanwhile, I was spending every spare moment on the campaign trail for my old friend, Richard Nixon. We knew he was a shoo-in against George McGovern early on, but it isn't good philosophy in politics or in life to count on anything. We worked hard, and in January 1969 I played at Nixon's inaugural gala. It was my fourth one, but this was the most enjoyable, because I had been with Nixon from the beginning.

Nixon was a true friend to black people. A lot of people don't know the things he did to help. One reason why he created the Small Business Administration was to help blacks. He fixed it so that blacks could go to the government and get money to start businesses—and boy, they got some money. I know guys who got their start from the SBA. And Nixon also helped out Howard University. Howard got a $75 million loan from the government when Nixon was president. That's how Howard got back on its feet and got all those big buildings and great teachers. Nixon really looked after blacks, but it wasn't in direct ways that people could understand.

Except for Nixon's inaugural gala, 1969 was business as usual. I played all the big jazz festivals in the U.S. in the summer and then spent the fall in Europe, playing Paris, London, Wien, Rotterdam, Berlin, Neuchatel. Reporters were starting to write articles about how I seemed to be ageless and unstoppable. But I have to confess that I was beginning to feel the effects of all those years on the road and especially of cutting up on stage. In the late spring of 1970 I started to have severe pain in my left shoulder and numbness in my left hand. This was serious, but I had dates to play and I hoped it would go away. When it didn't, I paid a visit to a chiropractor, and he did some massaging and I felt better. But then in early June I was playing in New Orleans. I was also having discussions with people down there at Xavier University and Dillard University about starting some jazz seminars. My shoulder started hurting again, and it got so bad I could barely hold the mallet in my left hand. So Al Hirt, the great New Orleans jazz trumpet player, referred me to a doctor in the city, Dr. Jack Wickstrom.

His diagnosis was "cervical arthrosis with disc degeneration." His treatment was to put me in traction two times a day. He even arranged for a Spinks Big Wheel Traction apparatus to be sent to me in New York so I could take it on the road with me. That, and a mild pain reliever, helped a lot. Two days after I left New Orleans I appeared on the "Tonight" show. After that we went to Antibes and Geneva.

I spent a lot of the fall of 1970 campaigning for Governor Rockefeller. I even composed a song for him called "The Rockefeller Rock." Some of the upstate audiences could be kind of reserved when we first started playing, but after they got a chance to warm up, they became the greatest jazz fans you ever saw. Rockefeller won that election, of course, and I'd played for every one of his campaigns since the first one in 1958.

Around the early part of 1971, I was busy making plans for the jazz seminars in New Orleans and also doing some more talking about opening a music school. By this time, I wasn't thinking about a chain of schools anymore, and I had decided to delay opening one school in Harlem. What made me change my mind had happened a couple of years back. I was talking up the idea to anyone who would listen, when a guy spoke up. His name was June Gunn and he was head of the St. Nicholas Park Community Council. He said to me, "Yes, we need your university. But more than that, we need housing."

I had to admit he was right. The black people in Harlem at that time couldn't get any kind of financing for housing or housing rehabilitation—no money from the banks or the government. And Governor Rockefeller was just putting into action his plan for Housing Redevelopment. Gunn said to me, "Hamp, you're close with Governor Rockefeller, ask him if we can get some housing in Harlem." So I said I'd see what I could do.

I spoke to the governor about it, and he got a guy named Edward

Logue from Boston to work with him on the idea. Governor Rockefeller started the State Urban Development Corporation, and Edward Logue became its president. Logue got together some architects and planners, and the first black architectural firm in New York City, Bond Ryder, came out of that.

The way it all worked was that a housing project had to have a nonprofit sponsor, and that sponsor had to come up with five percent of the cost of a development before any state or federal monies started to come in. So Gladys and I went to work. We put in our own money, and then helped raise the rest of the $750,000 needed to build more than 350 apartments at Eighth Avenue and 131st Street. The complex was going to be called the Lionel Hampton Houses.

Once I had that project under way, I started thinking again about my university. But I put that on the back burner while we traveled to Europe in March and played Stuttgart, Berlin, Paris, Zurich, and I don't know where else. Not long after that, we played some dates in Canada. I don't remember now, but it may have been that trip when one of the guys threw a bottle out of the bus window and it hit a cop, of all people. They impounded the whole bus! Even Bill Bergac couldn't get us out of that one.

Gladys wasn't with us at the time. We were playing one-nighters, and she knew that Bill could take care of things. Besides, she didn't like all of that hopping around. But we were scheduled to play Toronto for a week in late April–early May, and she was supposed to join us there. I kept waiting for her to come, and back in New York Bill Titone kept asking her when she was going to go up to Toronto. But she just kept putting it off for some reason. We don't know why. Maybe she wasn't feeling well. She'd been complaining for some time about her heart, said she had chest pains. She was taking medication, but I guess it wasn't working.

I'll never forget that phone call. I thought it might be Gladys, but it was Bill Titone on the line. He said, "Lionel, I want you to be very brave. Gladys passed away." I don't remember much after that. Bill tells me I just kept saying "Bill, Bill, Bill"—maybe a hundred times.

Later, Bill told me that the day had started out as usual. He'd driven over the George Washington Bridge from his house in New Jersey, and he'd picked up Gladys at the apartment, as he always did. He dropped her in front of the office building and then went to park the car in the garage on the corner. Then he went up to the office, and when he opened the door Gladys's little poodle, Candy, was running back and forth, all excited. He called out, "Gladys, Gladys," but there was no answer, and he went back to her office, and all he saw was two little black boots sticking out from behind the desk. She had fallen and hit her head on the edge of the desk. She'd had a massive heart attack. It took the ambulance only about two minutes to get there after Bill called, but the driver said she was already dead.

I walked around in a state of shock for days. I couldn't believe that Gladys was dead. We'd been together for so long—the previous November we'd celebrated our thirty-fourth anniversary at the 21 Club—and she'd looked after me for so long. I went through the motions. There was a wake at Benta's Funeral Parlor on St. Nicholas Avenue, conducted by Bishop Fulton J. Sheen, and I sat through that. Then there was a funeral at St. Mark's Methodist Church. I sat through that.

Our friends really rallied around me during that time. Teddy Wilson came to the funeral. So did a lot of guys who had played with me in the band over the years. Joey Adams, Honi Coles, Ruth Bowen, Rubel Blakely, who had been a vocalist with me. A lot of friends came. Percy Sutton, who was then borough president of Manhattan, came to the funeral to represent the city. President Nixon and Governor Rockefeller sent telegrams of condolence.

After the funeral in New York, Bill and I accompanied Gladys's body out to Los Angeles, where Gladys had wanted to be buried. She'd already bought the plots and ordered the marble crypts for us to be buried in, side by side. Another funeral was held out there. Lou Rawls sang "A Closer Walk with Thee" and Sarah Vaughan sang "I'll Be Seeing You." I sat through that. Then we all got into limousines to accompany the body to Rosemont Cemetery, and all of a sudden I knew I couldn't take it anymore. I said, "Bill, no more of this. I can't. You gotta take me out of here, back to the hotel." It meant breaking the line of cars, and nobody seemed to understand, but I didn't care. I didn't want to see Gladys's casket lowered into the ground.

Gladys is still with me. Not a day goes by that I don't think about her. Nothing has been the same since. Keeping the business going was no problem. Bill had worked with Gladys closely for almost ten years. And even if Bill hadn't been there, Gladys had always made sure that all the records were in order. She used to say to me, "Lionel, if anything should happen to me, don't worry. Everything will be like an open book." But Gladys and I were a team, the perfect team for what we did. She was the businesswoman and I was the musician. She was the boss offstage, I was the boss onstage. She ran interference for me—every creative person needs someone to do that for them. Life wasn't the same without Gladys. And it never will be.

11

LIFE AFTER GLADYS

*I*t took me quite a while to get over Gladys's death. I felt as if, with her gone, half my life was gone. I still feel that way. Everything reminded me of her, and I couldn't face staying in the apartment in the Doris E. Brooks Houses in Harlem anymore, because Gladys was everywhere in it. So I took a suite at the Americana Hotel downtown. I didn't have the energy to look for another place.

I got rid of all of Gladys's possessions, including her thirteen fur coats and all her diamonds. She had half a million dollars' worth of jewelry. She had one diamond ring that was worth a hundred thousand dollars—a blue-white diamond, ten carats. I was just hurting so that I didn't want anything. I gave away some things, sold others. It hurt too much to be reminded of her.

It was Bill Titone's wife, Cap, who found the apartment I'm in now. She found it and furnished it, all without me knowing anything about it. I was performing at Lincoln Center in a show sponsored by Timex called "Swing into Spring" with Doc Severinsen, Duke Ellington, Ella Fitzgerald, Count Basie, and the original Benny Goodman Quartet. After a rehearsal, I was walking with Bill and Cap along the street near Lincoln Center. I said, "Let's call a cab and go back to the hotel," and Cap stopped me and pointed to one of the buildings nearby and said, "You don't have to, you live right there. Here's the keys."

It's a nice place—twenty-eighth floor, three bedrooms. It cost a lot more than the apartment uptown—we never paid more than about sixty-five dollars a month up there—but I can afford it, thanks to Gladys. My bedroom overlooks the Hudson. There's plenty of room for my drums and vibes and a piano, and all my records, and the awards and plaques. I have a housekeeper and cook. It's more convenient to the downtown clubs and recording studios. But I have not forgotten Harlem. One of the things that kept me going that first year after Gladys died was the plans for the Lionel Hampton Houses.

In December of 1971, I put on a yellow hard hat and turned over the first spadeful of dirt at the ground-breaking ceremonies for the $13 million complex—355 apartments, 70 percent of them for moderate-income families and the rest for low-income families and the elderly. Later, I put that hard hat in a special place in my living room, because it was an important trophy—a symbol of the way Gladys and I had helped our neighbors who hadn't been as fortunate as us. To me, that hard hat was also a symbol that the Lionel Hampton Houses weren't just going to provide housing, but also jobs. We had worked out agreements so that there would be black construction workers wearing hard hats and getting on-the-job training.

The Lionel Hampton Community Development Corporation already had plans for another housing complex down the block. This one was going to be called the Gladys Hampton Houses. Plus, I had not given up on my dream for a college. I knew Gladys would have wanted me to keep working, and I did. Bill pushed me to get back onstage, and that was the best thing he could have done for me. We did cancel some dates, but Bill kept after me, and finally I said, "I'm ready to go to work, Bill. Let's go." Working was all I had, and I probably drove myself harder than ever before to fight off the sorrow of losing her.

One of the first engagements I played was in Chicago at the Blue Max Room. Bill and I were walking through the lobby, and we saw Mahalia Jackson talking to Leo Moore. She hugged and kissed me. She lived in Chicago. I invited her in to see the show, and she said, "No, no, can't go in there. I don't go to nightclubs. I just came by to say hello, but I can't go into nightclubs." Mahalia was true to her religion.

Then she pulled me aside and said, "Child, anyone that wishes you dead should not be around you. Leo said to me, 'I wish Lionel would have died instead of Gladys.' " Well, I was shocked. Imagine

Leo saying that when I'd been paying his salary all those years! Gladys and I had practically raised him since he was fourteen. I couldn't get it out of my mind, and it was four o'clock in the morning when I called Bill and told him to fire Leo. I was finished with him. Leo was all upset and waved a handful of pills around and threatened to commit suicide and everything, but he took his plane ticket and went on back to New York. He died not long after that—he was a heavy gin drinker.

I performed whenever and wherever I could, mostly with a small group. There was a time in the early seventies when jazz changed quite a bit, and it was hard for veterans—with the old sound—to get work. There were a bunch of kids around who weren't as attentive as they should have been. They called John Coltrane old-fashioned. Some even said Charlie Parker couldn't play. They were busy playing things in different keys. If you asked them what they were playing, they'd just say, 'Man, this is freedom.' They lost a lot, not having any respect for their predecessors.

I also didn't do much recording during that period. But my name was out there, just the same. RCA came out with a Vintage series, which was supposed to include all ninety-one sides I had recorded for Victor between 1937 and 1941. They got out volume 1, which had the first four complete sessions I ever did for them. But I don't know what became of volume 2, or the rest of what was supposed to be a boxed, six-record set.

I don't know what happened. Maybe other people got sick of hearing the young musicians criticize the older ones. Whatever happened, jazz was really making a comeback, and it seemed that every time I turned around I was getting offers to perform with guys I'd played with in the late thirties and forties. At the Newport Jazz Festival in July 1972, I had another reunion with Gene Krupa. Then the following year, the whole Benny Goodman Quartet were reunited again. This time the occasion was the Urban League's Thirty-third Annual Ball at the Waldorf-Astoria. It was a salute to me, not only for my long career in music, but also for my role as developer for the Lionel Hampton Houses. Duke Ellington and Benny Goodman were honorary chairmen, and Teddy Wilson, Gene Krupa, and Cab Calloway were honorary cochairmen. The members of the quartet didn't realize it at the time, but that was the last reunion we ever had. Gene died later that year. The next time the rest of us got together was in 1974 for "The World of Music Tribute to Gene Krupa" at the Felt Forum in New York.

Nineteen seventy-four was the first year I played a club in London. We played Ronnie Scott's in May, and we went over big. All the papers talked about my entertaining style, how I'd sit down at the drums and juggle four sticks at a time while the strobe lights played over the bandstand, how I'd laugh and roar and tell jokes. The way they carried on about it, you knew that London didn't see many real showmen anymore.

I had a bunch of young cats with me by then. Glen Drewes, my trumpet player, had just graduated from the Eastman School of Music in Rochester, and he could double as a concert pianist. Tom Gambino came out of Trenton State College, where he studied and taught. He could play flute, clarinet, and soprano and alto sax. Because I traveled with a small group, I needed musicians who were versatile, and I didn't have any trouble finding them. Most of them weren't even born yet when I was giving young cats like Dexter Gordon and Illinois Jacquet their first break.

I have to say, though, that a young kitten gave me a nice bit of play around that time. Bette Midler did a revue at the Minskoff Theater on Broadway in 1976, and she chose me to back her up. It was not so much her idea of camp as it was her appreciation of classic jazz that got the two of us together. She'd heard "Flying Home," and she wanted me to play "Flying Home," and she wanted to sing "Flying Home." The show was due to open in ten days, and I said "Bette, you don't have time to put out any publicity on me." She said, "You don't need any publicity. You get on the stage and make your own." So I went on and played for her, and that was a great engagement. We played ten weeks, and I like to think it was mutually beneficial—I helped give Bette legitimacy, which she really didn't need but which the press thought she did, and she helped to get my sound out to a whole new group of people.

I was still going to Europe several times a year. By now, George Wein was producing those European tours, and I was doing more recording in Europe than I was doing in the States during that period. I did some sides with Zoot Sims, Teddy Wilson, George Duvivier, and Buddy Rich around 1974, but I don't think I recorded at all in 1975. In May 1976 I recorded a bunch of sides in France—Paris, Saint Quentin. Billy Mackel was back with me for that trip. In May 1977 I was in France and Germany, and in Villengen and Toulouse I recorded with an all-star group that George Wein got together. It included Cat Anderson on trumpet, Paul Moon on alto sax, Eddie Chamblee (from the forties) on tenor sax, Milt Buckner on piano, Billy Mackel on guitar, Barry Smith on bass, and Frankie Dunlop on drums.

But a lot of my recordings were being issued anyway, around that time. Victor finally got it right with *The Complete Lionel Hamp-*

ton, in which all ninety-one small-band sides I had recorded for RCA between 1937 and 1941 were done chronologically, so that the different sides recorded in a particular session could be heard together for the first time. Stanley Dance did the liner notes, and Frank Driggs produced the whole thing. Listening to them, I felt like I was back in the Victor recording studios forty years before. *The New Yorker* reviewed them and said that Victor had finally erased more than twenty years of mistreatment it had subjected collectors of my records to.

Meanwhile, Pablo Records had come out with the piano solos and small-band dates of Art Tatum; Arista was bringing out old Charlie Parker, Don Byas (he played with me), and Red Norvo recordings. It was clear to me that the time was right for biographical jazz LPs. So I decided to do a Who's Who in Jazz series myself.

I wanted to make sure that the great musicians were recorded properly. I also wanted to be sure that blacks in music would handle some of their own business, that the world would know that they don't always have to depend on whites. Plus, I wanted to get some of that gutty jazz beat of the 1930s into contemporary recordings. I kept that beat going in my live performances, but I missed that beat in recordings. In one year, 1977, I recorded ten Who's Who LPs with jazz greats. I played vibes—or in one case vibes and piano—on each, and I had anywhere from five to ten instruments on each. I featured Cozy Cole, Earl Hines, Teddy Wilson (and Teddy Wilson, Jr., on drums), Woody Herman, Buddy Rich, Gerry Mulligan, Charlie Mingus, Dexter Gordon, and several others.

Each one was titled, *Lionel Hampton Presents . . .* , and some of them were great. *Lionel Hampton Presents Charles Mingus* had solos also by Woody Shaw on trumpet and Gerry Mulligan on baritone sax. It was like recreating the atmosphere of those classic small-band sides I did for Victor. I later had problems with distribution of those albums, but I am still proud of that project.

Charlie Mack, the studio engineer who had worked with me at Regent Sound and other studios back in the early sixties, had been out of touch for several years, but he came to the office of Glad-Hamp Records a couple of years after I did the Who's Who series. I hired him to make albums, tapes, whatever came up, and he's been with me ever since. To get himself back into the groove of my music, Charlie put on a headset and listened to albums and tapes from the last several years for about a month or two. He says that it was then that he realized I was a contemporary musician no matter what was happening in music, and that I was comfortable with whatever was happening. I fit in. The ten or so years away gave him that perspective.

He remembered when my big band was playing popular songs like "Little Bitty Pretty One." He saw how the melodic content of the pieces I played had changed. By 1980 I was playing Chick Corea tunes. The first album he worked on for me was *Chameleon*, which contained pieces written by Horace Silver, Herbie Hancock (the title song), Mike Foster, and others.

By now I wasn't able to hop around quite so much as I used to. But I was feeling positive every day. I still missed Gladys, but I could see that God had more for me to do. I read the Bible every day, and that gave me strength. I was also escorting ladies to different places, and that made me feel younger. Jewel Lafontant, an attorney, was one of those ladies. There have been several.

But my Fountain of Youth was, and always has been, performing. I am happiest when I am onstage or recording. I was getting a lot of chances to perform by the late 1970s because I'd been in the business so long I was being given all kinds of tributes. Plus, the old jazz sound was coming around again, and here I was, a guy who was associated with it, with the real thing. I had stayed out there and stayed with it while all the changes were coming through. I just kept on plugging. And then some of the young guys, like Chick Corea and Herbie Hancock, were playing in the old style. Dexter Gordon had Benny Bailey and Slide Hampton with him, and they used to play with me, and you could see my style in there. So between that new musical development and my longevity in the business, I was getting all these tributes.

The Amsterdam News gave me one at the Waldorf-Astoria in 1976. In March 1978 I was playing a gig at Dangerfield's with a quartet made up of Grady Tate on drums, Roland Hanna on piano, George Mraz on bass, and Frank Wess on flute and saxophones. We'd just gotten back from a tour of Yugoslavia, Bulgaria, Czechoslovakia, Romania, France, Spain, and the Virgin Islands. At the close of one set, Ossie Davis brought out a huge cake with fifty candles on it. His wife, Ruby Dee, wrote a poem for the occasion: "Among whom the gods bless, high on the list are the music people, who tune into celestial vibe-brations and give mortals a taste of immortal sensations. Paradise is to be the ultimate instrument, fulfilling God's desperate intent that we love each other. The music people—the Lionel Hampton kind of people—they give thanks for the gift and reflect the love."

In the summer of 1978, the city of New York had a Lionel Hampton day, and I got as many of my musicians from the old days together as I could, and we did a concert at Carnegie Hall. I received the city's highest citizenship award, the Bronze Medallion. It was for fifty years in music. So was the National Public Radio two-hour fiftieth-anniversary salute to me, which was part of its "Jazz Alive" series. Some of the other tributes were for forty years in music, but that's my fault, since nobody knew exactly when I was born or when I had started my professional career, and since I wasn't telling my age.

I played a sad tribute in 1978—to my old friend Nelson Rockefeller at his funeral. He'd gotten all the way to the vice presidency, and I, for one, had worked hard campaigning for him to be president. With Nixon out of politics, and Rockefeller dead, I started supporting George Bush, who I'd known since he was a teenager. I was a friend of his father, Senator Prescott Bush of Connecticut, from way back and used to play at his campaign rallies. Young George used to get Coca-Colas for me. Now he was a statesman himself, and I thought he should run for the Republican presidential nomination. He did the following year.

But back to Nelson Rockefeller for a moment. When he died, the Lionel Hampton Houses were just about completed, and plans for the Gladys Hampton Houses were well underway. He, more than anyone else, was responsible for both projects. I never could have done it without the Urban Development Corporation he started.

By the way, I had made arrangements for all income from the two projects to go into the Lionel and Gladys Hampton Scholarship Fund that I had set up. There was money to be made with those projects, but I wanted those houses to be a humanitarian thing.

I was now thinking about building housing in other cities, and I was talking with Los Angeles mayor Tom Bradley about doing the same kind of thing there. Times had changed, though, and now you needed federal money for those kinds of projects. Jimmy Carter was in the White House then. I liked the man. I played at his jazz party at the White House in June 1978. But I was hoping that in 1980 we could get a Republican administration in again.

Meanwhile, I was playing every chance I got, but I always made sure that when I went on the road, I had enough bookings to make it worthwhile. I had a group of guys in New York that I could count on—a guy who knew the first trumpet book, trombonists and sax players who knew their parts. They all fit right in and were available when I needed them. When I had special festival gigs to play, George Wein's office would always help me to put together all-star bands. I think back on the early days when we'd play for $250 for a whole band and then not have anyplace to go after that. Now, I turn down $10,000 to $15,000 bookings if they don't connect up with anything else.

In January of 1978 I had a good booking in Cannes, and it was there that I recorded with Chick Corea. We did *Chick and Lionel Live at Midem*. A lot of people said that we made an unikely combination, but maybe that was part of what made the combination so good. I really admired Chick's piano playing and composing. We did his composition "Sea Breeze," and the way we were able to get together shows on the recording of that piece. That isn't a well-known piece, and I believe I helped get it out to a wider public.

In the summer of 1978 I had a good long booking in Nice, France—something like six concerts in a week and a half. I'm glad I went, because I got a special bust of myself in the city's gardens, erected by the city of Nice.

It was George Wein's idea. There was a bust of Louis Armstrong in the garden, and so George said I should have one, since I'd been fifty years in show business. Now, the Nice people argued that they shouldn't put up such a bust until the musician had passed away, so they could have a plaque under it with the birth and death dates. But the mayor finally agreed that it would be nice to honor me when I was still alive. So they had a special dedication, and there's my bust in the garden, about twenty feet from Louis's.

By the way, the French have given me another honor. In Paris at the Meridien Hotel, there is a Jazz Club Lionel Hampton named in my honor.

I was doing a lot of jazz seminars at colleges and universities. I didn't have my own music school, but I could go to other schools to teach kids about music. I already had honorary degrees—from Pepperdine and Xavier (in Louisiana). In early 1979 I received an honorary degree from Howard University at the celebration of Charter Day, March 2, 1867, when the university was founded. I had given seminars at Howard. I remember one that was supposed to last one and a half hours and ended up being four. I couldn't eat or go anywhere, but for the kids hanging all over me, wanting to talk to me. I loved it.

For the Playboy Jazz Festival at the Hollywood Bowl and for the Newport Jazz Festival at Avery Fisher Hall in June 1979, I had Jerome Richardson, Arnett Cobb, Jimmy Cleveland, and Marshall Royal back with me—and this was going *way* back. I also played at a tribute to Billie Holiday at the Newport Jazz Festival. It was always fun playing music, but I don't mind telling you it was great playing with the old crowd.

After the Playboy Jazz Festival performance, I stayed out in Los Angeles for a few days, and while I was there, a guy invited me and Audrey Smaltz, my lady friend, to a nighttime Los Angeles Dodgers game against the Chicago Cubs. We had dinner in the Stadium Club, and then we took our box seats on the first base side. Then Audrey nudged me and pointed up at the message board behind the left-field seats. It said: "A Dodger Stadium Welcome to the Great Lionel Hampton." We had a great time that night, but too bad the Dodgers lost.

Audrey is a publicist, and she was a big help to me. She's the one who brought my coauthor and me together. A lot of good things that happened to me were because of her. She came into that apartment and saw to it that the people I was paying to take care of the place and of my clothes started doing it. She arranged my closets so I could find my performing clothes, and she made sure they were kept in order. She is one of the best-dressed women in the world. She is a strong-willed, independent lady, like Gladys. We went out for several years, but we had a little misunderstanding, and I don't take her out anymore.

When 1980 dawned, I got back into political campaigning in a big way because my longtime friend George Bush was running for president. George Bush and I go back a long way, to the forties, when he was a kid, and I played on the campaign trail for his father, Senator Prescott Bush, in Connecticut. Senator Bush also asked me to play at war bond rallies in various cities in Connecticut, and I'd take my band and play, and Senator Bush would make an appeal for the people to buy bonds. We sold a whole lot of bonds.

I watched George Bush's career. And when I needed help, he gave it to me. When I needed certain information about housing from HUD in Washington, D.C., he saw that I got it. At the time he was head of the CIA and chairman of the Republican party. I followed his career, kept up with every transition that he made, and when he announced that he was going to run for president, I jumped on his campaign bandwagon. I played for his campaign a few times. Meanwhile, I got elected as a Bush delegate from New York.

At the convention in Detroit, we were outnumbered by the Reagan delegates. George Bush wanted to pack up and go home. He told us, "There's no use holding out. I appreciate what you are doing, but we should turn our attention and support to Ronald Reagan." But I wasn't giving up that easily. I told him, "No, we're going to make you vice president, and from vice president you'll be president."

There was talk that Reagan would choose former president Ford to be his running mate, or maybe Henry Kissinger. But we Bush delegates decided it was going to be Bush. We went out and got a thousand signs made, and I got my gang together, and we put these signs all over the convention floor. Then we got all these sticker signs saying Bush for Vice President, and we walked around patting people on the back and leaving the stickers on them. We had a plague of publicity going for George Bush. And meanwhile, we were talking him up at all the committees. My coauthor remembers watching the convention and hearing John Chancellor of NBC say something like "There's a log-jam on the convention floor. There seems to be a Bush outbreak."

We did create a logjam, a big stumbling block. We tied up that convention so they couldn't do any business what with all the speculation about who was going to be vice president. Finally, Ronald Reagan had to come down to the convention floor himself, something that the winning candidate doesn't usually do that early. But he had to. He came down, and he announced that George Bush would be his vice president. Boy, the roof came off the place.

We got Bush in there. His campaign manager was James Baker, who is now Secretary of State, and Baker told Bush, "This man standing next to you, Lionel Hampton, has worked hard, and he is probably more responsible than anyone for you being vice president."

I campaigned for the ticket. I liked Reagan. When he was governor of California, he appointed a lot of blacks to jobs for the state. I pointed that out in my public statements. I also said in public, "There is no such thing as racism when it comes to the governor." I felt he would help the country a lot if people would give him a chance and let him do his thing. He was going to inherit an awful lot of economic problems. He was a conservative, but I don't pay any attention to those labels. I walk within the Republican party and do what I have to do, as long as Republicans are in it.

The Democrats use blacks just to get their vote. But when the time comes to compensate, they forget all about us. Republicans do good deeds for blacks without ballyhooing. I believe in a lot of the principles of Republicanism, like not being wasteful. A lot of federal agencies needed to be revamped because they were spending money wildly. I headed up the Black Republicans Committee for the Reagan-Bush ticket. Nancy Reagan came to New York to announce the formation of the Black Republicans Committee and the Senior Citizens Committee for Reagan-Bush. Gloria Swanson was named to head the Senior Citizens Committee. I qualified for that job, too.

I used my own money to buy ads in black publications like *Jet* to support the Reagan-Bush ticket. Republican party leaders thought that was a great idea. So many blacks were down on the party. I knew the best way to get the message across was to put it in *Jet*, because that's the Black Bible.

When Ronald Reagan was inaugurated, there were so many people they wanted to thank that they didn't have just one inaugural ball, they had several "satellite balls." I played at one of them.

About a month later, I was guest of honor at a benefit at Avery Fisher Hall at Lincoln Center in New York. I had the organizers invite George and Barbara Bush. They couldn't make it, but George sent a telegram that I am very proud to have:

DEAR LIONEL AND YOUR MANY FRIENDS:

BARBARA AND I ARE SORRY WE CANNOT BE WITH YOU TONIGHT AS YOU ARE GATHERED IN A GENEROUS AND PRAISEWORTHY CAUSE: SUPPORTING BOTH THE EMERSON INSTITUTE FOR ARTS AND THE ADDICT REHABILITATION CENTER. YOU ARE ALSO ASSEMBLED TO HONOR ONE OF OUR CLOSEST FRIENDS, LIONEL HAMPTON. WE HAVE KNOWN HAMP MANY YEARS. WHETHER HIS EFFORT HAS BEEN POLITICAL—SUCH AS HIS SUPPORT IN THE RECENT CAMPAIGN FOR PRESIDENT REAGAN AND ME—OR WHETHER IT HAS BEEN IN HIS CONSTANT FIGHT FOR A BETTER SOCIETY—SUCH AS HIS WORK FOR THE GLADYS HAMPTON HOMES HERE IN MANHATTAN—LIONEL HAS WON THE RESPECT OF ALL WHO KNOW HIM. MOST OF ALL, OF COURSE, LIONEL HAMPTON IS ONE OF THIS CENTURY'S GREAT MUSICAL INNOVATORS, WHOSE ACHIEVEMENTS WILL LAST FOREVER. THERE IS NO QUESTION IN THE MINDS OF ALL MUSICIANS, AS TO WHAT THIS MAN HAS DONE FOR THEIR ART, AND FOR AMERICA AS A LAND OF BOUNDLESS CREATIVITY. HAMP, CONGRATULATIONS UPON RECEIVING THE MONARCH I AWARD. YOUR GIFTS TO AMERICA AND HER MUSIC ARE YOUR LIVING MONUMENT. BARBARA JOINS ME IN SENDING BEST WISHES AS ALWAYS. GEORGE BUSH.

The following September the Reagans paid me just about the greatest honor I've ever had when they gave me a special reception at the White House. George Bush had a lot to do with that. It was his way of thanking me. About eight hundred people gathered on the south lawn of the White House, and President and Mrs. Reagan greeted everyone. Then we did a concert. Audrey Smaltz was sitting right next to the president, and Jewel Lafontant right next to her, and next to Jewel was Vice President Bush. Charley Pride was on the other side, next to Mrs. Reagan. After the concert, the president called me a great American, and I called him the greatest star in the world. I was deeply honored.

Later I had a private meeting with Vice President Bush, and then that evening the Kennedy Center had a benefit concert in my honor. I performed with a sixteen-piece band. I was saluted by Count Basie, Woody Herman, Betty Carter, Pearl Bailey, Tony Bennett, Stephanie Mills, Charley Pride, Stan Getz, Dave Brubeck, Louis Bellson, Clark Terry, Illinois Jacquet, Stanley Turrentine, Zoot Sims, and the Howard University Jazz Ensemble. I asked that the proceeds be used to establish a school of jazz in Harlem, under the auspices of the Lionel and Gladys Hampton Foundation.

I still had that dream for a music school in Harlem. But in the meantime the people said they needed housing more, and I was helping to provide that. A year before I was honored at the White House, I hosted the dedication of the Gladys Hampton Houses. We had a parade from 145th Street and Frederick Douglass Boulevard past the Lionel Hampton Houses and ending at the Gladys Hampton Houses at St. Nicholas Avenue and 130th Street. Then we had an outdoor concert. I just wish that Gladys had been alive to see the houses built and carrying her name. I had a special inscription placed on the cornerstone, something I had said often about Gladys: "God gave me the talent, but Gladys gave the inspiration."

The Gladys Hampton Houses were 205 low-income units, and they were designed by John James of Bond Ryder Associates, the same firm that designed the Lionel Hampton Houses (Max Bond was the architect for those). I had a hand in designing the deck in the courtyard area formed by the U-shaped buildings. I wanted different seating areas, sandboxes for children to play in, game tables, and a performance area for outdoor concerts. That's how the area was designed.

I like to have little outings for the kids in the houses. We have an Easter egg hunt, a Thanksgiving party, a Christmas party. I sponsor softball, baseball, and track teams for the boys and girls. I want to foster a sense of community for them, and that's why it's important to have welcoming public areas.

I had plans for more houses in Harlem and in other places, and with a Republican administration in the White House, I was hoping to get some federal money. It wasn't long before I had the Hampton Hills project going in Newark, New Jersey—ninety-one condominium units on six acres. Meanwhile, I was elected vice chairman of the New York County Republican Committee in October 1981, and about a year later I was part of an official American delegation to Swaziland and the funeral of King Sobhuza. Also on that trip was Carlos Campbell, the first black assistant commerce secretary.

The following year, I was appointed to New York City's Human

Rights Commission by Mayor Ed Koch, a Democrat, and honored by the National Conference of Black Mayors, almost all Democrats, in Washington, D.C. Just before I set off for Europe, I was also named United Nations music ambassador to the world by U.S. Ambassador to the United Nations Jeanne Kirkpatrick, a Republican. It was around this time that people started calling me vibes president, and I have to believe that it had something to do with my work in politics.

Musical highlights of those years included playing with Benny Goodman and Teddy Wilson at the Kool Jazz Festival in New York in the summer of 1982, playing a benefit for the American Shakespeare Festival in Stratford, Connecticut (Mrs. Reagan was honorary chairman) in September 1984, and being honored in a Grande Parade du Jazz in Nice in the summer of 1983. Also, there was the Japan tour and the album that came out of it, *Made in Japan*, which was released in 1983.

Another milestone was playing deep in the heart of Mississippi in 1982 and having the mayor and the governor declare a "Lionel Hampton Day," though it was no big deal to anyone who wasn't around in the old days. In some ways, it wasn't even a big deal for me. I was honored, but I had been treated well in Mississippi before. Still, I could see that great progress had been made in the South. There was no question about playing to integrated audiences nowadays, and the old days, when it was something you could stake your career on, seemed long ago and far away.

I had a personal milestone in 1981 when I played at a concert sponsored by Peace Train in New Haven, Connecticut. I really got into the mood that night, and I leaped off a bandstand that was several feet high, landed flat on my feet, and started jitterbugging with some women fans. By that time people were starting to talk about me like I was over the hill. One joke was, "How do you get Hamp to stop? Fly him home." I just wanted to remind them that I could fly myself home whenever I was ready to hang up the drumsticks and the vibes mallets.

I wasn't alone out there. Benny Goodman and Teddy Wilson were still performing—we had reunions annually at the jazz festivals. In 1984 I got together with Artie Shaw on a double bill at the Kool Jazz Festival in New York. As those of us who are left get older, there's more and more call for us to play.

In the meantime, I kept up my own schedule, playing the U.S.A. and Europe every year. In 1984 I was honored to receive the Medal of the City of Paris and to be serenaded by thirty of France's top jazz musicians. In 1985–1986 I did a "world tour" of Europe, Israel, and South America as a goodwill ambassador for the Reagan administration (I reported directly to Charles Wick, Director of the U.S. Information Agency) I took a seventeen-piece orchestra with me: Reynolds Mullins on piano; Richard Visone on drums; Patrick O'Leary on bass; Samuel H. Turner on percussion; Lee Romano, Vincent Cutro, Albert Bryant, and John Pendenza on trumpets; Chris Gulhaugen, John Gordon, Charles Stephens, and Robert Trowers on trombones; Thomas Chapin, Adam J. Brenner, Edward Miller, David M. Schumacher, and Gerard Weldon on saxophones.

In the U.S., I did as many college dates as I could, and along the way I collected more honorary degrees—I had ten by 1984—and endowed more music schools—four by 1984. That year, of course, I played a lot of gigs for the Republican party, including the convention in Dallas, where I was also a delegate from the Seventeenth Congressional District. By this time I was vice chairman of the Manhattan GOP. The following year State Senator Roy Goodman tossed out my name as a possible candidate for City Council president. I would have been willing to run, for the good of the party, but I was glad that someone else was chosen.

When you've been in the entertainment business as long as I have been, you start to get a lot of déjà-vus, or repeat performances. We were in Shreveport, Louisiana, in February 1986, and we did "When the Saints Go Marching In" as our finale. We marched through the aisles and the lobby, you know. I didn't expect a four-year-old kid to join us, but he was moved by the music and couldn't help it. He marched with us back up on the stage. Somebody called out, "He's the drummer for our church," and so when we got back up onstage, I lifted him up to the drums and placed my drumsticks in his little hands. The kid kept the beat, and even ended with a flourish. His name was Jamos Williams, but he reminded me so much of the four-year-old out of Nashville, Tennessee, whom I called "Hamp, Jr." about thirty years earlier.

Kids take to music so naturally. I've seen it again and again. That's why I've kept dreaming my dreams of music schools all across the country to teach young kids the rudiments that they need to add on to that natural rhythm and joy in music. I've been to a lot of places, and I've gone around to the public schools to find out just what kind of musical training kids are getting. More often than not, I find that they're not getting any training to speak of. Music education and art education are way down on the list of priorities.

I set up music scholarships at the University of Southern California, Duke, and a lot of other colleges. I was doing, formally, what I have always done professionaly—do all I can to teach young musicians. It was in 1986, I think, that Quincy Jones took out an ad in *Jazz Times* saluting me with "If it hadn't started with you, I wouldn't be nothin'."

At the University of Idaho I helped to set up a Jazz Festival Endowment Fund in the spring of 1985. The school had been hosting jazz festivals for almost twenty years, but this fund, which Chevron also helped get off the ground, was to make sure they would continue. The school thanked us by renaming the festival the University of Idaho Lionel Hampton–Chevron Jazz Festival.

Then Dr. Richard D. Gibb, president of the University of Idaho, wrote to me to ask if I'd help raise money for the construction of a new performing arts center for the school. They wanted to have it ready for 1989, when the school would celebrate its one hundredth anniversary. I agreed to be national campaign chairman. The facility would be called the Lionel Hampton Center for the Performing Arts.

We got to work raising money, and we had that facility built by the late winter of 1987. The dedication was February 28, and we had a huge all-star concert featuring Joe Williams, Clark Terry, Ray Brown, Al Grey, Carl Fontana, Benny Powell, Gene Harris, James Moody, and several others.

A special proclamation was issued:

PROCLAMATION

Whereas, Lionel Hampton, a Goodwill Ambassador for the United States of America, has done more for the understanding of all nations than perhaps any other human being;

Whereas, Lionel Hampton has achieved an international reputation for his musical achievements through dedication and commitment to his art form;

Whereas, Lionel Hampton, through his steadfast dedication to making jazz and through his infectious enthusiasm and profound sincerity for this art, has made a unique contribution to American music, and one to be cherished;

Whereas, the University of Idaho has developed an outstanding School of Music because of dedicated faculty and students;

Whereas, the University of Idaho School of Music is an aesthetic asset to the University and a cultural center for the community;

Therefore, the University of Idaho School of Music is hereby proclaimed the

—Lionel Hampton School of Music
—this day, February 28, 1987.

Robert Miller, Director
SCHOOL OF MUSIC
Galen Rowe, Dean
COLLEGE OF LETTERS AND SCIENCE
Richard D. Gibb, President
UNIVERSITY OF IDAHO

That was a proud day for me. That was a great school, with twenty-five full-time and eight part-time faculty, and a bunch of talented, dedicated students. Still is a great school. I give American jazz history workshops there regularly, and I've had guys in my band out of the University of Idaho, including arranger and trombone player Chris Gulhaugen. I always did like the Midwest, and I'm pleased to have such an important reason to go back there a lot.

I still haven't given up on my dream for the school of the arts in Harlem, but there are always so many other things to do.

In May 1987 I set off with a big band for a tour of Germany, Belgium, France, the Netherlands, Italy, Switzerland, and Monaco. During the summer I played the jazz festivals in the United States. In September I appeared with Frank Sinatra for the first time. He just called me up and asked me to be on the bill with him at Carnegie Hall. I played vibraphone and drums in front of his band for the first portion of the show—"Moonglow," "Flying Home," and some of the other things my bands did. It was such short notice that I didn't have time to practice my drum rudiments as much as I would have liked. Yes, after all these years I still practice. I like to practice every day.

I turned eighty years old in 1988. They had a seventy-fifth birthday party for me at Town Hall, with Bill Cosby as the host. That's because I'd been giving out my birth date as April 20, 1913, for so long. But when you get to be my age, five years one way or the other doesn't make much difference. To me, the most important thing was how old I felt, and believe me, I felt a lot younger than my years. The secret is keeping busy, and loving what you do. Plus, doing a lot of different things.

I was into all kinds of building projects. There were plans for more houses in Harlem. I was planning to take it from the Gladys Hampton Houses down to 126th Street. I had enough blocks to build about seven hundred units, so I was going to mix up the income levels and have some high-income apartments, too. And there would be a movie theater—movies seven times a week—which would help the teenagers by giving them something to do.

We had just finished ninety-one condominiums over in Newark, and the apartments were just about all filled. Now I was worrying about Atlanta, because I had 123 acres there, and it was too far away for me to oversee any building projects the way I like to oversee them. Atlanta University wanted that land, and I was thinking of selling it to the buyer they had lined up. If the guy couldn't come up with the money, then I'd just hold onto it. One thing about land— it doesn't go anywhere. And I wasn't depending on it for my next meal. Then there were the plans I had with some other guys who are big Republican contributors to develop some land down in Jamaica and bring gambling in. I was trying to interest Donald Trump in building a hotel down there.

Nineteen eighty-eight was also a busy year for me in politics. The time had finally come when I could work for George Bush and just about know he was going to be the Republican presidential nominee. It had been a long while coming, but I never doubted it. In fact, way back in the fall of 1985 I predicted that the next GOP ticket would be Bush and Jeanne Kirkpatrick, although if Kemp kept moving up I thought he might be in the VP spot. I was a delegate from New York, and I was also on the entertainment committee for the convention—first time there *was* an entertainment committee for the convention. There were only two of us. The other guy was Joe Canizeri, who runs a big advertising agency in Washington, D.C. He and I had worked together with Rockefeller. There was a lot of planning involved in that—what we wanted to do, what type of talent to get, and that kind of thing.

I had high hopes for a Republican victory in November. I believed that the country was better off after eight years of Reagan. The country had gone more conservative, and in my opinion there was no other way for it to go. Things were really getting out of hand. They talk about getting our teenagers tuned to a better way of life and good citizenship, and then they let all this filth in. There was a time when divorce was a damnable sin. Now a couple movie stars can shack up and have a kid out of wedlock, and they're heroes.

I wasn't happy about all the scandals in the Reagan administration, but it really stemmed from the free and loose way society had been going for a long time. Corruption, lack of morality—it's in the air. Conservatism is the only way to get back on the right track.

* * *

I was still playing music. I didn't ever intend to retire. Marshall Royal says that I'm liable to just topple off the bandstand one night while playing the vibes and everybody will say, "Well, that's the way he wanted to go out." I was still doing a lot of traveling, both in the U.S.A. and abroad, bringing the universal language to people. My first trip of 1988 was down to Washington, D.C., where I received a twenty-thousand-dollar Jazz Masters Fellowship from the National Endowment for the Arts, along with Billy Taylor and Art Blakey. The panel that decided who would get the awards cited my "mastery of swing and flawless execution of the mallets" along with my teaching work and work in the area of housing. In March I performed *King David Suite* at the Mariner's Temple Baptist Church in Manhattan. In early April I inaugurated a new jazz concert hall at South Street Seaport in Manhattan. In May I did a five-week tour of Europe with a big band.

I spent June, July, and August in the U.S. and Europe with a big band, with a small side trip to Tokyo. Here's the schedule:

June 16—Waldorf-Astoria Hotel, New York, N.Y.
June 20—Academy of Music, Philadelphia, Pa.
June 21—Heinz Hall, Pittsburgh, Pa.
June 24—Salute to Louis Armstrong, JVC Jazz Festival, New York, N.Y.
June 26—Pier Six Concert Pavilion, Baltimore, Md.
June 29—JVC Jazz Festival, Avery Fisher Hall, New York, N.Y.
July 2—Saratoga Performing Arts Festival, Saratoga, N.Y.
July 3—Finger Lakes Performing Arts Center, Rochester, N.Y.
July 6–21—Nice Grande Parade du Jazz, France
July 23—Tamiment Lodge, Tamiment, Pa.
July 27—Parsippany Hills High School, Parsippany, N.J.
July 28—Buccleuch Park, New Brunswick, N.J.
July 29–August 9—Tokyo, Japan
August 10—Paper Mill Playhouse, Milburn, N.J.
August 12—Art Park Theatre, Lewiston, N.Y.
August 13—Fort Adams State Park, Newport, R.I.
August 14–20—Republican Convention, New Orleans, La.
August 21–27—Disneyland, Los Angeles, Calif.
August 28—Rippling River Resort, Welches, Oreg.
August 29—Peter Britt Pavilion, Jacksonville, Oreg.
September 1—Grant Park, Chicago, Ill.
September 2–3—Earlham College, Richmond, Ind.
September 5—Steppingstone Park, Kings Point, N.Y.

September 9—Hudson River Jazz Cruise, New York, N.Y.
September 14—Hollywood Bowl, Los Angeles, Calif.
September 24–25—Paul Masson Winery, Saratoga, Calif.
September 30—Lincoln Center Library, New York, N.Y.

I keep contemporary. Go to one of my concerts and you'll hear the latest popular songs as well as the latest jazz tunes. But you'll also hear some of my old tunes. I like the music I have played over my entire career. Charlie Mack kids me that every time he plays one of my old albums for me, I want to reissue it. Sometimes he has to remind me that I don't own the rights to that particular album.

I love to listen to other people's music, too—Louis Armstrong, Benny Goodman, Coleman Hawkins, Benny Carter, Wynton Marsalis (Wynton is another phase of trumpet playing that started with Louis Armstrong and then Red Allen), Freddie Hubbard. But it's all jazz. It went from the classics to ragtime to Dixieland to swing to bebop to cool jazz, and whatever you hear today, it's gone—and this is what you're going to hear tomorrow.

I'm working on the newest incarnation of jazz right now. I call it Synco-Jazz. It's a new expression I'm putting out. It's syncopated jazz. But it's always jazz. You can put a new dress on her, a new hat on her, but no matter what kind of clothes you put on her, she's the same old broad.

DISCOGRAPHY

Despite its size, this discography should be regarded as selective, because it does not contain every recorded performance by Lionel Hampton in existence. His recordings with clarinetist/bandleader Benny Goodman are for the most part not listed, because D. Russell Connor, the acknowledged expert on Goodman, covers those recordings in his latest bio-discography *Benny Goodman: Listen to His Legacy* (Metuchen, N.J.: Scarecrow Press, 1988). Also not listed are a number of commercially unissued private recordings. Some Armed Forces Radio programs are listed, but not all of them.

When known, matrix numbers (indicating the master record from which duplicates are made) are listed to the right of the song titles. Under the song titles are catalog numbers following the designations 78, 45, EP, LP, or CD. This discography does not list every possible issue on which a title appears. In the case of 78s, the original issue number is given, along with the most recent LP issue(s). For titles first issued on LP, the most recent and hopefully still available issue(s) is listed. CDs (compact discs) are listed primarily when it's the only way a title can be currently obtained, but CD issues are given in some cases as an alternative to the LP. Of course, there is no guarantee that a recording which was available at the time of compilation will still be so later.

The sources consulted in the compilation of this discography include the standard works (Brian Rust's *Jazz Records: 1897–1942*, 5th ed.; Jorgen G. Jepsen's *Jazz Records: 1942–1962/69*; and Walter Bruyninckx's *Sixty Years of Recorded Jazz 1917–1977*); plus several specialized discographies.

177

The complier would like to thank the following individuals for their assistance: Ed Berger, Dan Morgenstern, Phil Schaap, and John Clement.

ABBREVIATIONS

acc	accordion	g	guitar
arr	arranger	h	harmonica
as	alto sax	ldr	leader
b	string bass	org	organ
bars	baritone sax	p	piano
bcl	bass clarinet	perc	percussion
bgs	bongos	ss	soprano sax
bj	banjo	stg	Hawaiian steel guitar
bsx	bass sax	tim	timbales
btb	bass trombone	tb	trombone
btp	bass trumpet	tp	trumpet
cel	celeste	ts	tenor sax
cgs	conga drums	tu	tuba
cl	clarinet	tymp	tympani
cnt	cornet	u	ukulele
cond	conductor	v	vocalist
d	drums	vib	vibraphone
elb	electric bass guitar	vn	violin
elp	electric piano	vtb	valve trombone
fhr	French horn	w	washboard
fl	flute	x	xylophone
flgh	flugelhorn		
Au	Australian	G	German
D	Danish	It	Italian
Du	Dutch	J	Japanese
E	English	N	Norwegian
Eu	Europe	Sw	Swedish
F	French		

April 16, 1929—Culver City, CA
Paul Howard's Quality Serenaders: *Hampton* (d, v), Paul Howard (ts, dir), George Orendorff (tp), Lawrence Brown (tb, arr), Charlie Lawrence (cl, as, arr), Harvey Brooks (p), Thomas Valentine (bj, g), James Jackson (tu).

Overnight Blues   50830-1-2
78: Victor (rejected)

Quality Shout   50831-1-2-3
78: Victor (rejected)

Note: Discographies have listed this session and the sessions of April 28 and 29, 1929, as taking place in Hollywood, CA, and the 1930 sessions as taking place in Culver City, CA, whereas the reverse is true, as the studio record cards show. In 1929 Victor owned no studios on the Pacific Coast, and they rented talking-film studio facilities in Culver City from cinema producer Hal Roach. By the following year Victor had established its own studios in Hollywood. (This information from liner notes of RCA (F) FXM1 7106.)

April 28, 1929—Culver City, CA
Paul Howard's Quality Serenaders: *Hampton* (d, v), Paul Howard (ts, dir), George Orendorff (tp), Lawrence Brown (tb, arr), Charlie Lawrence (cl, as, arr), Harvey Brooks (p), Thomas Valentine (bj, g), James Jackson (tu).

The Ramble   50868-1
78: Victor V-38068 LP: RCA (F) FXM1 7106

Moonlight Blues – LH (v)   50869-2
78: Victor V-38068 LP: RCA (F) FXM1 7106,
Franklin Mint Record Society 39

Charlie's Idea   50870-2
78: Victor V-38070 LP: RCA (F) FXM1 7106

April 29, 1929—Culver City, CA
Paul Howard's Quality Serenaders: *Hampton* (d, v), Paul Howard (ts, dir), George Orendorff (tp), Lawrence Brown (tb, arr), Charlie Lawrence (cl, as, arr), Harvey Brooks (p), Thomas Valentine (bj, g), James Jackson (tu).

Overnight Blues   50830-4
78: Victor V-38070 LP: RCA (F) FXM1 7106

Overnight Blues   50830-5
78: not issued LP: RCA (F) FXM1 7106,
Meritt 1

Quality Shout   50831-5
78: Victor V-38122 LP: RCA (F) FXM1 7106

Stuff   50877-1
78: Victor V-38122 LP: RCA (F) FXM1 7106

October 21, 1929—Culver City, CA
Paul Howard's Quality Serenaders: *Hampton* (d), Paul Howard (ts, dir), George Orendorff and Earl Thompson (tp), Lawrence Brown (tb), Charlie Lawrence (cl, as, arr), Lloyd Reese (cl, as), Reginald Foresythe (p), Thomas Valentine (bj, g), James Jackson (tu).

Harlem   54477-1-2
78: Victor (rejected)

Cuttin' Up   54478-1-2
78: Victor (rejected)

February 3, 1930—Hollywood, CA
Paul Howard's Quality Serenaders: *Hampton* (d, p, v), Paul Howard (ts, dir), George Orendorff and Earl Thompson (tp), Lawrence Brown (tb), Charlie Lawrence (cl, as, arr), Lloyd Reese (cl, as), Reginald Foresythe (p), Thomas Valentine (bj, g), James Jackson (tu).

Harlem   54477-3
78: Victor 23354 LP: RCA (F) FXM1 7106

Cuttin' Up – LH (v)   54478-3
78: Victor 23420 LP: RCA (F) FXM1 7106

New Kinda Blues – unidentified trio (v)   54585-1
78: Victor 22660 LP: RCA (F) FXM1 7106

California Swing – LH (v)   54586-2
78: Victor 23354 LP: RCA (F) FXM1 7106

June 25, 1930—Hollywood, CA
Paul Howard's Quality Serenaders: *Hampton* (d), Paul Howard (ts, dir), George
Orendorff and Earl Thompson (tb), Lawrence Brown (tb), Charlie Lawrence (cl,
as, arr), Lloyd Reese (cl, as), Reginald Foresythe (p), Charlie Rousseau (g), James
Jackson (tu).

Burma Girl   54847-3
78: not issued LP: Victor LPM-10117,
RCA (F) FXM1 7106

Gettin' Ready Blues   54848-1
78: Victor 23420 LP: RCA (F) FXM1 7106

July 21, 1930—Los Angeles, CA
Louis Armstrong and His Sebastian New Cotton Club Orchestra: *Hampton* (d),
Louis Armstrong (tp, v), Leon Elkins (tp, ldr), Lawrence Brown (tb), Leon
Herriford and Willie Stark (as), William Franz (ts), L. Z. Cooper or Harvey
Brooks (p), Ceele Burke (bj, stg), Reggie Jones (tu).

I'm a Ding Dong Daddy (from Dumas) – LA (v)   404403-A
78: Okeh 41442 LP: Columbia CL 854,
Swaggie (Au) S1265, CBS (F) 88003

I'm in the Market for You – LA (v)   404404-C
78: Okeh 41442 LP: Swaggie (Au) S1265, CBS (F) 88003

Confessin' (That I Love You) – LA (v)   404405-A
78: Okeh 41448 LP: Columbia CL 854,
Swaggie (Au) S1265, CBS (F) 88003

If I Could Be with You One Hour Tonight – LA (v)   404406-A
78: Okeh 41448 LP: Columbia CL 854, Swaggie (Au) S1265,
CBS (F) 88003

October 9, 1930—Los Angeles, CA
Louis Armstrong and His Sebastian New Cotton Club Orchestra: *Hampton* (d),
Louis Armstrong (tp, v), George Orendorff and Harold Scott (tp), Luther
"Sonny" Craven (tb), Les Hite (as, bars, ldr), Marvin Johnson (as), Charlie Jones
(cl, ts), Henry Prince (p), Bill Perkins (bj, g), Joe Bailey (b).

Body and Soul – LA (v)   404411-D
78: Okeh 41468 LP: Columbia CL 854, Swaggie (Au) S1265,
CBS (F) 88004

October 16, 1930—Los Angeles, CA
Louis Armstrong and His Sebastian New Cotton Club Orchestra: *Hampton* (d,
vib), Louis Armstrong (tp, v), George Orendorff and Harold Scott (tp), Luther

"Sonny" Craven (tb), Les Hite (as, bars, ldr), Marvin Johnson (as), Charlie Jones (cl, ts), Henry Prince (p), Bill Perkins (bj, g), Joe Bailey (b, tu).

Memories of You – LA (v)   404412-D
78: Okeh 41463 LP: Swaggie (Au) S1265,
CBS (F) 88004, Franklin Mint Record Society 39

You're Lucky to Me – LA (v)   404413-C
78: Okeh 41463 LP: Swaggie (Au) S1265, CBS (F) 88004

Note: Some discographies list a take E for matrices 404412 and 404413, but those takes do not exist.

December 23, 1930—Los Angeles, CA
Louis Armstrong and His Sebastian New Cotton Club Orchestra: *Hampton* (d), Louis Armstrong (tp, v), George Orendorff and Harold Scott (tp), Luther "Sonny" Craven (tb), Les Hite (as, bars, ldr), Marvin Johnson (as), Charlie Jones (cl, ts), Henry Prince (p), Bill Perkins (bj, g), Joe Bailey (b, tu).

Sweethearts on Parade – LA (v)   404417-A
78: Columbia 2688-D LP: Swaggie (Au) S1265,
CBS (F) 88004

You're Driving Me Crazy – LA (v)   404418-B
78: Okeh 41478 LP: Swaggie (Au) S1265

You're Driving Me Crazy – LA (v)   404418-C
78: Okeh 41478 LP: Swaggie (Au) S1265, CBS (F) 88004

The Peanut Vendor – LA (v)   404419-B
78: Okeh 41478 LP: Swaggie (Au) S1265, CBS (F) 88004

Note: Opening dialogue on 404418 is by Louis Armstrong and Lionel Hampton.

March 9, 1931—Los Angeles, CA
Louis Armstrong and his Sebastian New Cotton Club Orchestra: *Hampton* (d, vib), Louis Armstrong (tp, v), George Orendorff and Harold Scott (tp), Luther "Sonny" Craven (tb), Les Hite (as, bars, ldr), Marvin Johnson (as), Charlie Jones (cl, ts), Henry Prince (p), Bill Perkins (bj, g) Joe Bailey (tu).

Just a Gigolo – LA (v)   404420-A
78: Okeh 41486 LP: Columbia KG 31564, Swaggie (Au) S1265,
CBS (F) 88004

Shine – LA (v)   404421-C
78: Okeh 41486 LP: Columbia CL 854, Swaggie (Au) S1265,
CBS (F) 88004

August 18, 1936—Los Angeles, CA
Louis Armstrong with the Polynesians: *Hampton* (d, vib), Louis Armstrong (tp, v), Sam Koki (stg), George Archer and Harry Baty (g, v), Andy Iona (u, v), Joe Nawahi (b).

To You, Sweetheart, Aloha – LA, GA, HB, AI (v)   DLA-581-A
78: Decca 914 LP: MCA 1326

On a Cocoanut Island – LA, GA, HB, AI (v)   DLA-582-A
78: Decca 914 LP: MCA 1326

August 24, 1936—Los Angeles, CA
Teddy Wilson and His Orchestra: *Hampton* (vib), Teddy Wilson (p), Gordon
Griffin (tp), Benny Goodman (cl), Vido Musso (ts), Allan Reuss (g), Harry
Goodman (b), Gene Krupa (d), Helen Ward [as Vera Lane] (v).

You Came to My Rescue – HW (v)   LA-1158-A
78: Brunswick 7739 LP: Hep (E) 1014

Here's Love in Your Eyes – HW (v)   LA-1159-A
78: Brunswick 7739 LP: Columbia CJ 40833, Hep (E) 1014

Benny Goodman (cl) out; Red Harper (v) replaces Ward:

You Turned the Tables on Me – RH (v)   LA-1160-A
78: Brunswick 7736

Sing, Baby, Sing – RH (v)   LA-1161-A
78: Brunswwick 7736

February 8, 1937—New York, NY
Lionel Hampton and His Orchestra: *Hampton* (vib, d, v), Ziggy Elman (tp),
Hymie Schertzer and George Koenig (as), Vido Musso and Arthur Rollini (ts),
Jess Stacy (p), Allan Reuss (g), Harry Goodman (b), Gene Krupa (d).

My Last Affair – LH (v)   04582-1
78: Victor 25527 LP: Bluebird AXM6-5536,
RCA (F) PM 42393, RCA (F) NL 89583

My Last Affair – LH (v)   04582-2
78: not issued LP: RCA (F) NL 89583

Jivin' the Vibes   04583-1
the original label reads: "Jivin' the Vibres"
78: Victor 25535 LP: Bluebird AXM6-5536,
RCA (F) PM 42393, RCA (F) NL 89583

The Mood That I'm In – LH (v)   04584-1
78: Victor 25527 LP: Bluebird AXM6-5536,
RCA (F) PM 42393, RCA (F) NL 89583

Stomp [aka "Hampton Stomp"]   04585-1
78: Victor 25535 LP: Bluebird AXM6-5536,
RCA (F) PM 42393, RCA (F) NL 89583

April 14, 1937—New York, NY
Lionel Hampton and His Orchestra: *Hampton* (vib, v), Cootie Williams (tp),
Lawrence Brown (tb), Mezz Mezzrow (cl), Johnny Hodges (as), Jess Stacy (p),
Allan Reuss (g), John Kirby (b), Cozy Cole (d).

Buzzin' 'Round with the Bee – LH (v)   07792-3R
78: Victor 25575 LP: Bluebird AXM6-5536,
RCA (F) PM 42393, RCA (F) NL 89583
CD: Bluebird 6458-2-RB

Whoa Babe – LH (v)   07793-3R
78: Victor 25575 LP: Bluebird AXM6-5536,
RCA (F) PM 42393, RCA (F) NL 89583,
RCA (Eu) CL 89806

Stompology   07794-1
78: Victor 25601 LP: Bluebird AXM6-5536,
RCA (F) PM 42393, RCA (F) NL 89583
CD: Bluebird 6458-2-RB

April 26, 1937—New York, NY
Lionel Hampton and His Orchestra: *Hampton* (vib, p, d, v), Buster Bailey (cl),
Johnny Hodges (as), Jess Stacy (p), Allan Reuss (g), John Kirby (b), Cozy
Cole (d).

On the Sunny Side of the Street – LH (v)   07864-1
78: Victor 25592 LP: Bluebird AXM6-5536,
RCA (F) PM 42393, RCA (F) NL 89583, RCA (Eu)
CL 89806, Franklin Mint Record Society 16
CD: Bluebird 6458-2-RB

Rhythm, Rhythm ["I Got Rhythm"]   07865-1
78: Victor 25586 LP: Bluebird AXM6-5536,
RCA (F) PM 42393, RCA (F) NL 89583

China Stomp ["Chinatown, My Chinatown"]   07866-1
78: Victor 25586 LP: Bluebird AXM6-5536,
RCA (F) PM 42393, RCA (F) NL 89583

I Know That You Know   07867-1
78: Victor 25592 LP: Bluebird AXM6-5536,
RCA (F) PM 42393, RCA (F) NL 89583

August 16, 1937—Hollywood, CA
Lionel Hampton and His Orchestra: *Hampton* (vib, p, d, v), Jonah Jones (tp),
Eddie Barefield (cl), Clyde Hart (p), Bobby Bennett (g), Mack Walker (b), Cozy
Cole (d).

I'm Confessin' – LH (v)   09644-1
78: Victor 25658 LP: Bluebird AXM6-5536,
RCA (F) PM 42393, RCA (F) NL 89583
CD: Bluebird 6458-2-RB

Drum Stomp ["Crazy Rhythm"]   09645-1
78: Victor 25658 LP: Bluebird AXM6-5536,
RCA (F) PM 42393, RCA (F) NL 89583

Piano Stomp ["Shine"]   09646-1
78: Victor 25666 LP: Bluebird AXM6-5536,
RCA (F) PM 42393, RCA (F) NL 89583, RCA (Eu)
CL 89806, Franklin Mint Record Society 39
CD: Bluebird 6458-2-RB

I Surrender Dear   09647-1
78: Victor 25666 LP: Bluebird AXM6-5536,
RCA (F) PM 42393, RCA (F) NL 89583

September 5, 1937—Hollywood, CA
Lionel Hampton and His Orchestra: *Hampton* (vib, p, v), Ziggy Elman (tp), Vido Musso (cl, ts), Arthur Rollini (ts), Jess Stacy (p), Allan Reuss (g), Johnny Miller (b), Cozy Cole (d).

The Object of My Affection – LH (v)   09680-1
78: not issued LP: RCA (F) NL 89583

The Object of My Affection – LH (v)   09680-2
78: Victor 25699 LP: Bluebird AXM6-5536,
RCA (F) PM 42393, RCA (F) NL 89583

Judy – LH (v)   09681-2
78: Victor 25699 LP: Bluebird AXM6-5536,
RCA (F) PM 42393, RCA (F) NL 89583

Baby, Won't You Please Come Home – LH (v)   09682-2
78: Victor 25674 LP: Bluebird AXM6-5536,
RCA (F) PM 42393, RCA (F) NL 89583

Everybody Loves My Baby – LH (v)   09683-2
78: Victor 25682 LP: Bluebird AXM6-5536,
RCA (F) PM 42393, RCA (F) NL 89583
CD: Bluebird 6458-2-RB

After You've Gone – LH (v)   09684-1
78: Victor 25674 LP: Bluebird AXM6-5536,
RCA (F) PM 42393, RCA (F) NL 89583

I Just Couldn't Take It, Baby – LH (v)   09685-1
78: Victor 25682 LP: Bluebird AXM6-5536,
RCA (F) PM 42393, RCA (F) NL 89583

January 18, 1938—New York, NY
Lionel Hampton and His Orchestra: *Hampton* (vib, v), Cootie Williams (tp), Johnny Hodges (as), Edgar Sampson (bars, arr), Jess Stacy (p), Allan Reuss (g), Billy Taylor (b), Sonny Greer (d).

You're My Ideal – LH (v)   018335-1
78: Victor 25771 LP: Bluebird AXM6-5536,
RCA (F) PM 42393, RCA (F) NL 89583

The Sun Will Shine Tonight – LH (v)   018336-1
78: Victor 25771 LP: Bluebird AXM6-5536,
RCA (F) PM 42393, RCA (F) NL 89583

Ring Dem Bells – LH (v)   018337-1
78: Victor 25889 LP: Bluebird AXM6-5536,
RCA (F) PM 42393, RCA (F) NL 89583,
Franklin Mint Record Society 39
CD: Bluebird 6458-2-RB

Don't Be That Way – ES (arr)   018338-1
78: Victor 26173 LP: Bluebird AXM6-5536,
RCA (F) PM 42393, RCA (F) NL 89583, RCA (Eu)
CL 89806 CD: Bluebird 6458-2-RB

July 21, 1938—New York, NY
Lionel Hampton and His Orchestra: *Hampton* (vib, v), Harry James (tp), Benny
Carter (cl, as, arr), Dave Matthews (as), Herschel Evans and Babe Russin (ts),
Billy Kyle (p), John Kirby (b), Jo Jones (d).

I'm in the Mood for Swing   024065-1
78: Victor 26011 LP: Bluebird AXM6-5536,
RCA (F) PM 42393, RCA (F) NL 89583, RCA (F)
PM 42406, RCA (Eu) CL 89806, Franklin Mint
Record Society 39 CD: Bluebird 6458-2-RB

Shoe Shiner's Drag   024066-1
78: Victor 26011 LP: Bluebird AXM6-5536,
RCA (F) PM 42393, RCA (F) NL 89583, RCA (Eu)
CL 89806 CD: Bluebird 6458-2-RB

Any Time at All – LH (v)   024067-1
78: Victor 26039 LP: Bluebird AXM6-5536,
RCA (F) PM 42393, RCA (F) NL 89583

Muskrat Ramble   024068-1
78: Victor 26017 LP: Bluebird AXM6-5536,
RCA (F) PM 42393, RCA (F) NL 89583, RCA (Eu)
CL 89806 CD: Bluebird 6458-2-RB

September 20, 1938–Chicago, IL
Lionel Hampton and Jess Stacy piano duet.

Space, Man
LP: MGM E/X-3789

October 11, 1938—Chicago, IL
Lionel Hampton and His Orchestra: *Hampton* (vib, p, v), Walter Fuller (tp),
Omer Simeon (cl, as), George Oldham (as), Budd Johnson and Robert Crowder
(ts), Spencer Odom (p), Jesse Simpkins (b), Alvin Burroughs (d).

Down Home Jump   025866-1
78: Victor 26114 LP: Bluebird AXM6-5536,
RCA (F) PM 42393, RCA (F) NL 89583
CD: Bluebird 6458-2-RB

Rock Hill Special   025867-1
78: Victor 26114 LP: Bluebird AXM6-5536,
RCA (F) PM 42393, RCA (F) NL 89583

Fiddle Diddle – LH (v)   025868-1
78: Victor 26173 LP: Bluebird AXM6-5536,
RCA (F) PM 42393, RCA (F) NL 89583

November 12, 1938—New York, NY
Eddie Condon and His Band: *Hampton* (d), Bobby Hackett (cnt), Vernon Brown
(tb), Pee Wee Russell (cl), Bud Freeman (ts), Joe Bushkin (p), Eddie Condon (g),
Artie Shapiro.

Sunday   23706-1
78: Commodore 515 LP: Commodore XFL 16568,
Commodore (G) 6.25526 AG, Mosaic MR 23-123

Sunday   23706-2
78: not issued LP: Commodore XFL 16568,
Commodore (G) 6.25526 AG, Mosaic MR 23-123

California, Here I Come   23707-1A
78: not issued LP: Commodore XFL 16568,
Commodore (G) 6.25526 AG, Mosaic MR 23-123

California, Here I Come   23707-2
78: Commodore 515 LP: Commodore XFL 16568,
Commodore (G) 6.25526 AG, Mosaic MR 23-123

April 3, 1939—New York, NY
Lionel Hampton and His Orchestra: *Hampton* (vib, v), Irving Randolph (tp),
Hymie Schertzer (bcl, as), Russell Procope (as), Jerry Jerome and Chu Berry (ts),
Clyde Hart (p), Allan Reuss (g), Milt Hinton (b), Cozy Cole (d).

I Can Give You Love – LH (v)   035392-1
78: Victor 26343 LP: Bluebird AXM6-5536,
RCA (F) PM 42393, RCA (F) NL 89481 (2)

High Society – Fred Norman (arr)   035393-1
78: Victor 26209 LP: Bluebird AXM6-5536,
RCA (F) PM 42393

It Don't Mean a Thing, If It Ain't Got That Swing – LH (v)   035394-1
78: Victor 26254 LP: Bluebird AXM6-5536,
RCA (F) PM 42393 CD: Bluebird 6458-2-RB

Johnny Get Your Horn and Blow it – LH (v)   035395-1
78: Victor 26343 LP: Bluebird AXM6-5536,
RCA (F) PM 42393

April 5, 1939—New York, NY
Lionel Hampton and His Orchestra: *Hampton* (vib, p, v), Chu Berry (ts), Clyde
Hart (p), Allan Reuss (g), Milt Hinton (b), Cozy Cole (d).

Sweethearts on Parade – LH (v)   035703-1
78: Victor 26209 LP: Bluebird AXM6-5536,
RCA (F) PM 42393, RCA (F) NL 89481 (2)

Shufflin' at the Hollywood   035704-1
78: not issued LP: Victor LPM-10024,
Bluebird AXM6-5536, RCA (F) PM 42393

Shufflin' at the Hollywood   035704-2
78: Victor 26254 LP: Bluebird AXM6-5536,
RCA (F) PM 42393, RCA (F) NL 89481 (2),
RCA (Eu) CL 89806, Franklin Mint Record
Society 39 CD: Bluebird 6458-2-RB

Denison Swing   035705-1
78: Victor 26233 LP: Bluebird AXM6-5536,
RCA (F) PM 42393, RCA (F) NL 89481 (2),
Franklin Mint Record Society 39

CD: Bluebird 6458-2-RB

Wizzin' the Wizz   035706-2
78: Victor 26233 LP: Bluebird AXM6-5536,
RCA (F) PM 42393, RCA (F) NL 89481 (2)

Note: RCA (F) NL 89481 (2) lists "Wizzin' the Wizz" as matrix no. 035706-1,
but aurally it's no different than the commonly listed matrix no. 035706-2.

June 9, 1939—New York, NY
Lionel Hampton and His Orchestra: *Hampton* (vib, d, v), Ziggy Elman (tp),
Hymie Schertzer (as), Russell Procope (as, ss), Jerry Jerome and Chu Berry (ts),
Clyde Hart (p), Danny Barker (g), Milt Hinton (b), Cozy Cole (d).

If It's Good (Then I Want It) – LH (v)   037614-1
78: not issued LP: Victor LPM 6702-5,
Bluebird AXM6-5536, RCA (F) PM 42393

Stand By! for Further Announcements (and More Good News) –   037615-1
LH (v)
78: Victor 26296 LP: Bluebird AXM6-5536,
RCA (F) PM 42393

Ain't Cha Comin' Home   037616-1
78: Victor 26362 LP: Bluebird AXM6-5536,
RCA (F) PM 42393, RCA (F) NL 89481 (2)
CD: Bluebird 6458-2-RB

Big Wig in the Wigwam – vocal by ensemble   037617-1
78: Victor 26296 LP: Bluebird AXM6-5536,
RCA (F) PM 42393

June 13, 1939—New York, NY
Lionel Hampton and His Orchestra: *Hampton* (vib, p, v), Rex Stewart (cnt),
Lawrence Brown (tb), Harry Carney (bars), Clyde Hart (p), Billy Taylor (b),
Sonny Greer (d).

Memories of You   037630-1
78: Victor 26304 LP: Bluebird AXM6-5536,
RCA (F) PM 42393

The Jumpin' Jive – LH (v)   037631-1
78: Victor 26304 LP: Bluebird AXM6-5536,
RCA (F) PM 42393

Twelfth Street Rag   037632-1
78: Victor 26362 LP: Bluebird AXM6-5536,
RCA (F) PM 42417 CD: Bluebird 6458-2-RB

September 11, 1939—New York, NY
Lionel Hampton and His Orchestra: *Hampton* (vib, v); Dizzy Gillespie (tp);
Benny Carter (as, arr); Coleman Hawkins, Chu Berry, Ben Webster (ts); Clyde
Hart (p); Charlie Christian (g); Milt Hinton (b); Cozy Cole (d).

When Lights Are Low   041406-1
78: Victor 26371 LP: Bluebird AXM6-5536,
RCA (F) PM 42417, RCA (Eu) CL 89806

CD: Bluebird 6458-2-RB

When Lights Are Low   041406-2
78: not issued LP: Bluebird AXM6-5536,
RCA (F) PM 42417, RCA (F) PM 42406,
Franklin Mint Record Society 39

One Sweet Letter From You – LH (v)   ·   041407-1
78: Victor 26393 LP: Bluebird AXM6-5536,
RCA (F) PM 42417 CD: Bluebird 6458-2-RB

Hot Mallets   041408-1
78: Victor 26371 LP: Bluebird AXM6-5536,
RCA (F) PM 42417, RCA (F) NL 89481 (2),
RCA (Eu) CL 89806, Franklin Mint Record
Society 41 CD: Bluebird 6458-2-RB

Early Session Hop   041409-1
78: Victor 26393 LP: Bluebird AXM6-5536,
RCA (F) PM 42417 RCA CD: Bluebird 6458-2-RB

October 12, 1939—New York, NY
Lionel Hampton and His Orchestra: *Hampton* (vib, v), Henry "Red" Allen (tp)
J. C. Higginbotham (tb), Earl Bostic (as), Clyde Hart (p), Charlie Christian (g),
Artie Bernstein (b), Sidney Catlett (d).

I'm on My Way from You – LH (v)   042941-1
78: Victor 26476 LP: Bluebird AXM6-5536,
RCA (F) PM 42417

Haven't Named It Yet   042942-1
78: Victor 26476 LP: Bluebird AXM6-5536,
RCA (F) PM 42417, Franklin Mint Record
Society 73

The Heebie-Jeebies Are Rockin' the Town – LH (v)   042943-1
78: Victor 26423 LP: Bluebird AXM6-5536,
RCA (F) PM 42417

The Heebie-Jeebies Are Rockin' the Town – LH (v)   042943-2
78: Victor 26423 LP: Bluebird AXM6-5536,
RCA (F) PM 42417

October 30, 1939—New York, NY
Lionel Hampton and His Orchestra: *Hampton* (vib, d, p, v), Ziggy Elman (tp),
Toots Mondello (cl, as), Ben Webster and Jerry Jerome (ts), Clyde Hart (p), Al
Casey (g), Artie Bernstein (b), Slick Jones (d).

The Munson Street Breakdown   043246-1
78: Victor 26453 LP: Bluebird AXM6-5536,
RCA (F) PM 42417

I've Found a New Baby   043247-1
78: Victor 26447 LP: Bluebird AXM6-5536,
RCA (F) PM 42417

I Can't Get Started   043248-1
78: Victor 26453 LP: Bluebird AXM6-5536,
RCA (F) PM 42417

Four or Five Times – LH (v)   043249-1
78: Victor 25477 LP: Bluebird AXM6-5536,
RCA (F) PM 42417

Gin for Christmas   043250-1
78: Victor 26423 LP: Bluebird AXM6-5536,
RCA (F) PM 42417

October 31, 1939—New York, NY
Ida Cox (v) acc. by Her All-Star Band: *Hampton* (d), Hot Lips Page (tp), J. C.
Higginbotham (tb), Edmond Hall (cl), James P. Johnson (p), Charlie Christian
(g), Artie Bernstein (b).

Deep Sea Blues   25509-1
78: Vocalion 05336 LP: Queen-Disc (It) Q-048

Deep Sea Blues   25509-2
78: not issued LP: Meritt 5

One Hour Mama   25511-1
78: not issued LP: Meritt 5

Note: Hampton does not appear on matrix no 25510, "Death Letter Blues."

October 31, 1939—New York, NY (same session; different studio)
Ida Cox (v) acc. by Her All-Star Band: *Hampton* (d), Oran "Hot Lips" Page (tp),
J. C. Higginbotham (tb), Edmond Hall (cl), Fletcher Henderson (p), Charlie
Christian (g), Artie Bernstein (b).

Four-Day Creep   26239-A
78: Vocalion 05298 LP: Queen-Disc (It) Q-048

Pink Slip Blues   26240-A
78: Vocalion 05258 LP: Queen-Disc (It) Q-048

Hard Times Blues   26241-A
78: Vocalion 05298 LP: Queen-Disc (It) Q-048

Take Him Off My Mind   26242-A
78: Vocalion 05258 LP: Queen-Disc (It) Q-048

December 21, 1939—New York, NY
Lionel Hampton and His Orchestra: *Hampton* (vib), Benny Carter (tp), Edmond
Hall (cl), Coleman Hawkins (ts), Joe Sullivan (p), Freddie Green (g), Artie
Bernstein (b), Zutty Singleton (d).

Dinah   046024-1
78: Victor 26557 LP: Bluebird AXM6-5536,
RCA (F) PM 42417

Dinah   046024-2
78: not issued LP: Victor LPV-501,
Bluebird AXM6-5536, RCA (F) PM 42417

My Buddy   046025-1
78: Victor 26608 LP: Bluebird AXM6-5536,
RCA (F) PM 42417

Singin' the Blues till My Daddy Comes Home   046026-1
78: Victor 26557 LP: Bluebird AXM6-5536,
RCA (F) PM 42417

February 26, 1940—Chicago, IL
Lionel Hampton and His Orchestra: *Hampton* (vib), Ziggy Elman (tp), Toots
Mondello and Buff Estes (as), Jerry Jerome and Budd Johnson (ts), Spencer
Odom (p), Ernest Ashley (g), Artie Bernstein (b), Nick Fatool (d).

Shades of Jade   044724-1
78: Victor 26604 LP: Bluebird AXM6-5536,
RCA (F) PM 42417

Till Tom Special   044725-1
78: Victor 26604 LP: Bluebird AXM6-5536,
RCA (F) PM 42417, Smithsonian DMM6-0610

Flying Home   044726-1
78: Victor 26595 LP: Bluebird AXM6-5536,
RCA (F) PM 42417 RCA (Eu) CL 89806

Save It Pretty Mama   044727-1
78: Victor 26595 LP: Bluebird AXM6-5536,
RCA (F) PM 42417

Tempo and Swing   004728-1
78: Victor 26608 LP: Bluebird AXM6-5536,
RCA (F) PM 42417

May 9, 1940—Los Angeles, CA
Fred Astaire (v, tap dancing) acc. by the Benny Goodman Orchestra: *Hampton*
(vib), Benny Goodman (cl), Johnny Guarnieri (p), Charlie Christian (g), Artie
Bernstein (b), Nick Fatool (d).

Just Like Taking Candy from a Baby   26809-A
78: Columbia 35517

May 10, 1940—Hollywood, CA
Lionel Hampton and His Orchestra: *Hampton* (vib, p, d), Nat "King" Cole (p),
Oscar Moore (g), Wesley Prince (b), Al Spieldock (d), Helen Forrest (v).

House of Morgan   049641-1
78: Victor 26751 LP: Bluebird AXM6-5536,
RCA (F) PM 42417

I'd Be Lost without You – HF (v)   049675-1
78: Victor 26751 LP: Bluebird AXM6-5536,
RCA (F) PM 42417

Central Avenue Breakdown   049676-1
78: Victor 26652 LP: Bluebird AXM6-5536,

RCA (F) PM 42417

Jack the Bellboy   049677-1
78: Victor 26652 LP: Bluebird AXM6-5536,
RCA (F) PM 42417

Ca. May/June 1940—Savoy Ballroom, New York, NY ("Make Believe Ballroom" jam session)
Hampton (d), Roy Eldridge (tp), Harry James (tp), Tommy Dorsey (tb), Coleman Hawkins (ts), and others.

King Porter Stomp
LP: Jazz Society AA 504

July 17, 1940—Hollywood, CA
Lionel Hampton and His Orchestra: *Hampton* (vib), Nat "King" Cole (p), Oscar Moore (g), Wesley Prince (b), Al Spieldock (d), Hampton Rhythm Boys (v).

Dough-Rey-Mi – HRB (v)   049932-1
78: Victor 26696 LP: Bluebird AXM6-5536,
RCA (F) PM 42417

Jivin' with Jarvis – HRB (v)   049933-1
78: Victor 26724 LP: Bluebird AXM6-5536,
RCA (F) PM 42417, RCA (Eu) CL 89806

Blue   049934-1
78: Victor 26724 LP: Bluebird AXMG-5536,
RCA (F) PM 42417, Franklin Mint Record
Society 49

I Don't Stand a Ghost of a Chance   049935-1
78: Victor 26696 LP: Bluebird AXM6-5536,
RCA (F) PM 42417

August 19, 1940—New York, NY
Hampton (vib), Douglas Daniels (tiple), Teddy Bunn (g), Hayes Alvis (b).

Tempo and Swing
LP: Jazz Panarama 2, Beppo 14800, Swing House (E) SWH-43

Flying Home
LP: Jazz Panarama 2, Beppo 14800, Swing House (E) SWH-43

August 21, 1940—New York, NY
Lionel Hampton and His Orchestra: *Hampton* (vib), Marlowe Morris (p), Teddy Bunn (g), Douglas Daniels (tiple, v), Hayes Alvis (b), Kaiser Marshall (d).

Just for Laffs   055532-1
78: Victor 26793 LP: Bluebird AXM6-5536,
RCA (F) PM 42417

Martin on Every Block   055533-1
78: Victor 26739 LP: Bluebird AXM6-5536,
RCA (F) PM 42417

Pig Foot Sonata   055534-1
78: Victor 26793 LP: Bluebird AXM6-5536,
RCA (F) PM 42417

Charlie Was a Sailor – DD (v)   055535-1
78: Victor 26739 LP: Bluebird AXM6-5536,
RCA (F) PM 42417

December 19, 1940—Hollywood, CA
Lionel Hampton and His Sextette: *Hampton* (vib), Marshall Royal (cl, as), Ray
Perry (vn), Sir Charles Thompson (p), Irving Ashby (g), Vernon Alley (b), Lee
Young (d, v), Evelyn Myers (v), Hampton Rhythm Girls (v).

Lost Love – LY & HRG (v)   055228-1
78: Victor 27278 LP: RCA (F) 741077

Lost Love – LY & HRG (v)   055228-2
78: Victor 27278 LP: Bluebird AXM6-5536,
RCA (F) PM 42417

I Nearly Lost My Mind – EM (v)   055229-1
78: Victor 27316 LP: Bluebird AXM6-5536,
RCA (F) PM 42417

Altitude   055230-1
78: Victor 27316 LP: Bluebird AXM6-5536,
RCA (F) PM 42417

Fiddle-Dee-Dee   055231-1
78: Victor 27364 LP: Bluebird AXM6-5536,
RCA (F) PM 42417

December 20, 1940—Hollywood, CA
Lionel Hampton and His Sextette: *Hampton* (vib, p, v), remaining personnel as
above.

Bogo Jo – LH & HRG (v)   055234-1
78: Victor 27341 LP: Bluebird AXM6-5536,
RCA (F) PM 42417

Open House   055235-1
78: Victor 27341 LP: Bluebird AXM6-5536,
RCA (F) PM 42417

Smart Alec   055236-1
78: Victor 27278 LP: Bluebird AXM6-5536,
RCA (F) PM 42417

Hampton replaces Thompson on piano:

Bouncing at the Beacon   055237-1
78: Victor 27364 LP: Bluebird AXM6-5536,
RCA (F) PM 42417

April 8, 1941—Chicago, IL
Lionel Hampton and His Orchestra: *Hampton* (vib, d, v), Karl George (tp),
Marshall Royal (cl, as), Ray Perry (vn), Sir Charles Thompson (p), Irving Ashby
(g), Vernon Alley (b), Shadow Wilson (d), Rubel Blakely (v).

Give Me Some Skin – LH & choir (v)   064055-2R
78: Victor 27409 LP: Bluebird AXM6-5536,
RCA (F) PM 42417

Now That You're Mine – RB (v)   064056-1
78: Victor 27529 LP: Bluebird AXM6-5536,
RCA (F) PM 42417

Chasin' with Chase   064057-1
78: Victor 27529 LP: Bluebird AXM6-5536,
RCA (F) PM 42417

Three-Quarter Boogie   064058-1
78: Victor 27409 LP: Bluebird AXM6-5536,
RCA (F) PM 42417, RCA (Eu) CL 89806

December 24, 1941—New York, NY
Lionel Hampton and His Orchestra: *Hampton* (vib, v); Karl George, Ernie Royal,
Joe Newman (tp); Fred Beckett, Sonny Craven, Harry Sloan (tb); Marshall Royal
(cl, as); Ray Perry (as, vn); Dexter Gordon, Illinois Jacquet (ts); Jack McVea
(bars); Milton Buckner (p); Irving Ashby (g); Vernon Alley (b); George Jenkins
(d); Rubel Blakely (v).

Just for You – RB (v)   70100-A
78: Decca 18265

Southern Echoes – LH (v)   70101-A
78: Decca 18285 LP: MCA (F) 510 140

My Wish – RB (v)   70102-A
78: Decca 18265

Nola   70103-A
78: Decca 18285

March 2, 1942—New York, NY
Lionel Hampton Sextet: probable personnel—*Hampton* (vib, v), Marshall Royal
(cl, as), Ray Perry (bars, vn), Milton Buckner (p), Irving Ashby (g), Vernon Alley
(b), George Jenkins (d).

Royal Family   70416-A
78: not issued LP: MCA 1315, Ajazz-470, Affinity
(E) AFS 1037

I Can't Believe That You're in Love with Me   70417-A
78: not issued LP: MCA 1315, Ajazz-470

Blues in the News   70418-A
78: not issued LP: MCA 1315, Ajazz-470

Exactly Like You – LH (v)   70419-A
78: not issued LP: MCA 1315, Ajazz-470

May 26, 1942—New York, NY
Lionel Hampton and His Orchestra: *Hampton* (vib); Eddie Hutchinson, Manny
Klein, Ernie Royal, Jack Trainer (tp); Fred Beckett, Sonny Craven, Harry Sloan
(tb); Marshall Royal (cl, as); Ray Perry (as, vn); Eddie Barefield, Illinois Jacquet

(ts); Jack McVea (bars); Milt Buckner (p); Irving Ashby (g); Vernon Alley (b); Lee Young (d) Rubel Blakely (v).

Now I Know – RB (v) 70771-A
78: Decca 18535 LP: Ajazz-470

Half a Loaf Is Better Than None – RB (v) 70772-A
78: Decca 18535 LP: Ajazz-470

Flying Home – LH (arr) 70773-A
78: Decca 18394 LP: MCA 2-4075, MCA 1315,
Smithsonian DMM6-0610, Ajazz-470,
Affinity (E) AFS 1000

In the Bag 70774-A
78: Decca 18394 LP: MCA 1315, Ajazz-470,
Affinity (E) AFS 1017

December 29, 1943—New York, NY
Dinah Washington (v) with Lionel Hampton Sextet: *Hampton* (d, p), Joe Morris (tp), Rudy Rutherford (cl), Arnett Cobb (ts), Milt Buckner (p), Vernon King (b), Fred Radcliffe (d).

Evil Gal Blues LHS 1
78: Keynote K605 LP: Keynote (J) 830 121-1

I Know How to Do It LHS 2
78: Keynote K606 LP: Keynote (J) 830 121-1

Salty Papa Blues LHS 3
78: Keynote K606 LP: Keynote (J) 830 121-1

Homeward Bound LHS 4
78: Keynote K605 LP: Keynote (J) 830 121-1

January 18, 1944—New York, NY (Metropolitan Opera House)
Esquire All-American Jazz Stars: *Hampton* (vib), Roy Eldridge (tp), Jack Teagarden (tb), Barney Bigard (cl), Coleman Hawkins (ts), Art Tatum (p), Al Casey (g), Oscar Pettiford (b), Big Sid Catlett (d).

Tea for Two VP472
LP: Radiola 2MR-5051

Note: Some discographies list Hampton on "Esquire Bounce," but he does not play on this number. The announcer introduces him with other members of the group before "Esquire Bounce," and Hampton plays a two-bar break.

January 18, 1944—Metropolitan Opera House, New York, NY
Esquire All-American Jazz Stars: *Hampton* (vib), Louis Armstrong (tp), Roy Eldridge (tp), Barney Bigard (cl), Coleman Hawkins (ts), Art Tatum (p), Al Casey (g), Oscar Pettiford (b), Big Sid Catlett (d).

Flying Home (Part 1) JDB102
LP: Radiola 2MR-5051

Flying Home (Part 2) JDB103
LP: Radiola 2MR-5051

Note: "Flying Home" is also known as "Flying on a V-Disc."

January 18, 1944—Metropolitan Opera House, New York, NY
Lionel Hampton (d) and Big Sid Catlett (d).

Drum Duet
LP: Radiola 2MR-5051

January 18, 1944—Metropolitan Opera House, New York, NY
Esquire All-American Jazz Stars: *Hampton* (vib), Red Norvo (vib), Louis
Armstrong (tp), Roy Eldridge (tp), Jack Teagarden (tb), Barney Bigard (cl),
Coleman Hawkins (ts), Art Tatum (p), Al Casey (g), Oscar Pettiford (b), Big Sid
Catlett (d).

Jammin' the Blues
LP: Radiola 2MR-5051

National Anthem
LP: Radiola 2MR-5051

Notes: "Jammin' the Blues" is also known as "Jammin' the Vibes" and "Vibes
Blues."

March 2, 1944—New York, NY
Lionel Hampton and His Orchestra: *Hampton* (vib, p); Cat Anderson, Lammar
Wright, Jr., Roy McCoy, Joe Morris (tp); Al Hayse, Mitchell "Booty" Wood,
Fred Beckett (tb); Earl Bostic, Gus Evans (as); Al Sears, Arnett Cobb (ts);
Charles Fowlkes (bars); Milt Buckner (p); Eric Miller (g); Vernon King (b);
Fred Radcliffe (d).

Loose Wig – Frank Davenport (arr)   71825-A
78: Decca 18669 LP: MCA 1315, Ajazz-470

Chop Chop – JM (arr)   71826-A
78: Decca 18613 LP: MCA 1315, Ajazz-470

Flying Home (No. 2)   71827-A
78: Decca 23639 LP: MCA 1315, Ajazz-470,
Affinity (E) AFS 1000

Hamp's Boogie-Woogie   71828-A
78: Decca 18613 LP: MCA 2-4075, MCA 1315,
Ajazz-470, Affinity (E) AFS 1000

March 10, 1944—New York, NY
Lionel Hampton and His Orchestra: *Hampton* (vib), remaining personnel same as
above.

Flying Home (Parts 1 & 2)   VP540/41
78: V-Disc 188 LP: Caracol 440

The Major and the Minor   VP616
78: V-Disc 229 LP: Caracol 440

I Wonder Boogie   VP617
78: V-Disc 229

1944—New York, NY
Lionel Hampton and His Orchestra: *Hampton* (vib), remaining personnel same as
3-2-44.

All On
78: not issued LP: Jazz Club 121, Jazz Society (F) AA543

Design for Jivin'
78: not issued LP: Jazz Club 121, Jazz Society (F) AA543

March 19, 1944—New York, NY
Lionel Hampton and His Orchestra: *Hampton* (vib), Dinah Washington and Rubel Blakely (v), remaining personnel same as 3-2-44.

The Music Stopped – RB (v)
LP: Black Jack (G) LP 3001

Don't Believe Everything You Dream
LP: Black Jack (G) LP 3001

Now I Know – RB (v)
LP: Black Jack (G) LP 3001

There'll Be a Jubilee – DW (v)
LP: Black Jack (G) LP 3001

No Love, No Nothing – DW (v)
LP: Black Jack (G) LP 3001

Chop Chop
LP: Black Jack (G) LP 3001

Your Guess Is As Good As Mine
LP: Black Jack (G) LP 3001

Holiday For Strings
LP: Black Jack (G) LP 3001

1944 (probably early)—New York, NY
Lionel Hampton and His Orchestra: personnel same as above.

Design for Jivin'
LP: Black Jack (G) LP 3001

Major and Minor
LP: Black Jack (G) LP 3001

Your Guess Is As Good As Mine – RB (v)
LP: Black Jack (G) LP 3001

Evil Gal Blues – DW (v)
LP: Black Jack (G) LP 3001

All On
LP: Black Jack (G) LP 3001

No New Romance
LP: Black Jack (G) LP 3001

Ca. May/June 1944—New York, NY
Lionel Hampton's Jubilee: *Hampton* (vib, p, d); Al Killian, Joe Morris, Dave Page, Lammar Wright, Jr., Wendell Culley (tp); Al Hayse, Mitchell "Booty" Wood, John Morris, Andrew Penn (tb); Herbie Fields (cl, as, ss); Gus Evans (as); Arnett Cobb, Jay Peters (ts); Charlie Fowlkes (bars); Milt Buckner, Sugar Chile

Robinson (p); Billy Mackell (g); Charlie Harris, Ted Sinclair (b); Fred Radcliffe, Joey Preston (d); Dinah Washington, Madeline Green (v).

Loose Wig
LP: Joyce LP-5008

Caldonia Boogie
LP: Joyce LP-5008

Sugar's Boogie-Woogie
LP: Joyce LP-5008

Moonglow
LP: Joyce LP-5008

I'm Gonna Love That Guy – MG (v)
LP: Joyce LP-5008

Chasin' the Chase
LP: Joyce LP-5008

Nola
LP: Joyce LP-5008

Million-Dollar Smile – DW (v)
LP: Joyce LP-5008

Lady Be Good
LP: Joyce LP-5008

June 16, 1944—Trianon Ballroom, South Gate, CA (broadcast)
Lionel Hampton and His Orchestra: *Hampton* (vib); Wendell Culley, Snooky Young, Joe Morris, Dave Page, Lammar Wright, Jr. (tp); Vernon Porter, Fred Beckett, Andrew Penn, Sonny Craven, Allen Durham (tb); George Dorsey, Gus Evans (as); Arnett Cobb, Fred Simon (ts); Charlie Fowlkes (bars); Milt Buckner (p); Billy Mackel (g); Charlie Harris, Ted Sinclair (b); Fred Radcliffe (d); Rubel Blakely, Dinah Washington (v).

Theme
LP: Joyce LP-1055, Sandy Hook S.H. 2026

I'll Get By
LP: Joyce LP-1055, Sandy Hook S.H. 2026

Dearly Beloved
LP: Joyce LP-1055, Sandy Hook S.H. 2026

Idaho – RB (v)
LP: Joyce LP-1055, Sandy Hook S.H. 2026

Don't Believe Everything You Dream – RB (v)
LP: Joyce LP-1055, Sandy Hook S.H. 2026

The Music Stopped – RB (v)
LP: Sandy Hook S.H. 2026

Stardust
LP: Sandy Hook S.H. 2026

There'll Be a Jubilee – DW (v)
LP: Sandy Hook S.H. 2026

Linger Awhile
LP: Sandy Hook S.H. 2026

No Love, No Nothing – DW (v)
LP: Sandy Hook S.H. 2026

Moonglow, or How Am I to Know
LP: Sandy Hook S.H. 2026

Swanee River
LP: Sandy Hook S.H. 2026

October 16, 1944—Los Angeles, CA
Lionel Hampton and His Orchestra: same personnel as above, except Dinah
Washington (v) and Rubel Blakely (v) out.

Million-Dollar Smile   L3644
78: Decca 18719 LP: MCA 1315, Affinity (E)
AFS 1017, Franklin Mint Record Society 40

The Lamplighter   L3645
78: Decca 18910 LP: MCA 1315, Ajazz-470

Overtime   L3646-A
78: Decca 18669 LP: MCA 1315, Ajazz-470

Tempos Boogie   L3647
78: Decca 18910 LP: MCA 1315, Affinity (E) AFS 1000

October 16, 1944—Los Angeles, CA (Jubilee broadcast)
Lionel Hampton and His Orchestra: probably same personnel as above, except
add Dinah Washington (v).

Million-Dollar Smile – DW (v)
LP: Giants of Jazz GOJ 1014, Magic (E) AWE 18

Lady Be Good
LP: Giants of Jazz GOJ 1014, Magic (E) AWE 18

November 17, 1944—Los Angeles, CA
Lionel Hampton and His Orchestra: *Hampton* (vib); Snooky Young, Lammar
Wright, Jr., Dave Page, Joe Morris, Wendell Culley (tp); Vernon Porter, Andrew
Penn, Luther "Sonny" Craven, Allen Durham, Fred Beckett (tb); George Dorsey,
Gus Evans (as); Arnett Cobb, Fred Simon (ts); Charlie Fowlkes (bars); Milt
Buckner (p); Billy Mackel (g); Ted Sinclair, Charles Harris (b); Fred Radcliffe (d);
Rubel Blakely, Dinah Washington (v).

Chop Chop [aka "Shark Face"]
LP: Jazz Society (F) 605, Palm Club PC 08, Jazz Club LP 121

Trolley Song [aka "Hallicarnassus Lady"]
LP: Jazz Society (F) 605, Palm Club PC 08, Jazz Club LP 121,
Sunbeam SB 214

And Her Tears Flowed Like Wine – DW (v)
LP: Sunbeam SB 214

What a Difference a Day Made
LP: Palm Club PC 08

Hamp's Boogie
LP: Palm Club PC 08

Some Day – RB (v)
LP: not issued

January 22, 1945—New York, NY
Lionel Hampton and His Orchestra: *Hampton* (vib); Snooky Young, Lammar Wright, Jr., Dave Page, Joe Morris, Wendell Culley (tp); Vernon Porter, Andrew Penn, Luther "Sonny" Craven, Allen Durham, Fred Beckett, Al Hayse (tb); Herbie Fields (cl, as); Gus Evans (as); Arnett Cobb, Fred Simon (ts); Charlie Fowlkes (bars); Milt Buckner (p); Billy Mackel (g); Ted Sinclair, Charles Harris (b); Fred Radcliffe (d); Rubel Blakely, Dinah Washington (v).

Vibe Boogie   VP1125
78: V-Disc 404 LP: Palm Club PC 06, Caracol 440

Screamin' Boogie   VP1126
78: V-Disc 428 LP: Palm Club PC 06, Caracol 440

April 15, 1945—Carnegie Hall, New York, NY
Lionel Hampton and His Orchestra: *Hampton* (vib, p, d); Al Killian, Joe Morris, Dave Page, Lammar Wright, Jr., Wendell Culley, Dizzy Gillespie (tp); Abdul Hamid, Al Hayse, John Morris, Andrew Penn (tb); Herbie Fields (cl, as, ss); Gus Evans (as); Arnett Cobb, Jay Peters (ts); Charlie Fowlkes (bars); Milt Buckner, Leonard Feather (p); Billy Mackel (g); Charles Harris, Ted Sinclair (b); Fred Radcliffe (d); Dinah Washington (v).

Red Cross
LP: Decca DL 8088, MCA (F) 510142, Jasmine (E) JASM 1040

Hamp's Salty Blues
LP: Decca DL 8088, MCA (F) 510142, Jasmine (E) JASM 1040

I Know That You Know
LP: Decca DL 8088, MCA (F) 510142, Jasmine (E) JASM 1040

Loose Wig
LP: Decca DL 8088, MCA (F) 510142, Jasmine (E) JASM 1040

Hamp's Boogie-Woogie
LP: Decca DL 8088, MCA (F) 510142, Jasmine (E) JASM 1040

Oh Lady Be Good
LP: Decca DL 8088, MCA (F) 510142, Jasmine (E) JASM 1040

Evil Gal Blues – DW (v)
LP: Decca DL 8088, MCA (F) 510142, Jasmine (E) JASM 1040

Flying Home
LP: Decca DL 8088, MCA (F) 510142, Jasmine (E) JASM 1040

May 1945—New York, NY
Jam Session All-Stars: probable personnel—*Hampton* (p), Snooky Young (tp), Herbie Fields (cl, ts), Arnett Cobb (ts), Al Casey (g), Slam Stewart (b), Fred Radcliffe (d).

Five O'Clock Rise
78: Gilt Edge 3823

Fire Power
78: Gilt Edge 3823

May 4, 1945—New York, NY
Herbie Fields Hot Five: *Hampton* (d), Herbie Fields (cl, ts, as), John Mehegan (p), Al Casey (g), Slam Stewart (b), Al Hayse (v).

O.K. Sarge [0:14 false start] unissued	S5809-1
O.K. Sarge [0:16 false start] unissued	S5809-2
O.K. Sarge unissued	S5809-3
O.K. Sarge unissued	S5809-4
O.K. Sarge 78: Savoy 654	S5809-5
Comin' Home – AH (v) unissued	S5810-1
Comin' Home – AH (v) unissued	S5810-2
Stardust [0:14 false start] unissued	S5811-1
Stardust 78: Savoy 654	S5811-2
It's the Talk of the Town unissued	S5812-1

Note: Hampton listed on the label as "The Champ."

May 4, 1945—New York, NY
Hampton (p), Herbie Fields (ts), Al Casey (g), Slam Stewart (b).

Run Down [0:12 false start] unissued	S5813-1
Run Down unissued	S5813-2
Run Down 78: Savoy 591 LP: Savoy SJL 2208	S5813-3
Nuts to Notes [0:11 false start] unissued	S5814-1
Nuts to Notes unissued	S5814-2

Nuts to Notes [0:11 false start]   S5814-3
unissued

Nuts to Notes [1:21 incomplete take]   S5814-4
unissued

Nuts to Notes   S5814-5
78: not issued LP: Savoy SJL 2208

May 21, 1945—New York, NY
Lionel Hampton and His Septet: *Hampton* (vib, p), Wendell Culley (tp), Herbie
Fields (as), Arnett Cobb (ts), Johnny Mehegan (p), Billy Mackel (g), Charles
Harris (b), George Jones (d), Dinah Washington (v).

Doublin' with Dublin   72871
78: Brunswick (E) 04005 LP: MCA (F) 510063,
Affinity (E) AFS 1037

Ribs and Hot Sauce   72872-A
78: Decca 24513 LP: MCA (F) 510063,
Franklin Mint Record Society 40

Blow Top Blues – DW (v)   72873
78: Decca 23792 LP: MCA 2-4075, Franklin
Mint Record Society 40

Two-Finger Boogie   72874
78: Decca 23838 LP: MCA 2-4075

May 21, 1945—New York, NY
Lionel Hampton and His Orchestra: *Hampton* (vib, p); Wendell Culley, Joe
Morris, Al Killian, Lammar Wright, Jr., Dave Page (tp); Abdul Hamid, John
Morris, Al Hayse, Andrew Penn (tb); Herbie Fields, Gus Evans (as); Arnett Cobb,
Jay Peters (ts); Charlie Fowlkes (bars); Dardenelle Breckenbridge (p); Charles
Harris, Ted Sinclair (b); Fred Radcliffe (d); Dinah Washington (v).

Someday   72875
78: Decca (Sw) BM 30811 LP: Coral COPS 7186

Beulah's Boogie   72876
78: Decca 18719, Decca 23838 LP: MCA 1331,
MCA 2-4075, Affinity (E) AFS 1000

Playboy   72881
78: Decca (Sw) BM 30811 LP: Coral COPS 7186,
MCA (F) 510117

Punch and Judy   72882
78: Decca 23639 LP: Coral COPS 7186, MCA (F) 510112

May 30, 1945—New York, NY
Herbie Fields' Hot Seven: *Hampton* (p), Dave Page (tp), Jay Peters (ts), Herbie
Fields (cl), Billy Mackel (g), Charles Harris (b), George Jones (d).

Just Relaxin'   S5818-1
unissued

Just Relaxin' [1:37 incomplete take]   S5818-2
unissued

Just Relaxin'   S5818-3
78: Savoy 592

It Had to Be You   S5819-1
unissued

It Had to Be You   S5819-2
unissued

Camp Meeting   S5820-1
unissued

Camp Meeting [0:03 false start]   S5820-2
unissued

Camp Meeting   S5820-3
78: Savoy 591 LP: Savoy SJL 2224

Four O'Clock Blues   S5821-1
unissued

Four O'Clock Blues [1:51 incomplete take]   S5821-2
unissued

Four O'Clock Blues   S5821-3
unissued

Four O'Clock Blues [1:45 incomplete take]   S5821-4
unissued

Four O'Clock Blues   S5821-5
unissued

Four O'Clock Blues   S5821-6
78: Savoy 592 LP: Savoy SJL 2224

Note: On Savoy SJL 2224 the song titles "Camp Meeting" and "Four O'Clock
Blues" are reversed. What is labeled "Camp Meeting" plays take 6 of the "Four
O'Clock Blues." What is labeled "Four O'Clock Blues" plays take 3 of "Camp
Meeting."

November 26, 1945—New York, NY (Jubilee broadcast)
Lionel Hampton and His Orchestra: personnel probably similar to 5-21-45; Lena
Horne (v) added.

Loose Wig
LP: Giants of Jazz GOJ 1014

I Know That You Know
LP: Giants of Jazz GOJ 1014

As Long As You Live – L. Horne (v)
LP: Giants of Jazz GOJ 1014

Moonglow
LP: Giants of Jazz GOJ 1014

December 1, 1945—Los Angeles, CA
Lionel Hampton and His Orchestra: probable personnel—*Hampton* (vib); Joe
Morris, Wendell Culley, Dave Page, Jimmy Nottingham, Lammar Wright, Jr.,
(tp); Jimmy Wormick, Mitchell "Booty" Wood, Andrew Penn, Al Hayse (tb);
Bobby Plater, Ben Kynard (as); Arnett Cobb, Johnny Griffin (ts); Charlie Fowlkes
(bars); Milt Buckner (p); Billy Mackel (g); Charles Harris, Ted Sinclair (b);
George Jenkins (d).

Slide, Hamp, Slide   L4008
78: Decca 18754 LP: MCA 2-4075, Affinity (E)
AFS 1000

Hey-Ba-Ba-Re-Bop   L4009
78: Decca 18754 LP: MCA 2-4075,
Affinity (E) AFS 1000

December 3, 1945—New York, NY (Jubilee broadcast)
Lionel Hampton and His Orchestra: personnel probably same as above.

Swanee River
LP: Giants of Jazz GOJ 1014, Magic (E) AWE 18

Slide, Hamp, Slide
LP: Giants of Jazz GOJ 1014, Magic (E) AWE 18

Flying Home (No. 2)
LP: Giants of Jazz GOJ 1014, Magic (E) AWE 18

Ca. 1945—probably New York
Lionel Hampton and His Orchestra: personnel probably same as above.

The Mess Is Here
LP: Magic (E) AWE 18

Nola
LP: Magic (E) AWE 18

Moonglow
LP: Magic (E) AWE 18

Hamp's Boogie-Woogie
LP: Magic (E) AWE 18

January 21, 1946—New York, NY
Bing Crosby (v) acc. by Lionel Hampton and His Orchestra: *Hampton* (vib, p, v);
Joe Morris, Wendell Culley, Dave Page, Jimmy Nottingham, Lammar Wright, Jr.
(tp); Jimmy Wormick, Mitchell "Booty" Wood, Andrew Penn, Al Hayse (tb);
Bobby Plater, Ben Kynard (as); Arnett Cobb, Johnny Griffin (ts); Charlie Fowlkes
(bars); Milt Buckner (p); Billy Mackel (g); Charles Harris, Ted Sinclair (b);
George Jenkins (d).

Pinetop's Boogie-Woogie – BC (v)   73287-A
78: Decca 23843 LP: Coral COPS 7186, MCA (F) 510140

On the Sunny Side of the Street – BC & LH (v)   73288-A
78: Decca 23843 LP: Coral COPS 7186, MCA (F) 510140

January 29, 1946—New York, NY
Lionel Hampton and His Orchestra: *Hampton* (vib); Joe Morris, Dave Page,
Wendell Culley, Jimmy Nottingham, Lammar Wright, Jr. (tp); Jimmy Wormick,

Mitchell "Booty" Wood, Andrew Penn, Al Hayse (tb); Bobby Plater, Ben Kynard (as); Arnett Cobb, Johnny Griffin (ts); Charlie Fowlkes (bars); Milt Buckner (p); Billy Mackel (g); Charles Harris, Ted Sinclair (b); George Jenkins (d).

Rockin' in Rhythm (Part 1)   73324
78: Decca 24415 LP: MCA 2-4075,
Affinity (E) AFS 1000

Rockin' in Rhythm (Part 2)   73325
78: Decca 24415 LP: MCA 2-4075,
Affinity (E) AFS 1000

Gay Notes   73326
78: not issued LP: MCA 1351

Early 1946—New York, NY (broadcast)
Lionel Hampton and His Orchestra: personnel same as or similar to above; Sugar Chile Robinson (p) and Madeline Green (v) added.

Loose Wig
LP: Palm Club PC 08

Moonglow
LP: Palm Club PC 08

Chasing the Chase
LP: Palm Club PC 08

Caldonia Boogie
LP: Palm Club PC 08

Susie's Boogie-Woogie
LP: Palm Club PC 08

I'm Gonna Have That Guy – MG (v)
LP: Palm Club PC 08

January 30, 1946—New York, NY
Lionel Hampton and His Quartet: *Hampton* (vib, v), Dan Burley (p), Billy Mackel (g), Charles Harris (b), George Jenkins (d).

Tempo's Birthday   73327
78: not issued LP: MCA (F) 510140, Affinity (E) AFS 1037

Hamp's Salty Blues   73328-A
78: Decca 18830 LP: MCA (F) 510063

Ridin' on the L & N   73329-A
78: Decca 23839 LP: MCA (F) 510112, Affinity
(E) AFS 1037

Chord-A-Re-Bop   73330
78: Decca 18830 LP: MCA (F) 510112

Limehouse Blues   73331
78: Decca 23878 LP: MCA 2-4075, MCA (F) 510063

January 31, 1946—New York, NY
Lionel Hampton and His Orchestra: *Hampton* (vib); Joe Morris, Dave Page, Wendell Culley, Jimmy Nottingham, Lammar Wright, Jr. (tp); Jimmy Wormick,

Mitchell "Booty" Wood, Andrew Penn, Al Hayse (tb); Bobby Plater, Ben Kynard (as); Arnett Cobb, Johnny Griffin (ts); Charlie Fowlkes (bars); Milt Buckner (p); Billy Mackel (g); Charles Harris, Ted Sinclair (b); George Jenkins (d).

Cobb's Idea   73332
78: not issued LP: MCA 1351, Affinity (E) AFS 1000

Airmail Special (Part 1)   73333
78: Decca 18880 LP: MCA 2-4075, Affinity (E) AFS 1000

Airmail Special (Part 2)   73334
78: Decca 18880 LP: MCA 2-4075, Affinity (E) AFS 1000

Note: Guitarist/arranger Turk Van Lake confirmed that he arranged "Airmail Special."

June 23, 1946—Chicago, IL (Band Box broadcast)
Lionel Hampton and His Orchestra: personnel same as or similar to above.

Sergeant Miss
unissued

Chop Chop
unissued

Hey-Ba-Ba-Re-Bop – LH & band (v)
unissued

Hamp's Boogie-Woogie
LP: Swing House (E) SWH 8

Flying Home
unissued

Ca. June 1946—possibly Chicago
Lionel Hampton and His Orchestra: personnel same as or similar to above; Dinah Washington (v) added.

San Antonio Boogie in Rebop
unissued

Is You Is or Is You Ain't My Baby – DW (v)
unissued

Kiration Hop
unissued

Hey-Ba-Ba-Re-Bop – LH & band (v)
unissued

September 9, 1946—Los Angeles, CA
Lionel Hampton and His Orchestra: *Hampton* (vib); Wendell Culley, Duke Garrette, Jimmy Nottingham, Joe Wilder, Leo Shepherd (tp); Jimmy Wormick, Mitchell "Booty" Wood, Al Hayse, Andrew Penn (tb); Bobby Plater, Ben Kynard (as); Arnett Cobb, Johnny Griffin (ts); Charlie Fowlkes (bars); Milt Buckner (p); Billy Mackel (g); Joe Comfort, Charles Harris (b); Gene "Fats" Heard, Curley Hamner (d).

Playboy   L4287
78: Brunswick (E) 04322 LP: MCA 1351

Cobb's Idea   L4288
78: not issued LP: MCA 1351, MCA 2-4075

Tempo's Birthday   L4289
78: Decca 23696 LP: MCA (F) 510063

Adam Blew His Hat   L4290
78: Decca 24015 LP: MCA (F) 510063, Affinity (E) AFS 1037

September 17, 1946—Los Angeles, CA
Lionel Hampton and His Orchestra: personnel same as above.

The Pencil Broke   L4297
78: Decca 23696 LP: MCA (F) 510063, Affinity (E) AFS 1037

Empty Glass   L4298
78: not issued LP: MCA 1351, Affinity (E) AFS 1017

Hamp's Walkin' Boogie   L4299-A
78: Decca 23839 LP: MCA (F) 510112, Affinity (E) AFS 1000

September 23, 1946—Los Angeles, CA
Lionel Hampton and His Orchestra: personnel same as 9-9-46, except Jack
Kelson (cl) added.

Don't Let the Landlord Gyp You   L4300
78: Decca 23834 LP: MCA (F) 510117

I'm Mindin' My Business   L4301-A
78: Decca 23834 LP: MCA (F) 510112

Dig Those Vibes   L4302
78: not issued LP: MCA 1351, Affinity (E) AFS 1017

Reminiscing Mood   L4303
78: Decca 24015 LP: MCA (F) 510112

September 23, 1946—Los Angeles, CA
Lionel Hampton and His Octet: *Hampton* (vib, p), Joe Wilder (tp), Jack Kelson
(cl), Bobby Plater (as), Arnett Cobb (ts), Milt Buckner (p), Billy Mackel (g), Joe
Comfort (elb); Curley Hamner (d).

Robins in Your Hair   L4304
78: Decca 23792 LP: MCA (F) 510112

Double Talk   L4305
78: not issued LP: MCA 1351, Affinity (E) AFS 1017

S' Wonderful   L4306
78: not issued LP: MCA 1351

Jack the Fox Boogie   L4307
78: not issued LP: MCA 1351, MCA 2-4075,
Affinity (E) AFS 1017

Note: Joe Comfort's use of the electric bass guitar marks early appearance of this
instrument in a jazz group.

April 2, 1947—New York, NY
Lionel Hampton and His Hamptonians (quintet): *Hampton* (vib), Milt Buckner
(p), Billy Mackel (g), Charles Harris (b), Curley Hamner (d).

I Want to Be Loved – Hamptonians (v)   73843
78: Decca 23879 LP: Coral 6.22180, Coral PC 07502

How High the Moon   73844
78: Decca 24513 LP: MCA 2-4075, Affinity (E) AFS 1017

How High the Moon [alt. take]   73844-?
78: not issued LP: MCA (F) 510112

June 20, 1947—Culver City, CA (broadcast)
Lionel Hampton and His Orchestra: *Hampton* (vib); Wendell Culley, Duke
Garrette, Jimmy Nottingham, Kenny Dorham, Leo Shepherd (tp); Britt
Woodman, James Wormick, Sonny Craven, Andrew Penn (tb); Bobby Plater, Ben
Kynard (as); Morris Lane, John Sparrow (ts); Jack Kelson (as, cl); Charlie
Fowlkes (bars); Milt Buckner (p); Billy Mackel (g); Joe Comfort, Charles Harris
(b); Earl Walker (d); Wini Brown, Roland Burton, Herman McCoy and the
Hamp-Tones (v).

Hamp's Got a Duke
LP: Joyce LP 1055, Golden Era GE 15038, Sandy Hook S.H.
2026

Mamselle – RB (v)
LP: Joyce LP 1055, Golden Era GE 15038, Sandy Hook S.H.
2026

Beulah's Boogie
LP: Joyce LP 1055, Golden Era GE 15038, Sandy Hook S.H.
2026

Sunday Kind of Love – WB (v)
LP: Joyce LP 1055, Golden Era GE 15038, Sandy Hook S.H.
2026

I Know That You Know
LP: Joyce LP 1055, Golden Era GE 15038, Sandy Hook S.H.
2026

Chibaba Chibaba – Herman McCoy & the Hamp-Tones (v)
LP: Joyce LP 1055, Golden Era GE 15038, Sandy Hook S.H.
2026

That's My Desire
LP: Joyce LP 1055, Sandy Hook S.H. 2026

Eli Eli
LP: Joyce LP 1055, Sandy Hook S.H. 2026

Note: Sandy Hook S.H. 2026 gives July 20, 1947, as the date for this band
remote.

Ca. June/July 1947—Culver City, CA (broadcast)
Lionel Hampton and His Orchestra: personnel same as or similar to above; add
the Hamptonians (vocal group).

Oh Rock, Rock, Rock – LH & ensemble (v)
LP: Golden Era GE 15038

Swanee River
LP: Golden Era GE 15038

Confess – RB & the Hamptonians (v)
LP: Golden Era GE 15038

Hey Ba-Ba-Re-Bop – LH, WB, ensemble (v)
LP: Golden Era GE 15038

Memphis Blues
LP: Golden Era GE 15038

The New Look
LP: Golden Era GE 15038

Tempo's Birthday
LP: Golden Era GE 15038

August 4, 1947—Pasadena, CA (concert)
Lionel Hampton and His Just Jazz All-Stars: *Hampton* (vib), Charlie Shavers (tp), Willie Smith (as), Corky Corcoran (ts), Tommy Todd (p), Barney Kessel (g), Slam Stewart (b), Lee Young (d).

Stardust
78: Decca 11036/37/38/39 LP: MCA 198, Jasmine (E)
JASM 1044, Franklin Mint Record Society 40

Note: Hampton does not play on "The Man I Love," "One O'Clock Jump," and "Lady Be Good" from this concert.

August 4, 1947—Pasadena, CA (concert)
Lionel Hampton and His Just Jazz All-Stars: personnel same as above, except Milt Buckner (p) replaces Todd.

Perdido
LP: Gene Norman GNP 15

Shavers (tp), Smith (as), and Corcoran (ts) out:

That's My Desire
LP: Gene Norman GNP 15

Smith (as) and Corcoran (ts) out:

Central Avenue Breakdown
LP: Gene Norman GNP 15

Shavers (tp), Smith (as), and Corcoran (ts) out:

Hey-Ba-Ba-Re-Bop
LP: Gene Norman GNP 15

(Kaba's) Blues
LP: Gene Norman GNP 15

Hamp's Boogie-Woogie
LP: Gene Norman GNP 15

Add Shavers (tp), Smith (as), and Corcoran (ts):

Flying Home
LP: Gene Norman GNP 15

August 6, 1947—Los Angeles, CA
Lionel Hampton and His Orchestra: *Hampton* (vib); Wendell Culley, Duke
Garrette, Jimmy Nottingham, Kenny Dorham, Leo Shepherd (tp); Britt
Woodman, Jimmy Wormick, Sonny Craven, Andrew Penn (tb); Bobby Plater, Ben
Kynard (as); Morris Lane, John Sparrow (ts); Jack Kelson (cl, as); Charlie
Fowlkes (bars); Milt Buckner (p); Billy Mackel (g); Joe Comfort, Charles Harris
(b); Earl Walker (d); Wini Brown (v); the Hamptonians (v).

You Better Be Satisfied – the Hamptonians (v)	L4481
78: not issued LP: Coral 6.22180	

Hamp's Got a Duke	L4482
78: Decca 24248 LP: MCA 1331, Affinity (E) AFS 1017	

Gone Again – WB (v)	L4483
78: Decca 24248 LP: MCA 2-4075	

Three Minutes on Fifty-second Street	L4484
78: Decca 24429 LP: MCA 1331, Affinity (E) AFS 1017	

August 6, 1947—Los Angeles, CA
Lionel Hampton Sextet: *Hampton* (vib); Morris Lane (ts); Milt Buckner (p); Billy
Mackel (g); Charles Harris (b); Earl Walker (d).

One Little Tear Is Like an Ocean	L4485
78: Decca 24181 LP: Coral 6.22180	

I Miss You So	L4486
78: Decca 24181 LP: Coral 6.22180	

When Tonight Is Just a Memory	L4487
78: not issued LP: Coral 6.22180	

Possibly August 7, 1947—Hollywood, CA
The Leaders' Orchestra: *Hampton* (vib); Louis Armstrong (tp, v), Tommy Dorsey
(tb), Benny Goodman (cl), Charlie Barnet (ts), Mel Powell (p), Al Hendrickson
(g), Harry Babasin (b), Louie Bellson (d), Jeri Sullivan and the Golden Gate
Quartet (v), plus some unidentified musicians (possibly from Hampton's
orchestra).

A Song Was Born – LA (v)	M-233
LP: RCA (F) NL 89279, Pumpkin 109	

A Song Was Born – GGQ, JS, & LA (v)	M-233?
78: Victor (J) NB-6013 LP: RCA (F) FXM1 7083, RCA (F) NL 89279	

Possibly August 7, 1947—Hollywood, CA
The Leaders' Orchestra: same personnel as above, except Jeri Sullivan and the
Golden Gate Quartet (v) are out.

Goldwyn Stomp
LP: Pumpkin 109

August 1947–Hollywood, CA
The Leaders' Orchestra: personnel same as above, except Jeri Sullivan and the
Golden Gate Quartet (v) are added.

A Song Was Born (Part 1)–GGQ, JS, & LA (v)   3426
78: Capitol 10172

A Song Was Born (Part 2)   3427
78: Capitol 10172

Note: The title "A Song Was Born" is from the movie *A Song Is Born* , which
was released in 1948 but filmed the previous year. These sessions probably took
place in 1947 not 1948 as listed by most discographies. [This information is from
liner notes of RCA (F) NL 89279.]

November 3, 1947—Los Angeles, CA
Lionel Hampton and His Orchestra: *Hampton* (vib); Wendell Culley, Duke
Garrette, Snooky Young, Teddy Buckner, Leo Shepherd (tp); James Robinson,
Andrew Penn, Jimmy Wormick, Britt Woodman (tb); Jack Kelson (cl, as); Bobby
Plater, Ben Kynard (as); Morris Lane, John Sparrow (ts); Charlie Fowlkes (bsx);
Milt Buckner (p); Billy Mackel (g); Joe Comfort, Charles Mingus (b); Earl
Walker (d).

Goldwyn Stomp   L4528
78: Decca 24505 LP: MCA 1331

Red Top   L4529
78: Decca 24281 LP: MCA 2-4075, Affinity (E) AFS 1000

Giddy Up   L4530
78: Decca 24281 LP: MCA (F) 510117

November 10, 1947—Los Angeles, CA
Lionel Hampton and His Orchestra: personnel same as above, except Walter
Williams (tp) replaces Snooky Young.

Hawk's Nest   L4543
78: Decca 24505 LP: MCA 1331, Affinity (E)
AFS 1037

Mingus Fingers   L4544
78: Decca 24428 LP: MCA 1331, MCA 2-4075,
Affinity (E) AFS 1017, Smithsonian P6-19881,
Franklin Mint Record Society 40

Muchacho Azul   L4545
78: Decca 24428 LP: MCA 1331

Midnight Sun   L4546
78: Decca 24429 LP: MCA 2-4075, Affinity (E) AFS 1000

November 14, 1947—Los Angeles, CA
Lionel Hampton Sextet: *Hampton* (vib, v), Benny Bailey (tp), Morris Lane (ts),
Dodo Marmarosa (p), Billy Mackel (g), Charles Mingus (b), Earl Walker and
Curley Hamner (d).

Cherokee – LH (scat vocal)   L4560
78: Decca 24430 LP: MCA (F) 510181, Affinity (E) AFS 1037

No. 2 Re-bop and Be-bop   L4561
78: Decca 24430 LP: MCA (F) 510181

Zoo-Baba-Da-Oo-Ee – LH (v)   L4562
78: Decca 24431 LP: MCA (F) 510181

Benny Bailey (tp) and Earl Walker (d) out; Milt Buckner (p) replaces Marmarosa:

Be-bop's Turning Blue   L4563
78: Decca 24431 LP: MCA (F) 510181

May 1, 1948—Howard Theatre, Washington, DC (broadcast)
Lionel Hampton and His Orchestra: *Hampton* (vib, p, d, v); Fats Navarro, Teddy
Buckner, Wendell Culley, Leo Shepherd, Duke Garrette (tp); Britt Woodman,
Jimmy Wormick, Andrew Penn, Sonny Craven (tb); Ben Kynard, Bobby Plater
(as); Billy Williams, John Sparrow (ts); Charlie Fowlkes (bsx); Milt Buckner (p);
Charles Harris, Charles Mingus (b); Earl Walker (d).

Hot House
LP: Weka (Sw) jda-12-1, Cicala (It) BLJ 8015, Alamac QSR 2419

Adam Blew His Hat
LP: Alamac QSR 2419

Goldwyn Stomp
LP: Alamac QSR 2419

July 1, 1948—Geneva, NY (broadcast)
Lionel Hampton and His Orchestra: *Hampton* (vib); Teddy Buckner, Wendell
Culley, Leo Shepherd, Duke Garrette, Jimmy Nottingham (tp); Lester Bass (btp);
Britt Woodman, Jimmy Wormick, Sonny Craven (tb); Ben Kynard, Bobby Plater
(as); Billy "Smallwood" Williams, John Sparrow (ts); Charlie Fowlkes (bars);
Milt Buckner (p); Wes Montgomery (g); Charles Mingus (b); Earl Walker (d).

Adam Blew His Hat
LP: Weka jds-12-1, Cicala (It) BLJ 8015, Alamac QSR 2419

July 7, 1948—Geneva, NY (broadcast)
Lionel Hampton and His Orchestra: personnel same as above, except Billie
Holiday and Wynonie Harris (v), and Bobby Tucker (p) are added.

I Cover the Waterfront – BH (v), BT (p)
LP: Weka jds-12-1, Cicala (It) BLJ 8001

Good Rockin' Tonight – WH (v)
LP: Weka jds-12-1, Cicala (It) BLJ 8015

July 21, 1948—Geneva, NY (broadcast)
Lionel Hampton and His Orchestra: *Hampton* (vib); Teddy Buckner, Wendell
Culley, Leo Shepherd, Duke Garrette, Jimmy Nottingham (tp); Lester Bass (btp);
Britt Woodman, Jimmy Wormick, Sonny Craven (tb); Ben Kynard, Bobby Plater,
Johnny Board (as); Billy Williams, John Sparrow (ts); Charlie Fowlkes (bars);
Milt Buckner (p); Wes Montgomery (g); Charles Mingus (b); Earl Walker (d).

Brant Inn Boogie
LP: Weka jds-12-1, Cicala (It) BLJ 8015, Alamac QSR 2419

August 4, 1948—Peoria, IL (broadcast)
Lionel Hampton and His Orchestra: personnel similar to above.

Body and Soul [bass feature for Charles Mingus]
LP: Weka jds-12-1, Cicala (It) BLJ 8015, Alamac QSR 2419

August 11, 1948—Denver, CO (broadcast)
Lionel Hampton and His Orchestra: personnel similar to 7-21-48.

Satchmo's Blues
LP: Weka jds-12-1, Cicala (It) BLJ 8015, Alamac QSR 2419

October 15, 1948—Little Rock, AR (broadcast)
Lionel Hampton and His Orchestra: *Hampton* (vib, p, d, v); Benny Bailey, Duke
Garrette, Wendell Culley, Leo Shepherd (tp); Al Grey, Lester Bass, Jimmy
Wormick (tb); Johnny Board, Bobby Plater (as); Billy Williams, John Sparrow
(ts); Ben Kynard (bars); Milt Buckner (p); Wes Montgomery (g); Roy Johnson
(b); Earl Walker (d).

Dues in Blues
LP: Weka jds-12-1, Cicala (It) BLJ 8015, Alamac QSR 2419

1948—location unknown (broadcast)
Lionel Hampton and His Orchestra: *Hampton* (vib), same personnel as above,
except Lorraine (Betty) Carter (v) added.

Beulah's Boogie
LP: Weka jds-12-1, Cicala (It) BLJ 8015, Alamac QSR 2419

Calling Dr. Mancuso
LP: Weka jds-12-1, Cicala (It) BLJ 8015, Alamac QSR 2419

Jay Bird – BC (v)
LP: Weka jds-12-1, Cicala (It) BLJ 8015, Alamac QSR 2419

Re-bop
LP: Weka jds-12-1, Cicala (It) BLJ 8015, Alamac QSR 2419

January 24, 1949—New York, NY
Lionel Hampton and His Sextet: *Hampton* (vib, p, v), Benny Bailey and Duke
Garrette (tp), Johnny Board (as), Gene Morris (ts), Albert Ammons (p), Wes
Montgomery (g), Roy Johnson (b), Earl Walker (d), Sonny Parker and Betty
Carter (v).

Chicken Shack Boogie – LH (v)	74727
78: Decca 24574 LP: MCA 1331	
New Central Avenue Breakdown	74728
78: Decca 24607 LP: MCA 2-4075, MCA (F) 510112	
Benson's Boogie – SP & BC (v)	74729
78: Decca 24574 LP: MCA (F) 510112	

Note: Some discographies list the guitarist for this session as "John Leslie," but it
is actually Wes Montgomery, whose real name is John Leslie Montgomery.

January 28, 1949—New York, NY
Lionel Hampton and His Orchestra: *Hampton* (vib, p); Wendell Culley, Leo
Shepherd, Walter Williams, Benny Bailey, Duke Garrette (tp); Lester Bass, Al

Grey, Benny Powell, Jimmy Wormick (tb); Johnny Board, Bobby Plater (as); John Sparrow, Billy Williams, Gene Morris (ts); Ben Kynard (bars); Albert Ammons (p); Wes Montgomery (g); Roy Johnson (b); Earl Walker (d); Sonny Parker (v).

Hamp's Boogie (No. 2)   74730
78: Decca 24607 LP: MCA (F) 510112, Affinity (E) AFS 1000

Hamp's Gumbo – SP (v)   74731
78: not issued LP: MCA 1351

Beulah's Sister's Boogie   74732
78: Decca 24699 LP: MCA (F) 510112, Affinity (E) AFS 1000

Wee Albert   74733
78: Decca 24699 LP: MCA 1331, Affinity (E) AFS 1037

April 26, 1949—New York, NY
Lionel Hampton and His Orchestra: personnel same as above, except Doug Duke (p) replaces Ammons.

What's Happening Baby – SP (v)   74853
78: Decca 24642 LP: MCA (F) 510117

Drinking Wine Spo-dee-o-dee   74854
78: Decca 24642 LP: MCA (F) 510117

April 26, 1949—New York, NY
Lionel Hampton Quartet: *Hampton* (vib), Wes Montgomery (g), Roy Johnson (b), Earl Walker (d).

Moonglow   74855
78: not issued LP: MCA (F) 510181, Affinity (E) AFS 1037

May 10, 1949—New York, NY
Lionel Hampton and His Orchestra: *Hampton* (vib); Wendell Culley, Leo Shepherd, Walter Williams, Ed Mullens (tp); Lester Bass, Al Grey, Chippie Outcalt, Jimmy Wormick (tb); Johnny Board, Bobby Plater (as); John Sparrow, Billy Williams, Gene Morris (ts); Ben Kynard (bars); France Gadison (p); Wes Montgomery (g); Roy Johnson (b); Earl Walker (d); Betty Carter, the Hamp-Tones, Joe James, Sonny Parker (v).

The Hucklebuck – BC (v)   74897
78: Decca 24652 LP: MCA (F) 510117

Baby, You're Great – the Hamp-Tones (v)   74898

Note: the Hamp-Tones—John Wilson, Fred Hamilton, Raymond Johnson, Richard Palmer.

May 10, 1949—New York, NY
Hampton (vib), Wendell Culley (tp), Gene Morris (ts), Ben Kynard (bars), Doug Duke (org), Wes Montgomery (g), Roy Johnson (b), Earl Walker (d), Sonny Parker and Joe James (v).

Lavender Coffin – SP & JJ (v)   74899
78: Decca 24652 LP: MCA 1331, Affinity (E) AFS 1037

Autumn 1949—New York, NY
Lionel Hampton and His Orchestra: *Hampton* (vib, p), personnel similar to orchestra on 5-10-49.

Hamp's Bopology
78: Jazz Society A544

Hampology
78: Jazz Society A544

Flying Home (Part 1)
78: Jazz Society A561

Flying Home (Part 2)
78: Jazz Society A561

Beulah's Boogie (Part 1)
78: Jazz Society A588 LP: Jazz Club LP 121

Beulah's Boogie (Part 2)
78: Jazz Society A588 LP: Jazz Club LP 121

Jingle Boogie
78: Jazz Society A587

Drumology
78: Jazz Society A587

December 29, 1949—New York, NY
Lionel Hampton and His Orchestra: *Hampton* (vib); Walter Williams, Benny
Bailey, Ed Mullens, Duke Garrette, Leo Shepherd (tp); Al Grey, Benny Powell,
Jimmy Wormick, Paul Lee (tb); Bobby Plater, Jerome Richardson (as); Curtis
Lowe, Johnny Board, Billy "Smallwood" Williams (ts); Lonnie Shaw (bars); Doug
Duke (p, org); Wes Montgomery (g); Roy Johnson (b); Ellis Bartee (d); Sonny
Parker, unknown female (v).

Rag Mop	75636
78: Decca 24855 LP: MCA 1331, Affinity (E) AFS 1000	

For You My Love – SP (v)	75637
78: Decca 24855 LP: MCA (F) 510117	

Sky Blue – unknown female (v)	75638
78: not issued LP: Affinity (E) AFS 1037	

December 1949 & January 1950—Bop City, New York, NY
Lionel Hampton and His Orchestra: *Hampton* (vib, p, d); probable personnel of
the period—Walter Williams, Benny Bailey, Ed Mullens, Duke Garrette, Leo
Shepherd (tp); Al Grey, Benny Powell, Jimmy Wormick, Paul Lee (tb); Bobby
Plater, Jerome Richardson (as); Curtis Lowe, Johnny Board, Billy "Smallwood"
Williams (ts); Lonnie Shaw (bars); Doug Duke (p, org); Wes Montgomery (g);
Roy Johnson (b); Ellis Bartree (d); unknown female (v).

Mary Had a Little Lamb – unknown female (v)
LP: Alto AL 708

Hamp's Basement
LP: Alto AL 708

Shadows in the Night
LP: Alto AL 708

Hamp's Spectacle – LH (d) & RJ (b) only
LP: Alto AL 708

Symphony in Jazz
LP: Alto AL 708

Flying Home
LP: Alto AL 708

Jingle Boogie
LP: Alto AL 708

Hampology
LP: Alto AL 708

Bopology
LP: Alto AL 708

January 5, 1950—New York, NY
Lionel Hampton and His Orchestra: *Hampton* (vib); Walter Williams, Benny Bailey, Ed Mullens, Duke Garrette, Leo Shepherd (tp); Al Grey, Benny Powell, Jimmy Wormick, Paul Lee (tb); Bobby Plater, Jerome Richardson (as); Curtis Lowe, Johnny Board, Billy "Smallwood" Williams (ts); Lonnie Shaw (bars); Doug Duke (p, org); Wes Montgomery (g); Roy Johnson (b); Ellis Bartee (d); Sonny Parker, Little Jimmy Scott (v).

I've Been a Fool – LJS (v)   75664
78: Decca 24864 LP: Affinity (E) AFS 1037

How You Sound – SP (v)   75665
78: Decca 24911 LP: Coral 6.22421

I Almost Lost My Mind – SP (v)   75666
78: Decca 24864 LP: Coral 6.22421, MCA (J) 3527

January 25, 1950—New York, NY
Lionel Hampton and His Orchestra: personnel same as above, except Irma Curry (v) added.

Everybody's Somebody's Fool – LJS (v)   75743
78: Decca 27176 LP: MCA 2-4075, Affinity (E) AFS 1037

I'll Never Be Free – IC (v)   75744
78: Decca 24911 LP: Coral 6.22421

Sad Feelin' – SP (v)   75745
78: Decca 24946 LP: MCA 1331

Hamp's Gumbo – SP (v)   75746
78: Decca 24946 LP: MCA 1331, Affinity (E) AFS 1017

Please Give Me a Chance – LJS (v)   75752
78: not issued LP: Coral PC08226, Coral 6.22422

I Wish I Knew – JS (v)   75753
78: Decca 28711 LP: MCA 2-4075

Note: "JS" is probably Little Jimmy Scott.

January 26, 1950—New York, NY
Lionel Hampton and His Quintet: *Hampton* (vib), Jerome Richardson (fl), Doug
Duke (org), Wes Montgomery (g), Roy Johnson (b), Earl Walker (d).

Where or When   75754
78: Decca 27198 LP: Decca DL 8230

There Will Never Be Another You   75755
78: Decca 27198 LP: Decca DL 8230, Affinity (E) AFS 1037

March 23, 1950—New York, NY
Lionel Hampton and His Orchestra: *Hampton* (vib); Benny Bailey, Duke
Garrette, Ed Mullens, Leo Shepherd, Walter Williams (tp); Al Grey, Paul Lee,
Benny Powell, Jimmy Wormick (tb); Bobby Plater, Jerome Richardson (as);
Johnny Board, Lonnie Shaw, Curtis Lowe (ts); Ben Kynard (bars); Gus Domerette
(p); Rudy Mason (g); Roy Johnson (b); Ellis Bartee (d).

Turkey Hop (Part 1)   76021
78: Decca 24992 LP: MCA 1331, Affinity (E) AFS 1017

Turkey Hop (Part 2)   76022
78: Decca 24992 LP: MCA 1331, Affinity (E) AFS 1017

April 18, 1950—New York, NY
Lionel Hampton and His Orchestra: personnel same as above.

Birmingham Bounce   76168
78: not issued LP: Coral 6.22422, MCA/Coral PC08225

Jelly Roll   76169
78: not issued LP: Coral 6.22422, MCA/Coral PC08225

April 11 or 21, 1950—New York, NY
Lionel Hampton and His Orchestra: personnel same as 3-23-50, except Curley
Hamner (d) replaces Bartee; Sonny Parker (v), Fred Hamilton (v), and Roy
Johnson (v).

Birmingham Bounce – RJ & FH (v)   76205
78: Decca 27041 LP: MCA (F) 510117

Jelly Roll – SP (v)   76206
78: Decca 28230 LP: MCA (F) 510117

Cannonball Express   76207
78: Decca 27041 LP: MCA (F) 510117

July 25, 1950—Los Angeles, CA
Lionel Hampton and His Orchestra: *Hampton* (vib); Benny Bailey, Duke
Garrette, Ed Mullens, Leo Shepherd, Walter Williams (tp); Al Grey, Paul Lee,
Benny Powell, Jimmy Cleveland (tb); Bobby Plater, Jerome Richardson (as);
Johnny Board, Curtis Lowe, Gil Bernal (ts,); Ben Kynard (bars); Milt Buckner
(p); Billy Mackel (g); Roy Johnson (b, v); Curley Hamner (d); Sonny Parker (v).

Well, Oh Well – SP (v)   LA5757
78: Decca 27164 LP: MCA (F) 510117

Pink Champagne   LA5758
78: Decca 27164 LP: MCA (F) 510117

September in the Rain – GB (v)   LA5759
78: Decca 27176 LP: Coral 6.22422

July 26, 1950—Los Angeles, CA
Lionel Hampton and His Sextet: *Hampton* (vib), Buddy Cole (org), Milt Buckner
(p), Billy Mackel (g), Roy Johnson (b), Ellis Bartee (d).

Penthouse Serenade   LA5760
78: Decca 27372 LP: Coral 6.22423, Coral PC08226

Memories of You   LA5761
78: Decca 27374 LP: Coral 6.22423, Coral PC08226

You Go to My Head   LA5762
78: Decca 27373 LP: Coral 6.22423, Coral PC08226

September 14, 1950—Los Angeles, CA
Lionel Hampton and His Sextet: personnel same as above.

Moonglow   LA5835
78: Decca 27372 LP: MCA (F) 510117

I'll Remember April   LA5836
78: Decca 27375 LP: MCA (F) 510181, Affinity (E) AFS 1037

The Man I Love   LA5837
78: Decca 27373 LP: MCA (F) 510181, Affinity (E) AFS 1037

Time on My Hands   LA5838
78: Decca 27375 LP: MCA (F) 510181

Easy to Love   LA5839
78: Decca 27374 LP: MCA (F) 510117

Twentieth-Century Boogie   LA5840
78: not issued LP: MCA (F) 510181

October 13, 1950—Los Angeles, CA
Lionel Hampton and His Orchestra: *Hampton* (vib); Benny Bailey, Duke
Garrette, Ed Mullens, Leo Shepherd, Walter Williams (tp); Jimmy Cleveland, Al
Grey, Paul Lee, Benny Powell (tb); Bobby Plater, Jerome Richardson (as); Gil
Bernal, Johnny Board, Curtis Lowe (ts); Ben Kynard (bars); Milt Buckner (p);
Billy Mackel (g); Roy Johnson (b); Ellis Bartee (d); Sonny Parker (v).

Oh Babe – SP (v)   LA5880
78: Decca 27305 LP: MCA (F) 510117, Coral 6.22423

Who Cares?   LA5881
78: Decca 27305 LP: Coral 6.22423

October 27, 1950—Los Angeles, CA
Lionel Hampton and His Orchestra: personnel same as above, except Lonnie
Shaw (ts) replaces Bernal.

Boogie-Woogie Santa Claus – SP (v)   LA5895
78: Decca 27325 LP: MCA 1331, Jass 8, Affinity (E) AFS 1037

Merry Christmas Baby – SP (v)   LA5896
78: Decca 27325 LP: Stash ST-125

October 30, 1950—Los Angeles, CA
Lionel Hampton and His Orchestra: personnel same as 10-27-50, except add
Dave Howard (v).

June   LA5897
78: not issued LP: Coral 6.22423

Perdido – DH (v)   LA5898
78: Decca 27401 LP: Coral 6.22423

If You Ever Learn to Love   LA5899
78: Decca 28230 LP: Coral 6.22423

October 1950—Los Angeles, CA
Lionel Hampton and His Orchestra: personnel same as or similar to 10-27-50.

Apollo Boogie-Woogie (Part 1)
78: Bop (F) 5 LP: Jazz Club LP 121

Apollo Boogie-Woogie (Part 2)
78: Bop (F) 5 LP: Jazz Club LP 121

Habibi Bounce (Part 1)
78: Bop (F) 6 LP: Jazz Club LP 121

Habibi Bounce (Part 2)
78: Bop (F) 6 LP: Jazz Club LP 121

April 17, 1951—New York, NY
Lionel Hampton and His Orchestra: *Hampton* (vib); Benny Bailey, Ed Mullens,
Leo Shepherd, Idrees Sulieman, Walter Williams (tp); Jimmy Cleveland, Al Grey,
Paul Lee, Benny Powell (tb); Bobby Plater, Jerome Richardson (as); Gil Bernal,
Johnny Board, Curtis Lowe (ts); Ben Kynard (bars); Milt Buckner (p); Billy
Mackel (g); Roy Johnson (b); Ellis Bartee (d); Janet Thurlow (v).

I Can't Believe That You're in Love with Me – JT (v)   51S-157

Cool Train   51S-158
78: MGM 10979 LP: Verve VE2-2543

Gladysee Bounce   51S-159
78: MGM 11448 LP: Verve VE2-2543

Airmail Special   51S-160
78: not issued LP: Verve VE2-2543

May 8, 1951—New York, NY
Lionel Hampton and His Orchestra: *Hampton* (vib, v), personnel same as above,
except Milt Buckner plays organ and piano, and Sonny Parker and Irma Curry
(v) added.

Capitol Debut   51S-189
78: not issued

Gates Step Out – SP & IC (v)   51S-190
78: MGM 11371 LP: Verve VE2-2543

A Kiss Was Just a Kiss – SP & IC (v)   51S-191
78: MGM 11371 LP: Lion L 70064

Alone   51S-192
78: MGM 11448 LP: Verve VE2-2543

Love You Like Mad – LH (v)   51S-193
78: MGM 11176 LP: Verve VE2-2543

May 21, 1951—New York, NY
Lionel Hampton and His Orchestra: *Hampton* (vib, v); Quincy Jones (tp, arr);
Benny Bailey, Ed Mullens, Leo Shepherd, Walter Williams (tp); Jimmy Cleveland,
Al Grey, Paul Lee, Benny Powell (tb); Bobby Plater, Jerome Richardson (as); Gil
Bernal, Johnny Board, Curtis Lowe (ts); Ben Kynard (bars); Milt Buckner (org);
Billy Mackel (g); Roy Johnson (b); Ellis Bartee (d) Don Lamond (tymp).

Hannah, Hannah   51S-209
78: MGM 11039

Shalom, Shalom   51S-210
78: MGM 11039

Eli, Eli (Part 1)   51S-211
78: MGM 11339

Eli, Eli (Part 2)   51S-212
78: MGM 11339

Ca. August 1951—Malibu Beach, CA (concert)
Lionel Hampton and His Orchestra: *Hampton* (vib), personnel similar to above.

The following titles (of which the original are in brackets) were issued under the
pseudonyms on different labels, such as Tiara TMT 7528; Spin-O-Rama M 3077
("Stardust" as "Malibu Swing"); Coronet CX 159; Parade SP 377; Gala (E) GLP
371; Society (E) SOC 1006; Vogue (F) POP ZS 10035. Nearly all labels used the
pseudonyms and very seldom does the correct title appear on the labels.

[*Flying Home*] aka *First Song*
                June Moon
                Stoppin' Short
                Malibu Beach

[*Autumn in New York*] aka *Autumn*
                New York Fall

[*How High the Moon*] aka *Tribute*
                Starry Night
                Stellar P.M.

[*Out of Breath*] aka *Jet Ride*
                Out of Gass
                Cool Company
                Breathless Vibes

[*Hamp's Boogie-Woogie*] aka *Fascinating Furry*
Short of Breath
Jazz-a-ma-tazz

Ca. September 1951—Los Angeles, CA
Lionel Hampton and His Orchestra: *Hampton* (vib), personnel similar to 5-21-51, except unknown female vocalist (possibly Betty Carter) added.

T.V. Special
LP: Camay CA 3019, New World NW 5019

Midnight Sun
LP: Camay CA 3019, New World NW 5019

Cobb's Idea – BC [?] (v)
LP: Camay CA 3019, New World NW 5019

Vibe Boogie
LP: Camay CA 3019, New World NW 5019

Beulah's Boogie
LP: Camay CA 3019, New World NW 5019

Who Cares
LP: Camay CA 3019, New World NW 5019

Bongo Interlude
LP: Camay CA 3019, New World NW 5019

Airmail Special
LP: Camay CA 3019, New World NW 5019

October 16, 1951—Los Angeles, CA
Lionel Hampton and His Orchestra: *Hampton* (vib, v), Al Grey (tb), Johnny Board (ts), Floyd Dixon (p), Chuck Norris (g), Roy Johnson (b), Ellis Bartee (d), Sonny Parker (v).

Crying – SP (v)   51S-3155
78: MGM 11285 LP: Verve VE2-2543

Helpless – SP (v)   51S-3156
78: MGM 11108 LP: Lion L 70064

Jumpin' with G.H.   51S-3157
78: MGM 11765 LP: Verve VE2-2543

Sampson's Boogie   51S-3158
78: MGM 11108 LP: Verve VE2-2543

October 17, 1951—Los Angeles, CA
Lionel Hampton and His Orchestra: *Hampton* (vib, v); Benny Bailey, Quincy Jones, Ed Mullens, Leo Shepherd, Walter Williams (tp); Jimmy Cleveland, Al Grey, Paul Lee, Benny Powell (tb); Bobby Plater, Jerome Richardson (as); Gil Bernal, Johnny Board (ts); Curtis Lowe (ts, bars); Ben Kynard (bars); Milt Buckner (p); Billy Mackel (g); Roy Johnson (b); Ellis Bartee (d); Sonny Parker (v).

Gabby's Gabbin'   51S-3159
78: MGM 11765 LP: Verve VE2-2543

Don't Flee the Salty Scene – SP (v)   51S-3160
78: MGM 11227 LP: Verve VE2-2543

Kingfish   51S-3161
78: MGM 11227 LP: Verve VE2-2543

Oh Lady Be Good   51S-3162
78: MGM 11285 LP: Verve VE2-2543

Oh Rock – LH (v)   51S-3163
78: MGM 11176 LP: Verve VE2-2543

Probably October 17, 1951—Los Angeles, CA
Lionel Hampton and His Orchestra: personnel probably same as above.

Cry of the Blues
78: MGM 12986

Forbidden
78: MGM 12986

Note: some sources list this session as 1962 or 1963.

September 2, 1953—New York, NY
Norman Granz Jam Session: *Hampton* (vib); Dizzy Gillespie, Roy Eldridge (tp); Johnny Hodges (as); Illinois Jacquet, Flip Phillips, Ben Webster (ts); Oscar Peterson (p); Ray Brown (b); Buddy Rich (d).

Jam Blues   1280-3
LP: Verve MGV 8094

Blue Lou   1281-3
LP: Verve MGV 8062

Just You, Just Me   1282-3
LP: Verve MGV 8062

Hampton (vib), Oscar Peterson (p), Ray Brown (b), Buddy Rich (d):

Tenderly   1283-3
LP: Verve MGV 8094

Hampton (vib), Roy Eldridge (tp), Johnny Hodges (as), Illinois Jacquet and Flip Phillips (ts), Oscar Peterson (p), Ray Brown (b), Buddy Rich (d):

Jammin' for Clef   1284-3
LP: Verve MGV 8053

Blue Room   1285-2
LP: Verve MGV 8053

Note: "Tenderly" is a ballad feature for Hampton, but he also appears on "I Got It Bad and That Ain't Good" (a ballad feature for Hodges) and "She's Funny That Way" (a ballad feature for Eldridge).

September 2, 1953—New York, NY
Lionel Hampton Quartet: *Hampton* (vib), Oscar Peterson (p), Ray Brown (b), Buddy Rich (d).

Always LP: Verve (F) 813 091-1	1286-2
S'Wonderful LP: Verve (F) 813 091-1	1287-1
Air Mail Special LP: Verve (F) 813 091-1	1288-7
The Nearness of You LP: Verve (F) 813 091-1	1289-2
Soft Winds LP: Verve (F) 813 091-1	1290-1
Stompin' at the Savoy LP: Verve (F) 813 091-1	1291-1

Ca. September 1953—Paris, France
Lionel Hampton and His Orchestra: *Hampton* (vib); Clifford Brown, Art Farmer, Quincy Jones, Walter Williams (tp); Jimmy Cleveland, George Cooper, Al Hayse (tb); Gigi Gryce, Anthony Ortega (as); Clifford Solomon, Clifford Scott (ts); Oscar Estell (bars); George Wallington (p); Billy Mackel (g); Monk Montgomery (b); Alan Dawson, Curley Hamner (d); Sonny Parker, Annie Ross (v).

Opener
LP: IAJRC 31

Summertime
LP: IAJRC 31

On the Sunny Side of the Street
LP: IAJRC 31

On Rock
LP: IAJRC 31

How High the Moon
LP: IAJRC 31

Star Dust
LP: IAJRC 31

I Only Have Eyes for You
LP: IAJRC 31

Blue Boy
LP: IAJRC 31

September 28, 1953—Paris, France
Lionel Hampton and His Paris All-Stars: *Hampton* (vib), Walter Williams (tp), Al Hayse and Jimmy Cleveland (tb), Mezz Mezzrow (cl), Clifford Scott (ts), Claude Bolling (p), Billy Mackel (g), Monk Montgomery (elb), Curley Hamner (d).

Real Crazy
LP: Contemporary C3502, Vogue (F) 500752

Real Crazy (Complete Crazy)
78: Vogue (F) V5176 LP: Contemporary C3502

Real Crazy (More Crazy)
LP: Contemporary C3502

Real Crazy (More and More)
78: Vogue (F) V5181 LP: Contemporary C3502

September 28, 1953—Paris, France
Lionel Hampton and His Paris All-Stars: *Hampton* (vib, p), personnel same as above except Alix Combelle (ts) added.

Free Press Oui
LP: Contemporary C3502, Vogue (F) 500752

Blue Panassie
78: Vogue (F) V5151 LP: Contemporary C3502

Hampton replaces Bolling on piano:

Walkin' at the Trocadero
LP: Contemporary C3502, Vogue (F) 500752

September 28, 1953—Paris, France
Hampton (vib), Billy Mackel (g), Monk Montgomery (elb).

Always
LP: Blue Note BLP 5046, Vogue (F) 500752

September in the Rain
LP: Blue Note BLP 5046

I Only Have Eyes for You
78: Vogue (F) V5176 LP: Contemporary C3502, Vogue (F) 500752

November 11, 1953—Storyville Club, Copenhagen, Denmark
Lionel Hampton Jam Session: *Hampton* (p); Clifford Brown, Quincy Jones, Jorgen Ryg (tp); Jimmy Cleveland (tb); Anthony Ortega, Gigi Gryce (as); Clifford Scott (ts); Max Bruel (bars); unknown bass and drums.

Perdido unissued	CA113
All the Things You Are unissued	CA114
Indiana unissued	CA115

Hampton and Jorgen Bengston piano duet:

Anniversary Boogie unissued	CA116

Ca. 1953—no information

Tenderly
78: Panarama MH 98 LP: Fabulous 100009

Midnight Sun
78: Panarama MH 98 LP: Fabulous 100009

Smoke Gets in Your Eyes
LP: Fabulous 100009

Royal Swing
LP: Fabulous 100009

'Round about Midnight
LP: Fabulous 100009

November 30, 1953—Paris, France
Lionel Hampton and His Orchestra: *Hampton* (vib), Mezz Mezzrow (cl), Andre
Persiany (p), Buddy Banks (b), Curley Hamner (d).

Elmar the Stockbrocker	19.663
LP: Barclay (F) 80 988/989	

Serenade to Nicole's Mink Coat	19.664
LP: Barclay (F) 80 988/989	

Wailin' Panassie	19.665
LP: Barclay (F) 80 988/989	

Sweet Lorraine	19.666
LP: Barclay (F) 80 988/989	

November 30, 1953—Paris, France
Lionel Hampton and His Orchestra: *Hampton* (d), Mezz Mezzrow (cl), Andre
Persiany (p), Buddy Banks (b).

Crazy Hamp	19.667
LP: Barclay (F) 80 988/989	

November 30, 1953—Paris, France
Lionel Hampton and His Orchestra: *Hampton* (vib, x, tim), Mezz Mezzrow (cl),
Andre Persiany (p), Buddy Banks (b), Curley Hamner and Kansas Fields (d).

Mezz and the Hamp	19.668
LP: Barclay (F) 80 988/989	

November 30, 1953—Paris, France
Lionel Hampton and His Orchestra: *Hampton* (vib, p), Andre Persiany (p),
Buddy Banks (b), Curley Hamner (d).

Mister Fedor	19.669
LP: Barclay (F) 80 988/989	

November 30, 1953—Paris, France
Lionel Hampton and His Orchestra: *Hampton* (vib), Mezz Mezzrow (cl), Andre
Persiany (p), Buddy Banks (b), Kansas Fields (d).

Blues for the Hot Club de France	19.670
LP: Barclay (F) 80 988/989	

April 12, 1954—New York, NY
Lionel Hampton Quartet: *Hampton* (vib), Oscar Peterson (p), Ray Brown (b),
Buddy Rich (d).

Love for Sale   1548-1
LP: Verve (F) 813 091-1

April in Paris   1549-3
LP: Verve (F) 813 091-1

Just One of Those Things   1550-2
LP: Verve (F) 813 091-1

Stardust   1551-2
LP: Verve (F) 813 091-1

That Old Black Magic (Part 1)   1552-4
LP: Verve (F) 813 091-1 CD: Verve 833 287-2

That Old Black Magic (Part 2)   1552-5
LP: Verve (F) 813 091-1

This Can't Be Love   1553-1
LP: Verve (F) 813 091-1

Willow Weep for Me   1554-1
LP: Verve (F) 813 091-1

How High the Moon   1555-2
LP: Verve (F) 813 091-1

Blues for Norman   1556-2
LP: Verve (F) 813 091-1

I Can't Get Started   1557-1
LP: Verve (F) 813 091-1

Moonglow   1558-2
LP: Verve (F) 813 091-1

April 13, 1954—New York, NY
Lionel Hampton Quintet: *Hampton* (vib), Buddy De Franco (cl), Oscar Peterson
(p), Ray Brown (b), Buddy Rich (d).

It's Only a Paper Moon   1559-2
LP: Verve MGV 8106

The Way You Look Tonight   1560-1
LP: Verve MGV 8106

Flying Home   1561-?
LP: Verve MGV 8112

These Foolish Things   1562-2
LP: Verve MGV 8105

Don't Be That Way   1563-3
LP: Verve MGV 8105

Dinah   1564-2
LP: Verve MGV 8112

On the Sunny Side of the Street   1565-2
LP: Verve MGV 8113 CD: Verve 833 287-2

Je Ne Sais Pas   1566-1
LP: Verve MGV 8113 CD: Verve 833 287-2

July 22, 1954—Trianon Ballroom, Chicago, IL
Lionel Hampton and His Orchestra: *Hampton* (vib, p, d); Billy Brooks, Wallace
Davenport, Ed Mullens, Roy Slaughter (tp); George Cooper, Al Hayse, Harold
Roberts (ts); Jay Dennis, Bobby Plater (as); Elwyn Frazier, Jay Peters (ts); Oscar
Estell (bars); Dwike Mitchell (p); Billy Mackel (g); Peter Badie (b); Wilfred
Eddleton (d).

The Chase
LP: Columbia CL 711, CBS (Du) 21107

Stardust
LP: Columbia CL 711, CBS (Du) 21107

Mark VII
LP: Columbia CL 711, CBS (Du) 21107

Love for Sale
LP: Columbia CL 711, CBS (Du) 21107

Wailin' at the Trianon
LP: Columbia CL 711, CBS (Du) 21107

How High the Moon
LP: Columbia CL 711, CBS (Du) 21107

September 13, 1954—New York, NY
Lionel Hampton Quartet: *Hampton* (vib, v), Oscar Peterson (p), Ray Brown (b),
Buddy Rich (d, v).

It's a Blue World [long version]   1947-1
LP: Verve (F) 813 091-1

It's a Blue World [short version]   1947-4
78: Clef 89128 LP: Verve (F) 813 091-1

Rich and Brown out:

The High and the Mighty   1948-1
LP: Verve (F) 813 091-1 CD: Verve 833 287-2

Rich and Brown added:

When the Saints Go Marching In – LH & BR (v)   1949-?
LP: Verve (F) 813 091-1

Flying Home   1950-2
LP: Verve (F) 813 091-1 CD: Verve 833 287-2

Midnight Sun   1951-1
LP: Verve (F) 813 091-1

Tenderly   1952-1
LP: Verve (F) 813 091-1

Hallelujah   1953-2
LP: Verve (F) 813 091-1

Indiana   1954-2
LP: Verve (F) 813 091-1

September 15, 1954—New York, NY
Lionel Hampton Quintet: *Hampton* (vib, p, v), Oscar Peterson (p), Herb Ellis (g),
Ray Brown (b), Buddy Rich (d).

But Beautiful   1969-2
LP: Verve MGV 8228

Indiana   1970-4
LP: Verve MGV 8226

Hamp's Boogie-Woogie [long version]   1971-2
LP: Verve MGV 8228

Hamp's Boogie-Woogie [short version]   1971-3
78: Clef 89136 LP: Verve MGV 8275

Honeysuckle Rose [long version]   1972-1
LP: Verve MGV 8223

Honeysuckle Rose [short version]   1972-2
LP: Verve MGV 8223

China Boy   1973-1
LP: Verve MGV 8113 CD: Verve 833 287-2

A Foggy Day [long version]   1974-1
LP: Verve MGV 8223

A Foggy Day [short version]   1974-2
78: Clef 89136 LP: Verve MGV 8226, Verve MGV 8275

Our Love Is Here to Stay   1975-2
LP: Verve MGV 8228

Body and Soul   1976-1
LP: Verve MGV 8223

It's Only a Paper Moon   1977-2
LP: Verve MGV 8228

Sweethearts on Parade   1978-4
LP: Verve MGV 8228

Date with Oscar   1979-1
LP: Verve MGV 8228

**September 17, 1954—Bushnell Memorial Auditorium, Hartford, CT (Jazz at the
Philharmonic concert)**
Lionel Hampton– Buddy De Franco Sextet: *Hampton* (vib), Buddy De Franco
(cl), Oscar Peterson (p), Herb Ellis (g), Ray Brown (b), Buddy Rich (d).

How High the Moon
LP: Blue Star (F) GLP 3558, Verve (J) MV 9058/60

Body and Soul
LP: Blue Star (F) GLP 3558, Verve (J) MV 9058/60

Flying Home
LP: Verve 815146-1 Blue Star (F) 3558, Verve (J) MV 9058/60

Airmail Special
LP: Blue Star (F) GLP 3558, Verve (J) MV 9058/60

October 28, 1954—Amsterdam, Netherlands (concert)
Lionel Hampton and His Orchestra: *Hampton* (vib, p, d, v); Nat Adderley, Bill Brooks, Wallace Davenport, Ed Mullens (tp); Leon Comegys, Buster Cooper, Hal Roberts (tb); Jay Dennis, Bobby Plater (as); Elwyn Frazier, Jay Peters (ts); Joe Evans (bars); Dwike Mitchell (p); Billy Mackel (g); Peter Badie (b); Rufus Jones (d).

Stardust
LP: Philips B10157L, Contour 6870512

November 6, 1954—Düsseldorf, Germany (concert)
Lionel Hampton and His Orchestra: *Hampton* (vib, p, d, v), personnel same as above.

Introduction
LP: Philips B10157L, Contour 6870512

How High the Moon
LP: Philips B10157L, Contour 6870512

The Nearness of You
LP: Philips B10157L, Contour 6870512

Midnight Sun
LP: Philips B10157L, Contour 6870512

Lover Man
LP: Philips B10157L, Contour 6870512

Our Love Is Here to Stay
LP: Philips B10157L, Contour 6870512

Vibe Boogie
LP: Philips B10157L, Contour 6870512

Flying Home
LP: Philips B10157L, Contour 6870512

December 27, 1954—Industriehalle, Graz, Austria (concert)
Lionel Hampton and His Orchestra: *Hampton* (vib); Wallace Davenport, Julius Brooks, Ed Mullens, Nat Adderley (tp); Harold Roberts, Al Hayse, George Cooper (tb); Jay Dennis, Bobby Plater (as); Elwyn Frazier, Jay Peters (ts); Joe Evans (bars); Dwike Mitchell (p); Billy Mackel (g); Peter Badie (b); Wilfred Eddleton (d).

Theme
LP: First Heard (E) FH-54

Jam Blues
LP: First Heard (E) FH-54

Body and Soul
LP: First Heard (E) FH-54

The Chase
LP: First Heard (E) FH-54

Medium Blues
LP: First Heard (E) FH-54

Fast Blues
LP: First Heard (E) FH-54

December 27, 1954—Industriehalle, Graz, Austria (concert)
Lionel Hampton and His Orchestra: *Hampton* (vib, d), personnel same as above.

Airmail Special
LP: Swing House (E) SWH-45

Vibe Boogie
LP: Swing House (E) SWH-45

Jiving the Blues
LP: Swing House (E) SWH-45

Drums Feature
LP: Swing House (E) SWH-45

Medium Blues
LP: Swing House (E) SWH-45

How High the Moon
LP: Swing House (E) SWH-45

Vibe Boogie/Flying Home
LP: Swing House (E) SWH-45

March 18, 1955—Paris, France
Lionel Hampton Quartet: *Hampton* (vib), Michel Attenoux (cl), Raymond Fol
(p), Guy Pedersen (b), Moustache Galepides (d).

I've Found a New Baby
EP: Barclay (F) BEP 74007

Blues for the Hot Club de Lille
EP: Barclay (F) BEP 74007

March 19, 1955—Paris, France
Lionel Hampton and His French New Sound: *Hampton* (vib); Nat Adderley,
Benny Bailey, Bernard Hulin (tp); David Amram (fhr); Maurice Meunier (cl, ts);
William Boucaya (bars); Rene Urtreger (p); Sacha Distel (g); Guy Pedersen (b);
Baptiste "Mac Kac" Reilles (d); Christian Chevallier (arr).

Voice of the North   26.482
LP: Barclay (F) 80 988/989

Red Ribbon   26.483
LP: Barclay (F) 80 988/989

Crazy Rhythm   26.484
LP: Barclay (F) 80 988/989

Hampton (vib), Bernard Hulin (tp), Maurice Meunier (ts), Rene Urtreger (p),
Sacha Distel (g), Guy Pedersen (b), Baptiste "Mac Kac" Reilles (d) only:

I Cover the Waterfront   26.485
LP: Barclay (F) 80 988/989

Hampton (vib), Rene Urtreger (p), Sacha Distel (g), Guy Pedersen (b), Baptiste
"Mac Kac" Reilles (d) only:

Ala French   26.486
LP: Barclay (F) 80 988/989

Zebu
LP: Barclay (F) BLP 84004, EmArcy MG 36035

Night and Day
LP: Barclay (F) BLP 84005, EmArcy MG 36035

All the Things You Are
LP: Barclay (F) BLP 84005, EmArcy MG 36035

June 2, 1955—New York, NY
Mahalia Jackson (v) acc. by *Hampton* (vib), Mildred Falls (p), Ralph Jones (org),
Milt Hinton (b), Robert Prince (vib), with unknown orchestra.

No Room at the Inn
LP: Columbia CL 702, Columbia Special Products P 13347

The Holy Babe
LP: Columbia CL 702, Columbia Special Products P 13347

O Come All Ye Faithful
LP: Columbia CL 702, Columbia Special Products P 13347

Note: On two other titles from this session, "Joy to the World" and "Sweet Little
Jesus Boy," Hampton does not play.

July 31, 1955—Los Angeles, CA
Krupa-Hampton-Wilson Quartet: *Hampton* (vib), Teddy Wilson (p), Red
Callender (b), Gene Krupa (d).

Avalon   2360-4
LP: Verve (J) 23MJ 3072

I Got Rhythm   2361-6
LP: Verve (J) 23MJ 3072

Moonglow   2362-4
LP: Verve (J) 23MJ 3072 CD: Verve 833 287-2

Blues for Benny   2363-2
LP: Verve (J) 23MJ 3072

Just You, Just Me LP: Verve (J) 23MJ 3072	2364-4
The Man I Love LP: Verve (F) 813 091-1 CD: Verve 833 287-2	2365-1
Air Mail Special LP: Verve (J) 23MJ 3072 CD: 833 287-2	2366-2
Body and Soul LP: Verve (F) 813 091-1	2367-1

August 1, 1955—Los Angeles, CA
Lionel Hampton and Stan Getz: *Hampton* (vib), Stan Getz (ts), Lou Levy (p), Leroy Vinnegar (b), Shelly Manne (d).

Cherokee [breaks down during Hampton's solo] unissued	2368-5
Cherokee LP: Verve (J) MV 2534 CD: Verve 831 672-2	2368-6
Louise LP: Verve (J) MV 2534 CD: Verve 831 672-2	2369-1
Ballad Medley: East of the Sun/I Can't Get Started* LP: Verve (J) MV 2534 CD: Verve 831 672-2	2370-1
Jumpin' at the Woodside LP: Verve (J) MV 2534 CD: Verve 831 672-2	2371-1
Headache LP: not issued CD: Verve 831 672-2	2372-1
Gladys LP: not issued CD: Verve 831 672-2	2373-2
Gladys LP: Verve (J) MV 2534, Franklin Mint Record Society 40 CD: Verve 831 672-2, Verve 833 287-2	2373-3

Note: "Gladys" listed on session sheets as "Slew Foot."
 Unknown trombone player appears on the ballad medley, "Tenderly," and "Autumn in New York." He is probably from Hampton's big band at the time; it might be French horn player Willie Ruff.
 "Tenderly" and "Autumn in New York" are ballad features for Getz.

August 1, 1955—Los Angeles, CA
Hampton-Tatum-Rich: *Hampton* (vib), Art Tatum (p), Buddy Rich (d).

Perdido LP: Pablo 2310-720, Pablo 2625-0706	2374-2
Hallelujah LP: Pablo 2310-720, Pablo 2625-0706	2375-2

*Mystery trombone player appears on these titles!

I'll Never Be the Same LP: Pablo 2310-720, Pablo 2625-0706	2376-2
Love for Sale LP: Pablo 2310-775	2377-2
Love for Sale [alt. take] LP: Pablo 2310-775	2377-2
Body and Soul LP: Pablo 2310-775	2378-2
Please Be Kind LP: Pablo 2310-775	2379-1
What Is This Thing Called Love LP: Pablo 2310-720, Pablo 2625-0706	2380-2
Stars Fell on Alabama LP: Pablo 2310-775	2381-2
This Can't Be Love LP: Pablo 2310-775	2382-2
Lover Man LP: Pablo 2310-775	2383-1
Prisoner of Love LP: Pablo 2310-775	2384-2
Makin' Whoopee LP: Pablo 2310-720, Pablo 2625-0706	2385-1
More Than You Know LP: Pablo 2310-720, Pablo 2625-0706	2386-1
How High the Moon LP: Pablo 2310-720, Pablo 2625-0706	2387-2

August 2, 1955—Los Angeles, CA
Lionel Hampton Big Band: *Hampton* (vib, p, d, v); Billy Brooks, Wallace Davenport, Ed Mullens, Ed Preston (tp); Al Hayse, Arnett Sparrow, Hal Roberts (tb); Willie Ruff (fhr); James Araki, Bobby Plater (as); Eddie Chamblee, Retney Brauer (ts); Joe Evans (bars); Dwike Mitchell (p); Billy Mackel (g); Peter Badie (b); Rufus Jones (d); Isidore Hernandez (cgs).

Red River LP: Verve VE2-2543	2388-4
G.H.Q. LP: Verve VE2-2543	2389-6
Imagination 78: Clef 89165 LP: Verve VE2-2543	2390-6
Midnight Sun 78: Clef 89153 LP: Verve VE2-2543	2391-2
Airmail Special [short version] 78: Clef 89153 LP: Verve VE2-2543	2392-2

Airmail Special [long version]   2392-3
LP: Clef MGC 670

Flying Home [long version]   2393-1
LP: Verve VE2-2543 CD: Verve 833 281-2

Flying Home [short version]   2393-2
78: Clef 89165 LP: Verve MGV 8275

It's a Blue World   2394-1
LP: Verve VE2-2543

Swingin' on C   2395-3
LP: Verve VE2-2543

Shalom Shalom   2396-1
78: Clef 89154 LP: Clef MGC 670

The Blues Ain't News To Me – LH (v)   2397-5
LP: Verve VE2-2543

Note: Buddy Rich (d) replaces Rufus Jones on both versions of "Airmail Special" and "Flying Home."

August 3, 1955—Los Angeles, CA
Lionel Hampton Sextet: *Hampton* (vib), Willie Ruff (fhr), Dwike Mitchell (p), Billy Mackel (g), Peter Badie (b), Rufus Jones (d), Isidore Hernandez (cgs).

I Only Have Eyes for You   2398-6
LP: Verve VE2-2543

Song of the Vineyard   2399-1
78: Clef 89154 LP: Verve MGV 8019

Where or When   2400-1
LP: Verve MGV 8215

September 6, 1955—Los Angeles, CA
Lionel Hampton Sextet: *Hampton* (vib), Billy Brooks (tp), Eddie Chamblee (ts), Billy Mackel (g), Peter Badie (b), Rufus Jones (d), Vicki Lee (v).

Pig Ears and Rice   2486-2
LP: Verve VE2-2543

Baby Don't Love Me No More – VL (v)   2487-9
LP: Verve VE2-2543

All God's Chillun' Got Rhythm   2488-4
LP: Verve MGV 8215

September 7, 1955—Los Angeles, CA
Lionel Hampton's Jazz Giants: *Hampton* (vib), Harry Edison (tp), Art Tatum (p), Barney Kessel (g), Red Callender and John Simmons (b), Buddy Rich (d).

Plaid   2489-2
LP: Pablo 2310-731, Pablo 2625-0706

Somebody Loves Me   2490-2
LP: Pablo 2310-731, Pablo 2625-0706

Deep Purple   2491-5
LP: Pablo 2310-731, Pablo 2625-0706

What Is This Thing Called Love   2492-4
LP: Verve MGV 8215, Franklin Mint Record Society 40

September Song [long version]   2493-1
LP: Pablo 2310-731, Pablo 2625-0706

September Song [short version]   2493-3
78: Norgran 150

Verve Blues   2494-1
LP: Pablo 2310-731, Pablo 2625-0706

Note: John Simmons replaces Callender on bass on "Somebody Loves Me,"
"Deep Purple," and "Verve Blues." Guitarist Barney Kessel does not appear on
"September Song" and "Verve Blues."

January 28 & 30, 1956—Olympia, Paris, France (concert)
Lionel Hampton and His Orchestra: *Hampton* (vib, p, d, v); Billy Brooks, Dave
Gonsalves, Ed Mullens, Ed Preston (tp); Al Hayse, Walter "Phatz" Morris, Larry
Wilson (tb); Scoville Brown (cl, as); Bobby Plater (as, fl); Eddie Chamblee, Ricky
Brauer (ts); Curtis Lowe (bars); Oscar Dennard (p); Billy Mackel (g); Peter Badie
(b); Albert "June" Gardner (d); Robert Mosely (v).

Panama
LP: Versailles (F) 90M122, Festival 105

One O'Clock Jump
LP: Versailles (F) 90M122, Festival 105

Flyin' at the Olympia
LP: Versailles (F) 90M139, Festival 105

Paulette's Boogie
LP: Versailles (F) 90M142, Festival 105

Albuquerque Special
LP: Versailles (F) MED 4003, Festival 105

Gladys
LP: Versailles (F) MEDX 2003, Festival 105

Memories of You
LP: Versailles (F) MEDX 2003, Festival 105

Hallelujah
LP: Versailles (F) MEDX 2003, Festival 105

Battle of the Saxes
LP: Versailles (F) MEDX 2003, Festival 105

The Rice
LP: Versailles (F) 90M139, Festival 105

Blue One
LP: Versailles (F) MED 4003, Festival 105

10, Rue Caumartin
LP: Versailles (F) MEDX 2004, Festival 105

Add Curley Hamner (d):

Perdido
LP: Versailles (F) 90M122, Festival 105

Drums Fight
LP: Versailles (F) 90M122, Festival 105

Curley Hammer (d) out:

Rockin' at Olympia
LP: Versailles (F) 90M142, Festival 105

Hey-Ba-Ba-Re-Bop
LP: Versailles (F) 90M142, Festival 105

Blues for Sacha
LP: Versailles (F) MEDX 2004, Festival 105

Where or When
LP: Versailles (F) MEDX 2004, Festival 105

Patricia's Boogie
LP: Versailles (F) MEDX 2004, Festival 105

Clopin-Clopant – RM (v)
LP: Versailles (F) MEDX 2004, Festival 105

February 14, 1956—Tabarin, Vienna, Austria
Lionel Hampton meets Fatty George: *Hampton* (vib), Fatty George (cl), Bill Grah (p), Oskar Klein (g), Heinz Grah (b), Bob Blumenhoven (d).

How High the Moon
LP: Mastertone/Ex Libris JML 013, Black Jack (G) LP 3019

C Jam Blues
LP: Mastertone/Ex Libris JML 013

The Sheik of Araby
LP: Mastertone/Ex Libris JML 013

Add Willi Meerwaald (vtb) and Beryl Bryden (v, w); Oskar Klein switches to cornet:

Mama Don't Allow
LP: Mastertone/Ex Libris JML 013

Note: Several unissued masters exist from this session. Details are lacking as Mastertone files were destroyed.

May 1 & 2, 1956—Paris, France
Lionel Hampton and His Rhythm: *Hampton* (vib, p, arr), Oscar Dennard (p), Billy Mackel (g), Peter Badie (b), June Gardner (d).

Olee Dolee Doff
LP: Harmony HL 7115, Fontana (Du) 6433 029

It's a Long Way to Tipperary
LP: Harmony HL 7115, Fontana (Du) 6433 029

La Vie en Rose
LP: Harmony HL 7115, Fontana (Du) 6433 029

Toen Onze Mop Een Mopje Was
LP: Harmony HL 7115, Fontana (Du) 6433 029

Sarie Marais
LP: Harmony HL 7115, Fontana (Du) 6433 029

Tire L'Aiquille "Lai Lai Lai"
LP: Harmony HL 7115, Fontana (Du) 6433 029

Vieni Sul Mar
LP: Harmony HL 7115, Fontana (Du) 6433 029

Le Prisonier de Nantes
LP: Harmony HL 7115, Fontana (Du) 6433 029

Die Lorelei
LP: Harmony HL 7115, Fontana (Du) 6433 029

Zeg Kwezelken Wildet Gij Dansen
LP: Harmony HL 7115, Fontana (Du) 6433 029

Danny Boy
LP: Harmony HL 7115, Fontana (Du) 6433 029

I Kiss Your Little Hand, Madame
LP: Harmony HL 7115, Fontana (Du) 6433 029

May 3, 1956—Paris, France
Lionel Hampton and His All-Stars: *Hampton* (vib, p, v), Guy Lafitte (ts), Claude Bolling (p), Billy Mackel (g), Paul Rovere (b), Curley Hamner (d).

Panama
LP: Swing SW 8415, Pathé (F) 1727301

Sweethearts on Parade – LH (v)
LP: Swing SW 8415, Pathé (F) 1727301

Honeysuckle Rose – LH (v)
LP: Swing SW 8415, Pathé (F) 1727301

Body and Soul
LP: Swing SW 8415, Pathé (F) 1727301

Hamp Swings the Bells
LP: Swing SW 8415, Pathé (F) 1727301

Jazz Stars News
LP: Swing SW 8415, Pathé (F) 1727301

Bolling (p) out:

Jam for Brigitte
LP: Swing SW 8415, Pathé (F) 1727301

Add Bolling (p):

Genevieve
LP: Columbia (F) FP 1089, Pathé (F) 1727301

Blues for Lorraine
LP: Swing SW 8415

Guy Lafitte (ts) out:

What's New
LP: Swing SW 8415, Pathé (F) 1727301

Le Piege
LP: Swing SW 8415

May 5, 1956—Paris, France
Lionel Hampton and His All-Stars: *Hampton* (vib, p, v), Ed Mullens (tp), Eddie Chamblee (ts), Robert Mosely (p), Billy Mackel (g), Paul Rovere (b), Albert "June" Gardner (d).

St. Louis Blues – LH (v)
LP: Club Français du Disque (F) J80, Musidisc (F) 1068

Exactly Like You – LH (v)
LP: Club Français du Disque (F) J80, Musidisc (F) 1068

May 5, 1956—Paris, France
Lionel Hampton All-Stars: *Hampton* (vib, p, d, v), Ed Mullens (tp), Eddie Chamblee (ts), Jean-Claude Pelletier (p), Billy Mackel (g), Paul Rovere (b), Albert "June" Gardner (d).

Lullaby of Birdland
LP: Club Français du Disque (F) J79, Musidisc (F) 1064

Jammin' on High Society
LP: Club Français du Disque (F) J79, Musidisc (F) 1064

Blues for Monique – LH (v)
LP: Club Français du Disque (F) J79, Musidisc (F) 1064

Regina's Drag
LP: Club Français du Disque (F) J80, Musidisc (F) 1068

Just You, Just Me
LP: Club Français du Disque (F) J80, Musidisc (F) 1068

Hampton (vib), Robert Mosely (p), Benoit Quersin (b), June Gardner (d):

Love Is a Many-Splendored Thing
LP: Club Français du Disque (F) J79, Musidisc (F) 1064

June 28, 1956—Madrid, Spain
Lionel Hampton and His Orchestra: *Hampton* (vib), Dave Gonsalves (tp), Maria Angelicia (castanets), plus large band directed by Eddie Warner.

Bop City Flamenco
LP: Victor LPM 1422

Hot Club of Madrid Serenade
LP: Victor LPM 1422

Flamenco Soul
LP: Victor LPM 1422

June 28, 1956—Madrid, Spain
Lionel Hampton and His Orchestra: *Hampton* (vib, p, v); Dave Gonsalves, Billy Brooks, Ed Mullens, Ed Preston (tp); Al Hayse, Walter "Phatz" Morris, Larry Wilson (tb); Scoville Brown, Bobby Plater (as, cl, fl); Eddie Chamblee, Ricky Brauer (ts); Curtis Lowe (bars); Oscar Dennard, Robert Mosely (p); Peter Badie (b); June Gardner (d); Maria Angelicia (castanets).

Lovely Night in Spain
LP: Victor LPM 1422

The Bullfighter from Madrid
LP: Victor LPM 1422

I Got a Brand New Baby
LP: Victor LPM 1422

Hamp's Jazz Flamenco
LP: Victor LPM 1422

June 28, 1956—Madrid, Spain
Lionel Hampton and His Orchestra *Hampton* (vib), Tete Montoliu (p), Billy Mackel (g), Peter Badie (b), June Gardner (d), Maria Angelicia (castanets).

Spain
LP: Victor LPM 1422

Tenderly
LP: Victor LPM 1422

Toledo Blade
LP: Victor LPM 1422

Embraceable You
Unissued

July 16, 1956—Paris, France
Lionel Hampton and His Orchestra: *Hampton* (vib), personnel same as orchestra on 6-28-56, except Mosely (p) out and Gana M'Bo (bgs) added.

Let's Groove
unissued

Melancholy Feeling
unissued

Hamp's Special
unissued

Robert Mosely (org) added:

Gizmo
unissued

July 16, 1956—Paris, France
Lionel Hampton and His Orchestra: *Hampton* (vib), personnel same as orchestra
on 6-28-56, except Mosely (p) out and Gana M'Bo (bgs) added.

Fast Blues
unissued

Slow Blues
unissued

August 1956—New York, NY
Lionel Hampton Concert Hall All-Stars: *Hampton* (vib, marimba, p), Oscar
Dennard (p), Oscar Pettiford (b), Gus Johnson (d).

My Man
LP: Jazztone J-1040, Musidisc (F) 30 JA 5107

Too Much
LP: Jazztone J-1040, Musidisc (F) 30 JA 5107

Time for Lyons
LP: Jazztone (Eu) J-1238, Musidisc (F) 30 JA 5107

Loch Lomond
LP: Jazztone (Eu) J-1238, Musidisc (F) 30 JA 5107

Look, Four Hands
LP: Jazztone (Eu) J-1238, Musidisc (F) 30 JA 5107

Take the "A" Train
LP: Jazztone J-1040

August 1956—New York, NY
Lionel Hampton Concert Hall All-Stars: *Hampton* (vib, marimba, p), Ray
Copeland (tp), Jimmy Cleveland (tb), Lucky Thompson (ts), Oscar Dennard (p),
Oscar Pettiford (b), Gus Johnson (d).

Lionel's Choo-Choo
EP: Jazztone J-723

Romeo's Gone Now
EP: Jazztone J-723, Musidisc (F) 30 JA 5107

Dark Eyes
EP: Jazztone J-723, Musidisc (F) 30 JA 5107

Deep Purple
LP: Jazztone J-1040

Ghost of a Chance
LP: Jazztone J-1040, Musidisc (F) 30 JA 5107

Over the Rainbow
LP: Jazztone (Eu) J-1238

When You're Smiling
LP: Jazztone (Eu) J-1238

Copeland (tp) and Thomspon (ts) out:

Summertime
LP: Jazztone (Eu) J-1238

Add Copeland (tp) and Thompson (ts):

Reindeer
LP: Jazztone (Eu) J-1238, Musidisc (F) 30 JA 5107

Undecided
LP: Jazztone J-1040, Musidisc (F) 30 JA 5107

What's Your Hurry!
LP: Jazztone (Eu) J-1238

August 13 & 14, 1957—New York, NY
Lionel Hampton and His Orchestra: *Hampton* (vib, p, d, v), Bobby Plater (fl, as, ts, cl), Oscar Dennard (p), Billy Mackel (g), Julius Brown (b), Wilbert Hogan (d).

The Man I Love
LP: Audio Fidelity AF 1849/SD 5849

Just One of Those Things
LP: Audio Fidelity AF 1849/SD 5849

One Step from Heaven
LP: Audio Fidelity AF 1849/SD 5849

Darn That Dream
LP: Audio Fidelity AF 1849/SD 5849

Stardust
LP: Audio Fidelity AF 1849/SD 5849

Tracking Problem
LP: Audio Fidelity AF 1849/SD 5849

Lullaby of Birdland
LP: Audio Fidelity AF 1849/SD 5849

Blues for Stephen
LP: Audio Fidelity AF 1849/SD 5849

And the Angels Sing
LP: Audio Fidelity AF 1849/SD 5849

Our Love Is Here to Stay
LP: Audio Fidelity AF 1849/SD 5849

I Know That You Know
LP: Audio Fidelity AF 1849/SD 5849

Sometimes I'm Happy
LP: Audio Fidelity AF 1849/SD 5849

Thoughts of Thelma (Lazy Thoughts)
LP: Audio Fidelity AF 1849/SD 5849

Note: "Thoughts of Thelma" issued as "Thoughts of a Playboy" on Playboy PB 1958. Tune is actually "How High the Moon."

January 5 & 6, 1958—Stuttgart, Germany
Lionel Hampton and His Orchestra: *Hampton* (vib, p); Ed Mullens, Eddie
Williams, Dave Gonsalves, Arthur Hoyle, Macky Kasper (tp); Wade Marcus, Jr.,
Lou Blackburn, Lawrence Williams (tb); Leon Zachary, Leo Moore, Leroy
Thomas (as); Bobby Plater (as, fl); Andy McGhee, Gerald Weinkopf (ts); Lonnie
Shaw, Werner Baumgart (bars); Oscar Dennard (p); Billy Mackel (g); Julius
Brown (b); Wilbert Hogan, Curley Hamner (d); Cornelius "Pinocchio" James (v).

The Mess Is Here
LP: Bertelsmann 7034

Hamp's Boogie-Woogie
LP: Bertelsmann 7034

Flying Home
LP: Bertelsmann 7034

Our Love Is Here to Stay
LP: Bertelsmann 7034

My Prayer
LP: Bertelsmann 7034

Confirmation
LP: Bertelsmann 7034

Almost Paradise
LP: Bertelsmann 7034

Around about Midnight
LP: Bertelsmann 7034

New Orleans Woman – PJ (v)
LP: Bertelsmann 7034

The Move
LP: Bertelsmann 7034

Ca. 1958—Tel Aviv, Israel
Lionel Hampton (vib) acc. by large orchestra and vocal choir under the direction
of Regina Ben Amittay.

Song of the Negev
LP: Glad-Hamp GHLP 1001

Exodus
LP: Glad-Hamp GHLP 1001

April 30, 1958—"Timex Jazz Show," New York, NY
Hampton (vib), Louis Armstrong (tp, v), Jack Teagarden (tb, v), Gerry Mulligan
(bars), Ed Hall (cl), George Shearing (p), Mort Herbert (b), Danny Barcelona (d),
J. P. Morgan (v).

St. Louis Blues – LA & JPM (v)
LP: Kings of Jazz KLJ 20031

Basin Street Blues – JT (v)
LP: Kings of Jazz KLJ 20031

May 1958—New York, NY
Lionel Hampton (vib) acc. by large orchestra and vocal choir under the direction
of Regina Ben Amittay.

Hamp's Boogie-Woogie
LP: Kings of Jazz KLJ 20031

The Lady's a Tramp
LP: Kings of Jazz KLJ 20031

Real Gone and Crazy
LP: Kings of Jazz KLJ 20031

St. Louis Blues
LP: Kings of Jazz KLJ 20031

Ca. 1958—concert
Lionel Hampton and His Orchestra: *Hampton* (vib, p, d, v); Dave Gonsalves,
Arthur Hoyle, Ed Mullens, Ed Williams (tp); Slide Hampton, Larry Wilson,
Clarence Watson (tb); Bobby Plater, Leon Zachary (as); Elsie Smith (ts); Adam
Norris (bars); Oscar Dennard (p); Billy Mackel (g); Julius Brown (b); Wilbert
Hogan (d).

Stardust
LP: Ades JS 30 LA 501/30 LA 1001

Tenderly
LP: Ades JS 30 LA 501/30 LA 1001

Midnight Sun
LP: Ades JS 30 LA 501/30 LA 1001

The Nearness of You
LP: Ades JS 30 LA 501/30 LA 1001

'Round Midnight
LP: Ades JS 30 LA 501/30 LA 1001

How High the Moon
LP: Ades JS 30 LA 501/30 LA 1001

Gates Gone Blues
LP: Ades JS 30 LA 501/30 LA 1001

King David
LP: Ades JS 30 LA 501/30 LA 1001

Some discographies list an October 1958 "Art Ford TV Show" as a Lionel
Hampton item, but the vibraphone player has been identified as Harry Shepherd.

November 10, 1958—"Timex All-Star Jazz Show," New York, NY
Hampton/Krupa Quartet: *Hampton* (vib), Gene Krupa (d), Bob Haggart (b),
Donn Trenner (p).

How High the Moon
LP: Sounds Great SG-8011

Anita O'Day (v) and *Hampton* (v, vib) acc. by Les Brown and His Band of
Renown: Dick Collins, Wes Hensel, Frank Beach, Jerry Kadowitz (tp); Dick

Kenney, Roy Main, Jim Hill, Stumpy Brown (tb); Matt Utal, Ralph La Polla (as); Billy Usselton, Abe Aaron (ts); Butch Stone (bars); Donn Trenner (p); Tony Rizzi (g); Bob Borteaux (b); Lloyd Morales (d).

Let Me Off Uptown
LP: Sounds Great SG-8011

Hampton (vib, p) acc. by Les Brown and His Band of Renown.

Hamp's Boogie-Woogie
LP: Sounds Great SG-8011

Hampton (vib) plays on a medley of Hoagy Carmichael tunes. He is featured on a short rendition of "Stardust," and he plays behind vocalists Carmichael, Jane Morgan, Anita O'Day, Bob Crosby, and Louis Armstrong:

Hoagy Carmichael Medley
LP: Sounds Great SG-8011

Jam session featuring *Hampton* (vib), Gene Krupa and Chico Hamilton (d), Les Brown and His Band of Renown, the Bobcats, Louis Armstrong (tp).

One O'Clock Jump
LP: Sounds Great SG-8011

Note: Hampton does not take part in the rest of the show.

December 1, 1958—New York, NY
Lionel Hampton and His Orchestra: *Hampton* (vib, p, d, v); Edward Pazant, Bobby Plater (as); Andrew McGhee, Leon Zachary (ts); Lonnie Shaw (bars); Oscar Dennard (p); Billy Mackel (g); John Nixon, George Joyner (b); Wilbert Hogan (d).

Smoke Gets in Your Eyes — CO61900
LP: Columbia CL 1304/CS 8110

Satin Doll — CO61901
LP: Columbia CL 1304/CS 8110

Vibraholiday — CO61902
LP: Columbia CL 1304/CS 8110

The Nearness of You — CO61903
LP: Columbia CL 1304/CS 8110

My Prayer — CO61904
LP: Columbia CL 1304/CS 8110

Saxes out:

My Funny Valentine — CO61905
LP: Columbia CL 1304/CS 8110

'Round Midnight — CO61906
LP: Columbia CL 1304/CS 8110

The More I See You — CO61907
LP: Columbia CL 1304/CS 8110

But Beautiful   CO61908
LP: Columbia CL 1304/CS 8110

Just You, Just Me   CO61909
LP: Columbia CL 1304/CS 8110

Blues in Gold   CO61910
LP: Columbia CL 1304/CS 8110

White Christmas   CO61911
LP: Columbia CL 1893/CS 8693

The High and the Mighty   CO61912
LP: Columbia CL 1304/CS 8110

April 13, 1959—New York, NY
Lionel Hampton and His Orchestra: *Hampton* (vib, p, d, v); Ed Williams, Ed
Mullens, Arthur Hoyle, Dave Gonsalves, Donald Byrd, Cat Anderson (tp);
Clarence Watson, Lou Blackburn, Wade Marcus (tb); Bobby Plater, Ed Pazant
(as); Herman Green, Andrew McGhee (ts); Lonnie Shaw (bars); Wade Legge (p);
Billy Mackel (g); Lawrence Burgan (b); Charlie Persip, Wilbert Hogan (d);
possibly Pinocchio James (v).

Flying Home
LP: Audio Fidelity AF 1913

Hey Ba-Be-Re-Bop – LH & ensemble (v)
LP: Audio Fidelity AF 1913

Hamp's Boogie-Woogie
LP: Audio Fidelity AF 1913

Kidney Stew – PJ [?] (v)
LP: Audio Fidelity AF 1913

Hamp's Mambo
LP: Audio Fidelity AF 1913

Airmail Special
LP: Audio Fidelity AF 1913

Big Brass
LP: Audio Fidelity AF 1913

Red Top
LP: Audio Fidelity AF 1913

Night Train
LP: Audio Fidelity AF 1913

Elaine and Duffy
LP: Audio Fidelity AF 1913

Cutter's Corner
LP: Audio Fidelity AF 1913

Le Chat Noir
LP: Audio Fidelity AF 1913

Blue Lou
LP: Playboy PB 1959

March 10, 1960—New York, NY
Lionel Hampton and His Orchestra: *Hampton* (vib); Richard Hixson, Eddie Bert, Lou McGarity, Bobby Byrne (tb); Tommy Flanagan (p); Billy Mackel (g); George Duvivier (b); Osie Johnson (d).

For Better and Worse   CO54563
LP: Columbia CL 1486/CS 8277

What's New   CO54564
LP: Columbia CL 1486/CS 8277

Walkin' My Baby Back Home   CO54565
LP: Columbia CL 1486/CS 8277

Till You Return   CO54566
LP: Columbia CL 1486/CS 8277

Beulah's Boogie   ?CO54567
LP: CBS 88134

March 21, 1960—New York, NY
Lionel Hampton and His Orchestra: *Hampton* (vib); Eddie Bert, Richard Hixson, Sonny Russo, Bobby Byrne (tb); Tommy Flanagan (p); Skeeter Best (g); George Duvivier (b); Osie Johnson (d).

Skylark   CO54568
LP: Columbia CL 1486/CS 8277

Day by Day   CO54569
LP: Columbia CL 1486/CS 8277

Speak Low   CO54570
LP: Columbia CL 1486/CS 8277

My Foolish Heart   CO54571
LP: Columbia CL 1486/CS 8277

Poor Butterfly   CO54572
LP: Columbia CL 1486/CS 8277

March 23, 1960—New York, NY
Lionel Hampton (vib, x, cel), Tommy Flanagan (p), Billy Mackel (g), George Duvivier (b), Elvin Jones (d).

Blue Moon   CO64290
LP: Columbia CL 1486/CS 8277, Columbia CL 1610/CS 8410

I Can't Get Started   CO64291 [?]
LP: Columbia CL 1765/CS 8565

Ca. April 1960—New York, NY
Lionel Hampton All-Stars: *Hampton* (vib), Ram Ramirez (p, org), George Duvivier (b), Kenny Burrell (g), Osie Johnson (d).

Railroad No. 1   H0004
LP: Glad-Hamp GHLP 1001, Glad-Hamp GHLP 3050

Sometimes I'm Happy   H0005
45: Glad-Hamp 60005

Wild Bill Twist
LP: Glad-Hamp GHLP 1001, Glad-Hamp GHLP 3050

Note: "Railroad No. 1" and "Sometimes I'm Happy" are erroneously identified
as a live big band session at the Metropole Café (Dec. 1961).

Wailin'
45:Glad-Hamp 60009

The Wine Song
45:Glad-Hamp 60010

Let's Be Happy
45:Glad-Hamp 60010

1960—New York, NY
Hampton (vib), King Curtis (ts), Tommy Flanagan (p), Bucky Pizzarelli (g), Milt
Hinton (b), Ronnie Zito (d).

(Bruce's) Juice/More Juice
LP: Glad-Hamp GHLP 1001

Note: Label reads "Juice and More Juice."

Ca. 1960—New York, NY
Lionel Hampton and His Orchestra: *Hampton* (vib, p, d, v); Dave Gonsalves,
Virgil Jones, Floyd Jones, Andrew Wood (tp); Vincente Prudente, Haleem
Rasheed, George Jeffers (tb); Bobby Plater, Ed Pazant (as); Andrew McGhee,
Herman Green (ts); Lonnie Shaw (bars); Harold Mabern (p); Calvin Newborn
(g); Lawrence Burgan (b) Wilbert Hogan (d).

McGhee
LP: Glad-Hamp GHLP 1001

Playboy Theme
LP: Glad-Hamp GHLP 1001

Hava Nagila
LP: Glad-Hamp GHLP 1001

Lonesome Nights (aka "Take My Word")
LP: Glad-Hamp GHLP 1001

Wine Song
LP: Glad-Hamp GHLP 1001

March 25, 1961—Paris, France (concert)
Lionel Hampton and His Orchestra: *Hampton* (vib, p, d, v); Dave Gonsalves,
Virgil Jones, Floyd Jones, Andrew Wood (tp); Vincente Prudente, Haleem
Rasheed, George Jeffers (tb); Bobby Plater, Ed Pazant (as); Andrew McGhee,
Herman Green (ts); Lonnie Shaw (bars); Roland Hanna (p); Calvin Newborn (g);
Lawrence Burgan (b); Wayne Robinson (d).

Answer Me My Love
LP: Glad-Hamp GHLP 1005

How High the Moon
LP: Glad-Hamp GHLP 1003, Glad-Hamp GHLP 1005

Flying Home
LP: Glad-Hamp GHLP 1003

Summertime
LP: Glad-Hamp GHLP 1005

Little Bitty Pretty One
LP: Glad-Hamp GHLP 1005

America by Night
LP: Glad-Hamp GHLP 1005

March 26, 1961—Brussels, Belgium (concert)
Lionel Hampton and His Orchestra: *Hampton* (vib), personnel same as above.

Mr. John
LP: Glad-Hamp GHLP 1003

April 1961—Milan, Italy (concert)
Lionel Hampton and His Orchestra: *Hampton* (vib), personnel same as 3-25-61.

Mr. "J"
LP: Glad-Hamp GHLP 1003

April 11, 1961—New York, NY
Lionel Hampton (vib), unknown strings, Teo Macero and Jack Pleis (arr, cond).

Deep Purple LP: Columbia CL 1661/CS 8461	CO66584
On Green Dolphin Street LP: Columbia CL 1661/CS 8461	CO66585
Laura LP: Columbia CL 1661/CS 8461	CO66586
Star Eyes LP: Columbia CL 1661/CS 8461	CO66587
Ruby LP: Columbia CL 1661/CS 8461	CO66588
Over the Rainbow LP: Columbia CL 1661/CS 8461	CO66589
Do Nothin' Till You Hear from Me LP: Columbia CL 1661/CS 8461	CO66590
Stairway to the Stars LP: Columbia CL 1661/CS 8461	CO66591
Gone Again LP: Columbia CL 1661/CS 8461	CO66592

Blues I Got Coming Tomorrow   CO66593
LP: Columbia CL 1661/CS 8461

Once in a While   CO66594
LP: Columbia CL 1661/CS 8461

1961—Las Vegas, NV, or New York, NY
Lionel Hampton and His Orchestra: *Hampton* (vib); Virgil Jones, Floyd Jones,
Dave Gonsalves, Andrew Wood (tp); Lester Robertson, Haleem Rasheed, George
Jeffers (tb); Bobby Plater, Ed Pazant (as); Andrew McGhee, John Neely (ts);
Lonnie Shaw (bars); Kenny Lowe (p); Roland Faulkner (g); Lawrence Burgan (b);
Oliver Jackson (d); Pinocchio James (v).

Hamp Twist
LP: Glad-Hamp GHLP 1001, Glad-Hamp GHLP 3050

The Fabulous Flamingo Twist
LP: Glad-Hamp GHLP 1001, Glad-Hamp GHLP 3050

1961—Las Vegas, NV, or New York, NY
Lionel Hampton and His Orchestra: personnel similar to above.

Darktown Strutters Ball
45: Glad-Hamp 2002

Everybody Loves My Baby – PJ (v)
45: Glad-Hamp 2002

December 9, 1961—Metropole Café, New York, NY
Lionel Hampton and His Orchestra. Probable personnel: Hampton (vib); Dave
Gonsalves, Virgil Jones, Floyd Jones, Richard Williams (tp); Harleem Rasheed,
Vince Prudente, Lester Robinson (tb); Bobby Plater, Ed Pazant (as), Andrew
McGhee, John Neely (ts); Pepper Adams (bars); Kenny Lowe (p); Billy Mackel
(g); Lawrence Burgan (b); Wilbert Hogan (d).

At the Metropole
LP: Glad-Hamp GHLP 3050

Encore
LP: Glad-Hamp GHLP 3050

After You've Gone
LP: Glad-Hamp GHLP 1005

They Say It's Wonderful
LP: Glad-Hamp GHLP 1005

It's All Right with Me
LP: Glad-Hamp GHLP 1005

Take My Word
LP: Glad-Hamp GHLP 1005

McGhee
LP: Glad-Hamp GHLP 1005

January 11, 1962—New York, NY
Hampton (vib) acc. by unknown group.

It's Fun to Think
LP: Columbia CL 1791/CS 8591

January 11, 1962—New York, NY
Hampton (vib); Richard Hixson, Eddie Bert, Lou McGarity, Bobby Byrne (tb); Tommy Flanagan (p); Billy Mackel (g); George Duvivier (b); Osie Johnson (d).

White Christmas
LP: Columbia PC 36803 CD: Columbia MK 40166

April 10, 1962—New York, NY
Lionel Hampton and His Orchestra: *Hampton* (vib); Teo Macero (ts); Roland Hanna (p); Arvell Shaw, Lawrence Burgan (b); Al Dreares, Walter Perkins (d); Winslowe Barrajanos, Jose Paulo, Julio Colazzo (perc).

You're Cruel   CO70030
LP: Epic LA 16027/BA 17027

Macero (ts) out:

Answer Me My Love   CO70031
LP: Epic LA 16027/BA 17027

I'll Be Seeing You   CO70032
LP: Epic LA 16027/BA 17027

Like Someone in Love   CO70033
LP: Epic LA 16027/BA 17027

Where Are You   CO70034
LP: Epic LA 16027/BA 17027

April 17, 1962—New York, NY
Lionel Hampton and His Orchestra: *Hampton* (vib); Virgil Jones (tp); Teo Macero (ts); Roland Hanna (p, org); Edwin Woldin (p); Bucky Pizzarelli (g); Lawrence Burgan (b); Al Dreares (d); Winslowe Barrajanos, Jose Paulo, Julio Colazzo (perc).

Spring Is Here   CO70059
LP: Epic LA 16027/BA 17027

Edwin Woldin (p), Macero (ts), and Pizzarelli (g) out:

Hi Fly   CO70060
LP: Epic LA 16027/BA 17027

Woldin (p) out:

I Got It Bad   CO70061
LP: Epic LA 16027/BA 17027

One-Note Samba   CO70062
LP: Epic LA 16027/BA 17027

J.C. Cellar
LP: Columbia CL 1970/CS 8770

April 25, 1962—New York, NY
Lionel Hampton and His Orchestra: personnel same as 4-10-62.

Love Is a Many-Splendored Thing   CO70079
LP: Epic LA 16027/BA 17027

The Song of Moulin Rouge   CO70081
LP: Epic LA 16027/BA 17027

Three Coins in the Fountain   CO70093
LP: Epic LA 16027/BA 17027

Ca. 1962– 63—New York, NY
Lionel Hampton's All-Stars: *Hampton* (vib), Maury Wills (v), unknown (p), (org),
(b), (d).

Crawdad Hole   1037
45: Glad-Hamp 2009

Bye-Bye Blues   1038
45: Glad-Hamp 2009

Maybe Tomorrow
45: Cameo 204

Nothing's Impossible
45: Cameo 204

March 20, 1963—Silver Slipper Club, Las Vegas, NV
Lionel Hampton and Charlie Teagarden: *Hampton* (vib), Charlie Teagarden (tp),
Bill Harris (tb), Ronnie di Fillips (p), Carson Smith (b), Tom Montgomery (d).

Silver Slipper   DLA 13141
LP: Coral CRL (S7)57438, Affinity (E) AFS 1017

410 East   DLA 13142
LP: Coral CRL (S7)57438

Hamp's Vamp   DLA 13143
LP: Coral CRL (S7)57438

Blues for Little T   DLA 13144
LP: Coral CRL (S7)57438, Affinity (E) AFS 1017

Dancing on the Ceiling   DLA 13145
LP: Coral CRL (S7)57438, Affinity (E) AFS 1017

Memories of You   DLA 13148
LP: Coral CRL (S7)57438, Affinity (E) AFS 1017

How High the Moon   DLA 13149
LP: Coral CRL (S7)57438

I Can't Get Started   DLA 13150
LP: Coral CRL (S7)57438

Sermonette   DLA 13151
LP: Coral CRL (S7)57438

Masked Grandma   DLA 13152
LP: Coral CRL (S7)57438

The Deacon and the Elder   DLA 13154
LP: Coral CRL (S7)57438

September in the Rain   DLA 13156
LP: Coral CRL (S7)57438

September/October 1963—New York, NY
Lionel Hampton All-Stars: *Hampton* (vib, marimba), Bobby Plater (fl, as, bars),
Edwin Woldin (p), Jose Paulo (g, v), Lawrence Burgan (b), Don Michaels (d),
Danny Barrajanos (cgs), Carmen Costa (v).

Estranho
LP: Glad-Hamp GHLP 1004

Bossa Nova Jazz
LP: Glad-Hamp GHLP 1004

Recado
LP: Glad-Hamp GHLP 1004

Bossa Nova York
LP: Glad-Hamp GHLP 1004

Sambolero
LP: Glad-Hamp GHLP 1004

Same to You
LP: Glad-Hamp GHLP 1004

Some Day
LP: Glad-Hamp GHLP 1004

Palhacada
LP: Glad-Hamp GHLP 1004

Nota Sol
LP: Glad-Hamp GHLP 1004

St. Thomas
LP: Glad-Hamp GHLP 1004

Gladys' Bossa Nova
45: Glad-Hamp 2008

November 1963—Tokyo, Japan (concert)
Lionel Hampton and His Orchestra: *Hampton* (vib, d, v); Floyd Jones, Virgil
Jones, Yoshihiga Kato, Teruyky Fukushima (tp); Lester Robertson, Yasuo Maeda,
Kazou Usui (tb); Bobby Plater, Ed Pazant (as, fl); Andrew McGhee, Jiro Inagasky
(ts); Shinduje Tanaka (ts, bars); Masaky Kichuki (p); Lawrence Burgan (b); Floyd
Williams (d); Pinocchio James, Yakary Kuroda (v); P. Metro (arr).

Opening Theme (Big Slide)
LP: Glad-Hamp GHLP 1006

Sakura
LP: Glad-Hamp GHLP 1006

Midnight Sun
LP: Glad-Hamp GHLP 1006

Akirfa
LP: Glad-Hamp GHLP 1006

What'd I Say – YK (v)
LP: Glad-Hamp GHLP 1006

Vibe Boogie
LP: Glad-Hamp GHLP 1006

Happy Monk
LP: Glad-Hamp GHLP 1006

Medley: On the Sunny Side of the Street/After You've Gone
LP: Glad-Hamp GHLP 1006

Georgia on My Mind —PJ (v)
LP: Glad-Hamp GHLP 1006

Shojiiji
LP: Glad-Hamp GHLP 1006

Flying Home
LP: Groove Merchant GM 4400

January 1964—New York, NY
Lionel Hampton and His Orchestra: *Hampton* (vib); Virgil Jones, Al Bryant,
Wallace Davenport, Alex Rodriguez (tp); Quentin Jackson, Bernard McKinney,
Vince Prudente (tb); Bobby Plater, Ed Pazant (as); Andrew McGhee, Herman
Green (ts); Fred Jackson (bars); Kenny Lowe (p); Lawrence Burgan (b); Wilbert
Hogan (d); Duke Anderson (arr); Miyoko Hoshino (v).

Just in Time
LP: Glad-Hamp GHLP 1007

What a Little Moonlight Can Do [aka "What a Little Mambo
Can Do"]
LP: Glad-Hamp GHLP 1007

Hamabe No Uta
LP: Glad-Hamp GHLP 1007

Easy Living
LP: Glad-Hamp GHLP 1007

What Can You Lose
LP: Glad-Hamp GHLP 1007

So Great
LP: Glad-Hamp GHLP 1007

Here's Happiness
LP: Glad-Hamp GHLP 1007

Please Don't Talk about Me When I'm Gone
LP: Glad-Hamp GHLP 1007

Please Be Kind
LP: Glad-Hamp GHLP 1007

Indiana
LP: Glad-Hamp GHLP 1007

Ca. 1964 [?]
No details.

Midnight Sun   . R5KM7508
45: Glad Hamp 2019

Inside Out   R5KM7509
45: Glad Hamp 2019

August 1964—New York, NY
Lionel Hampton and His Jazz Inner Circle: *Hampton* (vib), Sy Mann (p),
Lawrence Burgan (b), Bob Mann (g), Floyd Williams (d), Carmen Costa (v).

Jazzland   R4KM0939
45: Glad-Hamp 2020 LP: Glad-Hamp GHLP 1009

Twilight in the City   R4KM0940
45: Glad-Hamp 2020 LP: Glad-Hamp GHLP 1009

The Ingenue
LP: Glad-Hamp GHLP 1009

Prelude to a Kiss
LP: Glad-Hamp GHLP 1009

What's New
LP: Glad-Hamp GHLP 1009

Little Girl Blue
LP: Glad-Hamp GHLP 1009

Jazz at the Fair
LP: Glad-Hamp GHLP 1009

Ca. 1964—New York, NY
Hampton (vib), Sevuca (g), Carmen Costa (perc, v, cabasa), and others.

Depuis Longtemps – [?] (v)
LP: Glad-Hamp GHLP 1009

How Insensitive – CC (v)
LP: Glad-Hamp GHLP 1009

Batida Differente
LP: Glad-Hamp GHLP 1009

Nuit de Mon Amour – [?] (v)

Ca. late 1964
No details but probably from same period as session above.

Glad-Hamp
LP: Versatile NED 1127

Groovin' Gates
LP: Versatile NED 1127

Bad Dude
LP: Versatile NED 1127

Uska Dara
LP: Versatile NED 1127

Close to You
LP: Versatile NED 1127

Willow Weep for Me
LP: Versatile NED 1127

Eubie's Boogie
LP: Versatile NED 1127

Easy Living
LP: Versatile NED 1127

Flying Home
LP: Versatile NED 1127

October 26, 28, & 29, 1964—New York, NY
Hampton (vib, p, v), Clark Terry (tp), Ben Webster (ts), Hank Jones (p, v), Milt Hinton (b), Osie Johnson (d).

Trick or Treat LP: Impulse A(S) 78	90188
Moon over My Annie LP: Impulse A(S) 100	90189
Pick-a-Rib LP: Impulse A(S) 78	90190
Ring Dem Bells – LH & HJ LP: Impulse A(S) 78	90191
Cute LP: Impulse A(S) 78	90192
Sweethearts on Parade – LH (v) LP: Impulse A(S) 78	90193
Vibraphone Blues – LH (v) LP: Impulse A(S) 78	90194
Tempo's Birthday LP: Impulse A(S) 78	90195
A Taste of Honey LP: Impulse A(S) 78	90196
Swingle Jingle LP: Impulse A(S) 78	90198

1965—New York, NY
Jazz All-Stars: *Hampton* (vib, p), Clark Terry (tp), Thad Jones (tp, flgh), J.J. Johnson (tb), Lucky Thompson (ss), Coleman Hawkins (ts), Hank Jones (p), Arvell Shaw (b), Osie Johnson (d).

Stardust
LP: Who's Who WWLP 21010

Midnight Blues
LP: Who's Who WWLP 21010, Glad Hamp GHS 1027

As Long As We're Here
LP: Who's Who WWLP 21010

Ca. 1966—New York, NY
Hampton (vib), John Hunt (tp), Ed Pazant (as, fl), Eddie Shu (as, mouth organ), Reynolds "Zeke" Mullins (p, org), Billy Mackel (g), Lawrence Burgan (b), Roy Burns (d).

Brazilian Summer   SK4M6579
45: Glad Hamp 2026

The Ingenue   SK4M6580
45: Glad Hamp 2026

Ca. summer 1966 (possibly 1965)—New York, NY
Hampton (vib), Reynolds "Zeke" Mullins (p), Billy Mackel (g), Lawrence Burgan (b), Wilbert Hogan (d).

The Price of Jazz
LP: Folkways FJ 2871

C Minor Blues
LP: Folkway FJ 2871

Tenderly
LP: Folkways FJ 2871

Note: On "C Minor Blues," Kenny Burrell (g) replaces Mackel, and unknown cellist added.

July 3, 1967—Newport Jazz Festival, Newport, RI
Lionel Hampton and His Orchestra: *Hampton* (vib, p, d, v); Snooky Young, Jimmy Nottingham, Joe Newman, Wallace Davenport (tp); Al Grey, Garnett Brown, Britt Woodman, Benny Powell (tb); Ed Pazant (as, fl, ts); George Dorsey (as); Dave Young, Frank Foster (ts); Jerome Richardson (bars); John Spruill (p); Billy Mackel (g); George Duvivier (b); Steve Little (d).

Turn Me Loose   UPA5-6344
LP: Victor LPM (S) 3891

Thai Silk   UPA5-6345
LP: Victor LPM (S) 3891

Greasy Greens [2 takes]   UPA5-6346
LP: Victor LPM (S) 3891

Tempo's Birthday   UPA5-6347
LP: Victor LPM (S) 3891

Misunderstood Blues   UPA5-6348
LP: Victor LPM (S) 3891

Meet Benny Bailey   UPA5-6349
LP: Victor LPM (S) 3891

Milt Buckner (p) replaces Spruill; Illinois Jacquet (ts) and Alan Dawson (d) added:

Medley: Hey Ba-Ba-Re-Bop/Hamp's Boogie-Woogie　　　　　　　UPA5-6350
LP: Victor LPM (S) 3891

Flying Home　　　　　　　　　　　　　　　　　　　　　　UPA5-6351
LP: Victor LPM (S) 3891, Franklin Mint Record Society 40

July 1967—Newport, RI
Lionel Hampton and His Orchestra: personnel same as 7-3-67.

Glad-Hamp
LP: Groove Merchant GM 4400

Blues for Gerty
LP: Groove Merchant GM 4400

Meet Ben Bailey
LP: Groove Merchant GM 4400

Ca. 1967 [?]
Hampton (vib), Reynolds "Zeke" Mullins (org), Billy Mackel (g), Bob Cranshaw (b), Ted Sommer (d), Jack Jennings (perc).

Here's That Rainy Day
LP: Groove Merchant GM 4400

Ca. 1967 [?]
Hampton (vib); Charles Cameleri, Dominick Alai (tp); Dennis Wilson (tb); Ray German, Benny Slovack, Ruce Schaffel (reeds); Reynolds "Zeke" Mullins (org); Billy Mackel (g); Bob Cranshaw (b); Ted Sommer (d); Jack Jennings (perc).

Raunchy Rita
LP: Groove Merchant GM 4400

Killer Joe
LP: Groove Merchant GM 4400

Psychedelic Sally
LP: Groove Merchant GM 4400

Lion's Den
LP: Groove Merchant GM 4400

October 1967—New York, NY
Lionel Hampton and His Jazz Inner Circle: *Hampton* (vib, p, d), Wallace Davenport (tp), Ed Pazant (as, fl), Dave Young (ts), John Spruill (b), Billy Mackel (g), Lawrence Burgan (b), Ronnie Cole (d).

Hamp Stamp　　　　　　　　　　　　　　　　　　　　　　TK4M5599
45: Glad Hamp 2035 LP: Glad-Hamp GHLP 1011

Tom Collins　　　　　　　　　　　　　　　　　　　　　　TK4M5600
45: Glad Hamp 2035 LP: Glad-Hamp GHLP 1011

King Cool
LP: Glad Hamp GHLP 1011

Don't Be So Mean
LP: Glad Hamp GHLP 1011

Japanese Lullaby
LP: Glad Hamp GHLP 1011

By By [AKA Bye Bye]
LP: Glad Hamp GHLP 1011

Sunshine Superman
LP: Glad Hamp GHLP 1011

Greasy Greens
LP: Glad Hamp GHLP 1011

Jazz at the Fair
LP: Glad-Hamp GHLP 1011

The Ingenue
LP: Glad-Hamp GHLP 1011

A & T
LP: Glad-Hamp GHLP 1011

Georgia on My Mind
LP: Glad Hamp GHLP 1011

January 3, 4, 9, & 12, 1968—New York, NY
Hampton (vib, p, d), John Spruill (p), Al Caiola (g), Richard Davis (b), Don Lamond (d).

Casa Bianca
LP: Company Discografica Italiana (It) CALP 2044

Canzone
LP: Company Discografica Italiana (It) CALP 2044

Mi va di cantare
LP: Company Discografica Italiana (It) CALP 2044

Canzone per te
LP: Company Discografica Italiana (It) CALP 2044

Cha vale per me
LP: Company Discografica Italiana (It) CALP 2044

Da bambino
LP: Company Discografica Italiana (It) CALP 2044

Deborah
LP: Company Discografica Italiana (It) CALP 2044

Gli ochhi miel
LP: Company Discografica Italiana (It) CALP 2044

Il posto mio
LP: Company Discografica Italiana (It) CALP 2044

Il re d'Ingliterra
LP: Company Discografica Italiana (It) CALP 2044

La farfalla impazzita
LP: Company Discografica Italiana (It) CALP 2044

La siepe
LP: Company Discografica Italiana (It) CALP 2044

La tramonta
LP: Company Discografica Italiana (It) CALP 2044

La vita
LP: Company Discografica Italiana (It) CALP 2044

La voce del silenzio
LP: Company Discografica Italiana (It) CALP 2044

La opera di Bartolomeo
LP: Company Discografica Italiana (It) CALP 2044

Le solita cose
LP: Company Discografica Italiana (It) CALP 2044

No amore
LP: Company Discografica Italiana (It) CALP 2044

Per vivere
LP: Company Discografica Italiana (It) CALP 2044

Quando m'innamoro
LP: Company Discografica Italiana (It) CALP 2044

Sera
LP: Company Discografica Italiana (It) CALP 2044

Stanotte sentirai una canzone
LP: Company Discografica Italiana (It) CALP 2044

Tu che non sorridi mai
LP: Company Discografica Italiana (It) CALP 2044

Un uomo piange solo per amore
LP: Company Discografica Italiana (It) CALP 2044

Foolin' Around
LP: Groove Merchant GM 4400

Note: The number on the sleeve of the Company Discografica Italiana LP reads "CALP 2043."

Probably early 1970s
Lionel Hampton and His Orchestra: *Hampton* (vib), personnel unknown.

Jamming the Session (Line For Lyons)
LP: Up Front UPF 153

Stella by Starlight
LP: Up Front UPF 153

Jamming Blues Homeward
LP: Up Front UPF 153

I Only Have Eyes for You – unknown female (v)
LP: Up Front UPF 153

Big Fine Girl – unknown male (v)
LP: Up Front UPF 153

Jumpin' the Beat
LP: Up Front UPF 153

My Baby Don't Leave Me – unknown vocalists
LP: Up Front UPF 153

Rollin' Pete – unknown male (v)
LP: Up Front UPF 153

More on the Jam [aka "Blues in the Closet"] [small combo: ts,
elp, g, elb, d]
LP: Up Front UPF 153

Ca. 1974
Hampton (vib, v), Zoot Sims (ts), Teddy Wilson (p), George Duvivier (b), Buddy
Rich (d).

Avalon
LP: Groove Merchant GM 3302

Airmail Special
LP: Groove Merchant GM 3302

Ham Hock Blues
LP: Groove Merchant GM 3302

Ring Dem Bells – LH (v)
LP: Groove Merchant GM 3302

Ca. 1974
Hampton (vib), Sal Nistico (ts), Joe Romano (ss), Kenny Barron (p), Jack Wilkins
(g, arr), Anthony Jackson and Bob Cranshaw, (b), Buddy Rich (d), Ted Sommer
and Stanley Kay (perc), Mike Abene (arr).

E.G. – MA (arr)
LP: Groove Merchant GM 3302

Zoot Sims (ts) added:

Fum – JW (arr)
LP: Groove Merchant GM 3302

May 25, 1976—Paris, France
Hampton (vib, v), Claude Gousset (tb), Michel Attenoux (as), Gerard Badini (ts),
Raymond Fol (p), Billy Mackel (g), Michel Gaudry (b), Sam Woodyard (d).

Ring Dem Bells – LH (v)
LP: Blue Star (F) 80706

Psychedelic Sally
LP: Blue Star (F) 80706

Hamp's Thing
LP: Blue Star (F) 80706

May 25, 1976–Paris, France
Hampton (vib, v), Dany Doriz (vib), Raymond Fol (p), Billy Mackel (g), Michel Gaudry (b), Sam Woodyard (d).

Seven Come Eleven
LP: Blue Star (F) 80706

May 26, 1976—Paris, France
Hampton (vib, v), Gerard Badini (ts), Reynolds Mullins (org), Raymond Fol (p), Billy Mackel (g), Michel Gaudry (b), Sam Woodyard (d).

Blue Lou
LP: Blue Star (F) 80706

Badini (ts) out:

On the Sunny Side of the Street – LH (v)
LP: Blue Star (F) 80706

Vibraphone Blues – LH (v)
LP: Blue Star (F) 80706

Ca. 1976—Saint Quentin, France
Lionel Hampton and Friends: *Hampton* (vib), Glen Drewes and Dominick Alai (tp), Keith O'Quinn (tb), Billie Drewes (as), Paul Moen (ts, ss), Freddy Foss (bars), Zeke Mullins (org), Billy Mackel (g), Gary Mazzaroppi (b), Frankie Dunlop (d), Sam Turner (perc).

Barbara
LP: Glad-Hamp GHS 1021

Chameleon
LP: Glad Hamp GHS 1021

Psychedelic Sally
LP: Glad Hamp GHS 1021

Raunchy Rita
LP: Glad Hamp GHS 1021

May 7, 1977—Villingen, Germany
Hampton (vib), Cat Anderson (tp), Paul Moen (as), Eddie Chamblee (ts), Milt Buckner (p), Billy Mackel (g), Barry Smith (b), Frankie Dunlop (d).

Avalon
LP: MPS 15469

Midnight Sun
LP: MPS 15469

How High the Moon
LP: MPS 15469

Medley: The Birth of the Blues/Old Man River
LP: MPS 15469

I'm Confessin'
LP: MPS 15469

Hamp's Boogie-Woogie
LP: MPS 15469

Funky Mama
LP: MPS 15469

Flying Home
LP: MPS 15469

May 15, 1977—Toulouse, France
Hampton (vib, d), Cat Anderson (tp), Paul Moen (as), Eddie Chamblee (ts), Milt Buckner (p), Billy Mackel (g), Barry Smith (b), Frankie Dunlop (d).

Liza
LP: Black and Blue (F) 33107

Lady Be Good – LH (v)
LP: Black and Blue (F) 33107

Birth of the Blues – LH (v)
LP: Black and Blue (F) 33107

The Fox
LP: Black and Blue (F) 33107

Old Man River
LP: Black and Blue (F) 33107

Lover
LP: Black and Blue (F) 33107

Shuffling for Jacques
LP: Black and Blue (F) 33107

1977—New York, NY
Hampton (vib), Hank Jones (p), Bucky Pizzarelli (g), George Duvivier (b), Grady Tate (d), Candido Camero (cgs).

Satin Doll
LP: Gateway GSLP 7020

Mr. P.C.
LP: Gateway GSLP 7020

I Wish You Love
LP: Gateway GSLP 7020

It Don't Mean a Thing If It Ain't Got That Swing
LP: Gateway GSLP 7020

Memories of You
LP: Gateway GSLP 7020

Old Man River
LP: Gateway GSLP 7020

How High the Moon
LP: Gateway GSLP 7020

1977—New York, NY
Hampton (vib), Hank Jones (p), Vinnie Bell (g), Milt Hinton (b), Grady Tate (d), Candido Camero (perc).

I Found a New Baby
LP: Who's Who WWLP 21008

Green Dolphin Street
LP: Who's Who WWLP 21008

Undecided
LP: Who's Who WWLP 21008

This Could Be the Start of Something Big
LP: Who's Who WWLP 21008

1977—New York, NY
Hampton (vib, p), Victor Paz (tp), Janice Robinson (tb), Frank Foster and Frank Wess (ts), Roland Hanna (p), Vinnie Bell (g), George Mraz (b), Grady Tate (d), Sam Turner (cgs).

Dizzy Spells
LP: Who's Who WWLP 21008

1977—probably New York, NY
Hampton (vib), Zeke Mullins (p), Billy Mackel (g), Lawrence Burgan (b), Roy Burns (d).

Fantanique
LP: Who's Who WWLP 21010

C Minor Blues
LP: Who's Who WWLP 21010

Tenderly
LP: Who's Who WWLP 21010

Running Home
LP: Who's Who WWLP 21010

Estranho
LP: Who's Who WWLP 21010

1977—New York, NY
Hampton (vib, v), Hank Jones (p), Bucky Pizzarelli (g), George Duvivier (b), Grady Tate (d), Candido Camero (cgs).

Volare
LP: Who's Who WWLP 21014

Ain't Misbehavin' – LH (v)
LP: Who's Who WWLP 21014

Blues for Hamp
LP: Who's Who WWLP 21014

1977—New York, NY
Hampton (vib), Bill Doggett (org, elp, ldr), Norris Turney and Charles Williams (as), David Brooks (ts), Larry Luger (g), Larry Troit (b), Howard Overton (d), Sam Turner (cgs).

Bill's Honky Tonk
LP: Who's Who WWLP 21002

Pots A-Cookin'
LP: Who's Who WWLP 21002

I Wish You Love
LP: Who's Who WWLP 21002

Dig the Thing
LP: Who's Who WWLP 21002

Dug's Pad
LP: Who's Who WWLP 21002

Midnight Sun
LP: Who's Who WWLP 21002

Flying Home
LP: Who's Who WWLP 21002

Charlie's Alley
LP: Who's Who WWLP 21002

1977—New York, NY
Hampton (vib), Marty Napoleon (p, ldr), Cozy Cole (d, ldr), Arvell Shaw (b), Joe Muranyi (cl), Johnny Letman (tp), Russell "Big Chief" Moore (tb).

Cabaret
LP: Who's Who WWLP 21003

Some Day You'll Be Sorry
LP: Who's Who WWLP 21003

Louis' Dream
LP: Who's Who WWLP 21003

Short Ribs
LP: Who's Who WWLP 21003

Mack the Knife
LP: Who's Who WWLP 21003

Do You Know What It Means to Miss New Orleans
LP: Who's Who WWLP 21003

Black and Blue
LP: Who's Who WWLP 21003

Back Home Again in Indiana
LP: Who's Who WWLP 21003

Hello Dolly
LP: Who's Who WWLP 21008

Jeepers Creepers
LP: Who's Who WWLP 21008

Sleepy Time Down South
LP: Who's Who WWLP 21012

September 26, 1977—New York, NY
Hampton (vib), Earl Hines (p, ldr), Milt Hinton (b), Grady Tate (d), Sam Turner (cgs).

Earl's Pearl
LP: Who's Who WWLP 21004, Legends of Music (J) RJL-2647

If It's True
LP: Who's Who WWLP 21004, Legends of Music (J) RJL-2647

Rosetta
LP: Who's Who WWLP 21004, Legends of Music (J) RJL-2647

One Night in Trinidad
LP: Who's Who WWLP 21004, Legends of Music (J) RJL-2647

Ginger Man
LP: Who's Who WWLP 21008, Legends of Music (J) RJL-2647

I Know That You Know
LP: Who's Who WWLP 21004, Legends of Music (J) RJL-2647

If I Had You
LP: Who's Who WWLP 21004, Legends of Music (J) RJL-2647

St. Louis Blues
LP: Who's Who WWLP 21004, Legends of Music (J) RJL-2647

Chicago
LP: Who's Who WWLP 21004, Legends of Music (J) RJL-2647

Fatha Meets Gates
LP: Who's Who WWLP 21014, Legends of Music (J) RJL-2647

October 7, 1977—New York, NY
Hampton (vib), Teddy Wilson (p, ldr), Gerry Fuller (cl), George Duvivier (b), Teddy Wilson, Jr. (d), Sam Turner (cgs).

Misty
LP: Who's Who WWLP 21014, Legends of Music (J) RJL-2644

One O'Clock Jump
LP: Who's Who WWLP 21009, Legends of Music (J) RJL-2644

I Can't Get Started with You
LP: Who's Who WWLP 21009, Legends of Music (J) RJL-2644

Dizzy Spells
LP: Who's Who WWLP 21009, Legends of Music (J) RJL-2644

Limehouse Blues
LP: Who's Who WWLP 21009, Legends of Music (J) RJL-2644

The Man I Love
LP: Who's Who WWLP 21009, Legends of Music (J) RJL-2644

Liza
LP: Who's Who WWLP 21009, Legends of Music (J) RJL-2644

Prelude to a Kiss
LP: Who's Who WWLP 21009, Legends of Music (J) RJL-2644

Sweet Sue
LP: Who's Who WWLP 21009, Legends of Music (J) RJL-2644

Ca. September/October 1977—New York, NY
Hampton (vib), Woody Herman (cl, ss, as, v, ldr), Roland Hanna (p), Al Caiola (g), George Mraz (b), Richie Pratt (d), Candido Camero (cgs).

Body and Soul
LP: Who's Who WWLP 21013

Rose Room
LP: Who's Who WWLP 21013

Early Autumn
LP: Who's Who WWLP 21013

Caldonia – WH (v)
LP: Who's Who WWLP 21013

Mood Indigo
LP: Who's Who WWLP 21013

Ca. October 1977—New York, NY
Hampton (vib); Buddy Rich (d, ldr); Steve Marcus, Gary Pribek, Paul Moen (ts); Barry Kiener (p), Tom Warrington (b), Candido Camero (cgs), Jon Hendricks (v).

Moment's Notice
LP: Who's Who WWLP 21006

Second Tune
LP: Who's Who WWLP 21006

Buddy's Cherokee
LP: Who's Who WWLP 21006

Take the "A" Train
LP: Who's Who WWLP 21006

I'll Never Be the Same
LP: Who's Who WWLP 21006

Latin Silk
LP: Who's Who WWLP 21006

Buddy's Rock
LP: Who's Who WWLP 21012

My Funny Valentine
LP: Who's Who WWLP 21012

Hamp, Rich, Dido Blues – JH (v)
LP: Who's Who WWLP 21012

Note: Jon Hendricks was not scheduled to be on this session, but he just happened to be in the studio and did the vocal on "Hamp, Rich, Dido Blues."

Ca. October 1977—New York, NY
Hampton (vib), Gerry Mulligan (bars, ss, ldr), Hank Jones (p), George Duvivier (b), Grady Tate (d), Candido Camero (cgs).

Apple Core
LP: Who's Who WWLP 21007

Song for Johnny Hodges
LP: Who's Who WWLP 21007

Blight of the Fumble Bee
LP: Who's Who WWLP 21007

Gerry Meets Hamp
LP: Who's Who WWLP 21007

Blues for Gerry
LP: Who's Who WWLP 21007

Line for Lyons
LP: Who's Who WWLP 21007

Limelight
LP: Who's Who WWLP 21012

Walkin' Shoes
LP: Who's Who WWLP 21012

November 6, 1977—New York, NY
Hampton (vib), Charles Mingus (b, v, ldr), Jack Walrath and Woody Shaw (tp), Ricky Ford (ts), Paul Jeffrey (ts, arr), Gerry Mulligan (bars, ss), Peter Matt (fhr), Bob Neloms (p), Dannie Richmond (d).

Remember Rockefeller at Attica (Part 1)
LP: Who's Who WWLP 21005

Remember Rockefeller at Attica (Part 2)
LP: Who's Who WWLP 21005

Peggy's Blue Skylight
LP: Who's Who WWLP 21005

Carolyn "Kekki" Mingus
LP: Who's Who WWLP 21005

Slop
LP: Who's Who WWLP 21005

Fables of Faubus – CM (v)
LP: Who's Who WWLP 21005

Duke Ellington's Sound of Love
LP: Who's Who WWLP 21005

Farwell Farewell
LP: Who's Who WWLP 21005

So Long Eric
LP: Who's Who WWLP 21014

Note: "Remember Rockefeller at Attica" retitled "Just for Laughs" for issue.

Ca. November 1977—New York, NY
Hampton (vib), Dexter Gordon (ts, ss, ldr), Hank Jones (p), Bucky Pizzarelli (g), George Duvivier (b), Oliver Jackson (d), Candido Camero (cgs).

Cute
LP: Who's Who WWLP 21011, Glad-Hamp GHS 1027

They Say That Falling in Love Is Wonderful
LP: Who's Who WWLP 21011

Lullaby of Birdland
LP: Who's Who WWLP 21011, Glad-Hamp GHS 1027

I Should Care
LP: Who's Who WWLP 21011, Glad-Hamp GHS 1027

Seven Come Eleven
LP: Who's Who WWLP 21011, Glad-Hamp GHS 1027

Blues for Gates
LP: Who's Who WWLP 21011, Glad-Hamp GHS 1027

Lullabye [sic] *of the Leaves*
LP: Who's Who WWLP 21014, Glad-Hamp GHS 1027

Ca. 1978—New York, NY
Hampton (vib, marimba), Teo Macero (ts, arr, cond), George Young (saxes, woodwinds), Mike Nock (keyboards), John Scofield (g), Richard Laird (b), Al Foster (d), George Devens (perc), Lynn Williamson (v).

How Deep Is Your Love
LP: Philips 9199739, Laurie LES-6003

More Than a Woman
LP: Philips 9199739, Laurie LES-6003

You Should Be Dancing
LP: Philips 9199739, Laurie LES-6003

Stayin' Alive
LP: Philips 9199739, Laurie LES-6003

Jive Talkin'
LP: Philips 9199739, Laurie LES-6003

Night Fever
LP: Philips 9199739, Laurie LES-6003

Ca. 1978—New York, NY
Hampton (vib), Teo Macero (ts), George Young (woodwinds, saxes), Mike Nock (Moog synthesizer), John Scofield (g), Herb Bushler (b), Al Foster (d), Phil Kraus (perc), Pauletta Pearson, Lynn Williamson (v).

We Go Together
LP: Laurie LES-6004

Sandy
LP: Laurie LES-6004

You're the One That I Want
LP: Laurie LES-6004

Hopelessly Devoted to You
LP: Laurie LES-6004

Born to Hand Jive
LP: Laurie LES-6004

Grease
LP: Laurie LES-6004

Open Up
LP: Laurie LES-6004

January 22, 1978—MIDEM, Cannes, France
Hampton (vib), Chick Corea (p), Oliver Jackson (d), remaining musicians unknown.

Sea Breeze
LP: Who's Who WWLP 21016, Toledo (G) INT 147.528

Moment's Notice
LP: Who's Who WWLP 21016, Toledo (G) INT 147.528

Come Rain or Shine
LP: Who's Who WWLP 21016, Toledo (G) INT 147.528

Fiesta Piano Solo
LP: Who's Who WWLP 21016, Toledo (G) INT 147.528

I Ain't Mad at You
LP: Who's Who WWLP 21016, Toledo (G) INT 147.528

Note: Al Vicutti (tp) and Ron Moss (tb) were overdubbed in the studio at a later date.

May 10, 1978—Copenhagen, Denmark
Hampton (vib), Svend Asmussen (vn), Rune Ofwerman (p), Niels Henning Orsted Pedersen (b), Ed Thigpin (d).

Flying Home
LP: Sonet (E) SNTF 779

Midnight Sun
LP: Sonet (E) SNTF 779

Rose Room
LP: Sonet (E) SNTF 779

Airmail Special
LP: Sonet (E) SNTF 779

Avalon
LP: Sonet (E) SNTF 779

As Time Goes By
LP: Sonet (E) SNTF 779

May 13, 1978—De Muzeval, Emmen, Netherlands
Hampton (vib), Joe Newman and Victor Paz (tp), Eddie Chamblee (as), Paul Moen (ts), Wild Bill Davis (org, p), Billy Mackel (g), Barry Smith (b), Frankie Dunlop (d).

Airmail
LP: Timeless (Du) SJP 120

Big Bad Henry
LP: Timeless (Du) SJP 120

Moment's Notice
LP: Timeless (Du) SJP 120

No Me Esqueca
LP: Timeless (Du) SJP 120

Giant Steps
LP: Timeless (Du) SJP 120

Rodney Round Robin
LP: Timeless (Du) SJP 120

Flying Home
LP: Timeless (Du) SJP 120

Hamp's Boogie-Woogie
LP: Timeless (Du) SJP 120

July 1, 1978—Carnegie Hall, New York, NY
Lionel Hampton's 50th Anniversary Concert: *Hampton* (vib); Cat Anderson, Jimmy Maxwell, Joe Newman (tp, flgh); Doc Cheatham (tp); Eddie Bert, John Gordon, Benny Powell (tb); Bob Wilber (cl); Charles McPherson (as); Earle Warren (as, cl, fl); Arnett Cobb, Paul Moen (ts); Pepper Adams (bars); Ray Bryant (p); Billy Mackel (g); Chubby Jackson (b); Panama Francis (d).

On the Sunny Side of the Street
LP: Sutra SU2 1006

Hamp's the Champ
LP: Sutra SU2 1006

Stompin' at the Savoy
LP: Sutra SU2 1006

Flyin' Home
LP: Sutra SU2 1006

Hamp's Boogie-Woogie
LP: Sutra SU2 1006

Tea for Two
LP: Sutra SU2 1006

I'm Confessin' (That I Love You)
LP: Sutra SU2 1006

Misty
LP: Sutra SU2 1006

Avalon
LP: Sutra SU2 1006

More Than You Know
LP: Sutra SU2 1006

Runnin' Wild
LP: Sutra SU2 1006

May 20, 1979—Concertgebouw, Haarlem, Netherlands
Hampton (vib, p, d, v), Joe Newman and Wallace Davenport (tp), Curtis Fuller
(tb), Steve Slagle (as), Paul Moen (ts), Paul Jeffrey (bars), Wild Bill Davis (org, p),
Gary Mazzaroppi (b), Richie Pratt (d).

Glad Hamp
LP: Timeless (Du) SJP 133

Ol' Man River
LP: Timeless (Du) SJP 133

Greasy Greens
LP: Timeless (Du) SJP 133

Mr. P.C.
LP: Timeless (Du) SJP 133

Hamp's Got the Blues
LP: Timeless (Du) SJP 133

Salsa, Ein Buergermeister de François
LP: Timeless (Du) SJP 133

July 8, 1979—Orange, France
Lionel Hampton and His Orchestra: *Hampton* (vib, v); Cat Anderson, Wallace
Davenport, Joe Newman, Roy Roman (tp); Curtis Fuller, Benny Powell, Kai
Winding (tb); Arnett Cobb, Ernie Wilkins, Paul Moen, Paul Jeffrey, Cecil Payne
(saxes); Zeke Mullins (p); Chubby Jackson (b); Oliver Jackson (d); Sammy
Turner (perc).

Sweethearts on Parade – Ernie Wilkins (arr)
LP: Glad-Hamp GHS 1024

November 6, 1979—Zagreb, Yugoslavia
Lionel Hampton Quintet: *Hampton* (vib, v), Cat Anderson (tp), Wild Bill Davis
(org), Gary Mazzaroppi (b), Richie Pratt (d).

If the Blues Was Whiskey – LH (v)
LP: Glad-Hamp GHS 1024

Cat Anderson (tp) out:

Misty
LP: Glad-Hamp GHS 1024

February 1980—New York, NY
Lionel Hampton and his Orchestra: *Hampton* (vib); Barry Ries, Walt Johnson, Bob O'Jeda, Roy Roman (tp); Oscar Brashear (flgh); Curtis Fuller, Jimmy Cleveland, Tom McIntosh, Maurice Spears, George Bohanon (tb); Jack Kelso, Paul Moen, Herman Riley, Roger Hogan, Bill Green (saxes); Zeke Mullins (p); Wild Bill Davis (org); Gary Bell (g); Richie Pratt (d); Amos Hunt (hands over mouth), Sammy Turner (perc).

Wail for the Cat
LP: Glad-Hamp GHS 1022, Timeless (Du) SJP 163

May 3, 1980—Basel, Switzerland
Lionel Hampton and his Orchestra: *Hampton* (vib); Joe Newman, Wallace Davenport, Roy Roman, Stephen Gut (tp); Curtis Fuller, Richard Caruso (tb); Paul Moen, Steve Slagle, Kevin Brown (saxes); Wild Bill Davis (org); Gary Mazzaroppi (b); Frankie Dunlop (d).

Cherokee —Roberta Como (arr)
LP: Glad-Hamp GHS 1024

Midnight Sun —Ernie Wilkins & Frank Como (arr)
LP: Glad-Hamp GHS 1026, Amos LP-5435

Oleo —Hampton (arr)
LP: Glad-Hamp GHS 1026, Amos LP-5435

Break Out
LP: Amos LP-5435

Hamp
LP: Amos LP-5435

You and Me —Frank Como (arr)
LP: Amos LP-5435

Dynamo —Hampton (arr)
LP: Amos LP-5435

Shadow of Your Smile —Hampton (arr)
LP: Amos LP-5435

Spring in Switzerland
LP: Amos LP-5435

October 1980—Los Angeles, CA
Lionel Hampton and His Orchestra: *Hampton* (vib); Barry Ries, Walt Johnson, Bob O'Jeda (tp); Oscar Brashear (flgh); Jimmy Cleveland, Tom McIntosh, Maurice Spears, George Bohanon (tb); Jack Kelso, Paul Moen, Herman Riley, Roger Hogan, Bill Green (saxes); Zeke Mullins (p); Bob Saravia (b); Wild Bill Davis (org); Gary Bell (g); Frankie Dunlop (d); Sammy Turner (perc).

Ko-Ko
LP: Glad-Hamp GHS 1022, Timeless (Du) SJP 163

Tap Step
LP: Glad-Hamp GHS 1022, Timeless (Du) SJP 163

Hamp and Dex
LP: Glad-Hamp GHS 1022, Timeless (Du) SJP 163, Glad Hamp
GHS 1027

Dr. Lambchop
LP: Glad-Hamp GHS 1022, Timeless (Du) SJP 163

Leonard Feather (p) replaces Zeke Mullins:

Heavy-Hearted Blues
LP: Glad-Hamp GHS 1022, Timeless (Du) SJP 163

Note: "Hamp and Dex" issued on Glad-Hamp GHS 1027 as "Hamp Celebrates Dexter."

September 2, 1981—Aurex Jazz Festival, Osaka, Japan
Lionel Hampton and His All-Star Big Band, featuring Woody Herman: *Hampton* (vib, p, d, v); Pete Candoli, Wallace Davenport, Billy Brooks, Johnny Walker (tp); Buster Cooper, Garnett Brown, Ed Neumeister (tb); Woody Herman (cl); Jack Kelso (as); Yoshi Malta (as, ss); Ricky Ford (ts); Tom Chapin (ts, fl); Kenny Rogers (bars); Zeke Mullins (p); Chubby Jackson (b); Frankie Dunlop (d).

Air Mail Special
LP: Eastworld (J) EWJ-80207

Sakura '81
LP: Eastworld (J) EWJ-80207

Stardust
LP: Eastworld (J) EWJ-80207

Hamp's Boogie-Woogie
LP: Eastworld (J) EWJ-80207

Valve Job
LP: Eastworld (J) EWJ-80254

September 3, 1981—Aurex Jazz Festival, Osaka, Japan
Lionel Hampton and his All-Star Big Band featuring Woody Herman: personnel same as above.

Sweet Georgia Brown
LP: Eastworld (J) EWJ-80207

I Can't Get Started
LP: Eastworld (J) EWJ-80207

Rose Room
LP: Eastworld (J) EWJ-80207

In the Mood
LP: Eastworld (J) EWJ-80207

At the Woodchopper's Ball
LP: Eastworld (J) EWJ-80254

September 3, 1981—Osaka, Japan
Lionel Hampton and His Orchestra: *Hampton* (vib, v); Johnny Walker, Pete Candoli, Wallace Davenport, Billy Brooks (tp); Ed Neumeister, Buster Cooper,

Garnett Brown (tb); Yoshi Malta, Tom Chapin, Jack Kelso, Ricky Ford, Kenny Rogers (saxes); Zeke Mullins (p); Chubby Jackson (b); Frankie Dunlop (d); Sammy Turner (perc).

Lady Be Good
LP: Glad-Hamp GHS 1024

Sweet Georgia Brown – LH (v)
LP: Glad-Hamp GHS 1024

Moonglow
LP: Glad-Hamp GHS 1024

Air Mail Special
LP: Glad-Hamp GHS 1026

Greasy Greens
LP: Glad-Hamp GHS 1026

Note: First three titles arranged by Frank Como.

September 5, 1981—Osaka, Japan
Lionel Hampton and His Orchestra: personnel same as October 1980.

In the Mood
LP: Timeless SJP 1C3

September 6, 1981—Aurex Jazz Festival, Osaka, Japan
Lionel Hampton and his All-Star Big Band featuring Woody Herman: personnel same as 9-2-81.

Dexter
LP: Eastworld (J) EWJ-80207

January 26, 1982—New York, NY
Hampton (vib), Axel Zwingenberger (p), Arvell Shaw (b), Panama Francis (d).

Mr. Freddie Blues
LP: Telefunken (G) 6.25427

The Sheik of Araby
LP: Telefunken (G) 6.25427

Central Avenue Breakdown
LP: Telefunken (G) 6.25427

January 28, 1982—New York, NY
Hampton and Axel Zwingenberger, piano duet; Arvell Shaw (b); Panama Francis (d).

Central Avenue Breakdown
LP: Telefunken (G) 6.25427

January 28, 1982—New York, NY
Hampton (vib, v), Axel Zwingenberger (p), Illinois Jacquet and George Kelly (ts), Irvin Stokes (tp), Sam Hurt (tb), Arvell Shaw (b), Panama Francis (d).

Whisky Blues
LP: Telefunken (G) 6.25427

New York Shuffle
LP: Telefunken (G) 6.25427

March 16, 1982—New York, NY
Hampton (vib, v), George Kawaguchi (d), Arnett Cobb (ts), Kenny Barron (p),
Milt Hinton (b).

How High the Moon
LP: Paddle Wheel (J) K28P-6170

Secret Love
LP: Paddle Wheel (J) K28P-6170

Star Dust
LP: Paddle Wheel (J) K28P-6170

Air Mail Special
LP: Paddle Wheel (J) K28P-6170

Sweet Georgia Brown
LP: Paddle Wheel (J) K28P-6170

Hamp Meets George – LH (v)
LP: Paddle Wheel (J) K28P-6170

Note: Sam Turner (perc) appears on "Air Mail Special" and "Hamp Meets
George."

May 3, 1982—Doorwerth, Netherlands
Lionel Hampton Big Band: *Hampton* (vib, v); Axel Zwingenberger (p); John
Marshall, Barry Ries, John Walker, Vince Cutro (tp); John Gordon, Charles
Stephens (tb); Chris Gulhaugen (btb); Yoshi Malta, Tom Chapin (as); Arnett
Cobb, Ricky Ford (ts); Glenn Wilson (bars); Ralph Hamperian (b); Duffy
Jackson (d); Sam Turner (perc).

Graffitti Express
LP: Telefunken (G) 6.25427

Hamp's Boogie-Woogie
LP: Telefunken (G) 6.25427

May 3, 1982—Doorwerth, Netherlands
Hampton (vib), Axel Zwingenberger (p), Arnett Cobb and Ricky Ford (ts), Barry
Reis and John Walker (tp), Ralph Hamperian (b), Duffy Jackson (d).

Jivin' in Jazzland
LP: Telefunken (G) 6.25427

Ca. 1982/83—France
Hampton (vib), Michel Attenoux (ss), Henri Salvador (g, v), Arnett Cobb (ts),
Christian Donnadieu (p), Pierre Nicolas (b), Moustache Galepides (d), others
unknown.

La Première Fille —HS (v)
LP: Philips (F) 812 386-1

L'Orage
LP: Philips (F) 812 386-1

June 1, 2 & 3, 1983—Kosei-Nenkin Kaikan Hall & Shibuya Kokaido Hall, Tokyo, Japan
Lionel Hampton and His Orchestra: *Hampton* (vib); Vince Cutro, John Marshall, Barry Ries, Johnny Walker (tp); John Gordon, Chris Gulhaugen, Charles Stephens (tb); Tom Chapin, Ricky Ford, Paul Jeffrey, Yoshi Malta, Glenn Wilson (saxes); John Colianni (p); Todd Coolman (b); Duffy Jackson (d); Sam Turner (perc).

Air Mail Special
LP: Timeless (Du) SJP 175

Advent
LP: Glad-Hamp GHS 1023, Timeless (Du) SJP 175

Stardust/Moonglow
LP: Timeless (Du) SJP 175

Mess Is Here
LP: Timeless (Du) SJP 175, Glad-Hamp GHS 1026

Interpretations Opus 5
LP: Glad-Hamp GHS 1023, Timeless (Du) SJP 175

Minor Thesis
LP: Glad-Hamp GHS 1023, Timeless (Du) SJP 175

Jodo
LP: Glad-Hamp GHS 1023, Timeless (Du) SJP 175

Valve Job
LP: Timeless (Du) SJP 175, Glad-Hamp GHS 1026

Evidence
LP: Glad-Hamp GHS 1023

Sans Souci
LP: Glad-Hamp GHS 1023

Sakura '82
LP: Glad-Hamp GHS 1026

April 13, 16, or 17, 1984—New York, NY
Frank Sinatra (v) acc. by a large studio orchestra conducted by Quincy Jones. Personnel includes: *Hampton* (vib), Joe Newman (tp), Urbie Green (tb), George Benson (g), Major Holley (b), Frank Foster (ts, arr), and others.

Mack the Knife – FF (arr)
LP: Qwest 25145-1

After You've Gone – FF (arr)
LP: Qwest 25145-1

Note: Aural evidence shows that Hampton does not appear on the other titles recorded at these sessions.

Summer 1984—Probably New York
Hampton (vib); Fred McFarland (synthesizers & drum machine).

Vibramatic
Glad-Hamp GHS 4001

Note: This is a 12″ 33 ⅓ rpm single play disc with the same tune on both sides.
Side A is the club version which plays (7:42). Side AA is a shorter version (5:32).

Ca. 1984/85—Probably New York, NY
Teo Macero (ldr, arr, cond); *Hampton* (vib); Dave Valentin (fl); Dave Liebman
(ss); Alex Foster (as); Gato Barbieri, Bill Evans, John Stubblefield (ts); Mike Nock
(Fender Rhodes, Mini Moog); Jorge Dalto (p); Larry Coryell, Ryo Kawasaki (g);
Lincoln Goines (elb); Buddy Williams (d); Carol Steele (perc).

The Man with the Horn
LP: Doctor Jazz FW 40111

Slow and Easy
LP: Doctor Jazz FW 40111

Acoustical Suspension
LP: Doctor Jazz FW 40111

Hey Man, What's Happenin'?
LP: Doctor Jazz FW 40111

Sun Rays (Violet Blue)
LP: Doctor Jazz FW 40111

March 13 & 14, 1985—New York, NY
Lionel Hampton and His Orchestra, featuring Sylvia Bennett: *Hampton* (vib,
synthesizer); Vince Cutro, John Pendenza, Al Bryant, Lee Romano (tp); Charles
Stephens, Robert Trowers, John Gordon, Chris Gulhaugen (tb); Tom Chapin,
Adam Brenner, Doug Miller, Gerry Weldon, Dave Schumacher (saxes); Alan
Simon (p); Pat O'Leary (b); Rick Visone (d); Sam Turner (perc); Sylvia Bennett
(v).

Sentimental Journey – Roberta Como (arr)
LP: Atlantic 81644-1

Don't Get Around Much Anymore – Chris Gulhaugen (arr)
LP: Atlantic 81644-1

The Lady Is a Tramp – Mike Lewis (arr)
LP: Atlantic 81644-1

Undecided – Chris Gulhaugen (arr)
LP: Atlantic 81644-1

It Don't Mean a Thing (If It Ain't Got That Swing) – Mike
Lewis (arr)
LP: Atlantic 81644-1

It's All Right with Me – Mike Lewis (arr)
LP: Atlantic 81644-1

Lullabye of Birdland – Chris Gulhaugen (arr)
LP: Atlantic 81644-1

Almost Like Being in Love – Chris Gulhaugen (arr)
LP: Atlantic 81644-1

Avalon – Pete Yellin (arr)
LP: Atlantic 81644-1

March 10, 1988—New York City
Hampton (vib), Bobby Scott (p), Joe Beck (g), Bob Cranshaw (b), Grady Tate (d).

Bye Bye Blues
CD: Musicmasters CIJD 60168K Cassette: Musicmasters CIJD
40168L

Someday My Prince Will Come
CD: Musicmasters CIJD 60168K Cassette: Musicmasters CIJD
40168L

Take the "A" Train
CD: Musicmasters CIJD 60168K Cassette: Musicmasters CIJD
40168L

Blues For Jazz Beaux
CD: Musicmasters CIJD 60168K Cassette: Musicmasters CIJD
40168L

Walkin' Uptown
CD: Musicmasters CIJD 60168K Cassette: Musicmasters CIJD
40168L

April 8, 1988—New York City
Hampton (vib), Bobby Scott (p), Joe Beck (g), Anthony Jackson (elb), Chris
Parker (d).

Honeysuckle Rose
CD: Musicmasters CIJD 60168K Cassette: Musicmasters CIJD
40168L

Mostly Blues
CD: Musicmasters CIJD 60168K Cassette: Musicmasters CIJD
40168L

Limehouse Blues
CD: Musicmasters CIJD 60168K Cassette: Musicmasters CIJD
40168L

Gone With the Wind
CD: Musicmasters CIJD 60168K Cassette: Musicmasters CIJD
40168L

ADDITIONS

Since I chose not to list Hampton's recordings with Benny Goodman, I would
like to point out the following in-print items for the reader:

Benny Goodman: The RCA Years [16-LP set]
Bluebird 5704-1-RB [features Hamp with the Goodman Quartet
and Big Band, 1936 – 39]

Benny Goodman Live at Carnegie Hall
Columbia J2C 40244 [the famous 1938 Carnegie Hall concert,
featuring Hamp with the Goodman Quartet]

The following items have always been considered Lionel Hampton items, but my
source tells me they aren't:
Lionel Hampton/*Them Changes* (Brunswick BL 754182)
Lionel Hampton/*Please Sunrise* (Brunswick BL 754190)
Lionel Hampton/*There It Is* ! (Brunswick BL 754198)
Lionel Hampton/*Stop, I Don't Need No Sympathy* (Brunswick BL 754203)
Lionel Hampton/*Off into a Black Thing* (Brunswick BL 754213)

Compiled by

Vincent H. Pelote
Librarian
Institute of Jazz Studies
Rutgers University

INDEX

Count Basie, 68, 72, 81, 141–142
Crawford, Joan, 49, 143
Creswell, Nelson. *See* Dr. Chops
Crown, Jackie, 102, 103–104
Crump, Rastus, 36
Cuber, Ronnie, 148

D
Dallas (Tex.), 63–64
Dankworth, Johnny, 118, 121
David (King), 119
Davis, Miles, 90
Davis, Sammy, Jr. (half brother), 5–6, 23
Davis, Sammy, Jr. (performer), 79–80, 112, 134, 135
Davis, Samuel (stepfather), 5, 11, 13, 15
Decca Records, 80, 81, 86, 88, 89
Dennis, Emmett J. (Jay), 105
Deuchar, Jimmy, 118
DeVaughan, Beazie, 54
Dr. Chops (Nelson Creswell), 43–44, 50
Down Beat magazine, 58, 59, 65, 66, 153
Durham, Al, 45, 55

E
Eckhardt, Father Stephen, 18
Eckstein, Billy, 92
Eisenhower, Dwight, 97–98, 115, 119, 120, 124
Elkins, Leon, 34
Ellington, Duke, 35, 47, 56, 72
Ertegun, Ahmet, 93
Ervine, Sam, 46, 47, 51, 53

Esquire magazine, 89
Evans, Herschel, 77

F
Faith healing, 8, 9, 17
Feather, Leonard, 71, 88, 89, 90
Fields, Herbie, 90
Flamingo Hotel (Las Vegas), 134–135, 140
"Flying Home," 68, 70, 79, 81, 146, 161
Ford, Pherebia Morgan, 5, 17
Frank Sebastian's Cotton Club, 34–36, 38–39
Freedomland (N.Y.), 135

G
Garrick's Show Bar, 85–86
Ghana, 123
Gibb, Richard D., 172
Gillespie, Dizzy, 70
Glad-Hamp Records, 131, 140–141, 146, 150
Glad Records, 130–131
Gladys Hampton Houses, 164, 169
Glaser, Joe, 72, 74, 76, 77, 83, 85, 86, 98–99, 105–106, 114, 115, 122, 123–124, 141
Glenn, Tyree, 48, 54
Godfrey, Arthur, 135–136
Goldwater, Barry, 143
Goodman, Benny, 52–72 *passim*, 109, 112, 132, 133
Gordon, Dexter, 78, 80–81, 82
Granz, Norman, 104, 109, 114–115
Great Britain, 116–118